THE **COMPLETE**
IDIOT'S
GUIDE® TO

Book Proposals & Query Letters

by Marilyn Allen and Coleen O'Shea

ALPHA
A member of Penguin Group (USA) Inc.

ALPHA BOOKS

Published by the Penguin Group

Penguin Group (USA) Inc., 375 Hudson Street, New York, New York 10014, USA

Penguin Group (Canada), 90 Eglinton Avenue East, Suite 700, Toronto, Ontario M4P 2Y3, Canada (a division of Pearson Penguin Canada Inc.)

Penguin Books Ltd., 80 Strand, London WC2R 0RL, England

Penguin Ireland, 25 St. Stephen's Green, Dublin 2, Ireland (a division of Penguin Books Ltd.)

Penguin Group (Australia), 250 Camberwell Road, Camberwell, Victoria 3124, Australia (a division of Pearson Australia Group Pty. Ltd.)

Penguin Books India Pvt. Ltd., 11 Community Centre, Panchsheel Park, New Delhi—110 017, India

Penguin Group (NZ), 67 Apollo Drive, Rosedale, North Shore, Auckland 1311, New Zealand (a division of Pearson New Zealand Ltd.)

Penguin Books (South Africa) (Pty.) Ltd., 24 Sturdee Avenue, Rosebank, Johannesburg 2196, South Africa

Penguin Books Ltd., Registered Offices: 80 Strand, London WC2R 0RL, England

Copyright © 2011 by Marilyn Allen and Coleen O'Shea

International Standard Book Number: 978-1-61564-045-4
Library of Congress Catalog Card Number: 2010910363

13   12   11   8   7   6   5   4   3   2   1

Interpretation of the printing code: The rightmost number of the first series of numbers is the year of the book's printing; the rightmost number of the second series of numbers is the number of the book's printing. For example, a printing code of 11-1 shows that the first printing occurred in 2011.

Printed in the United States of America

Note: This publication contains the opinions and ideas of its authors. It is intended to provide helpful and informative material on the subject matter covered. It is sold with the understanding that the authors and publisher are not engaged in rendering professional services in the book. If the reader requires personal assistance or advice, a competent professional should be consulted.

The authors and publisher specifically disclaim any responsibility for any liability, loss, or risk, personal or otherwise, which is incurred as a consequence, directly or indirectly, of the use and application of any of the contents of this book.

Most Alpha books are available at special quantity discounts for bulk purchases for sales promotions, premiums, fund-raising, or educational use. Special books, or book excerpts, can also be created to fit specific needs.

For details, write: Special Markets, Alpha Books, 375 Hudson Street, New York, NY 10014.

Publisher: *Marie Butler-Knight*

Associate Publisher: *Mike Sanders*

Senior Managing Editor: *Billy Fields*

Acquisitions Editor: *Tom Stevens*

Development Editor: *Lynn Northrup*

Production Editor: *Kayla Dugger*

Copy Editor: *Jan Zoya*

Cover Designer: *Kurt Owens*

Book Designers: *William Thomas, Rebecca Batchelor*

Indexer: *Celia McCoy*

Layout: *Ayanna Lacey*

Proofreader: *John Etchison*

Contents

Part 1:   Before You Start Writing 1

1   **Does Your Book Project Have What It
Takes?** 3

Making Your Dream a Reality 4

It Starts with a Query 5

Pre-Query "Musts" for Fiction 6

Pre-Query "Musts" for Nonfiction........................ 7

Originality Is Key 7

Credibility Makes a Difference 9

To Market, to Market 10

The Next Step: The Book Proposal.....................11

Creating a Platform...13

What's in a Name? 15

Using a Subtitle..*16*

Keep It Easy to Find with Keywords....................*17*

2   **Test-Run Your Project**.................................19

Why Waste Time on Feedback? 19

Get Thee to a Writers' Group 20

Clear Goals and Procedures................................ *20*

A Compatible Culture.. *20*

Work, Not Play...*21*

Location, Location, Location...............................*21*

Rules to Criticize By *22*

When It's Not Working *23*

Writers' Conferences: Writing with Benefits.....................23

Rules of Engagement.. *24*

Finding the Best Writers' Conference...................*25*

Researching the Right Writers' Conference........................ *26*

Part 2:   The Query Letter................................... 27

3   **Query Letter Basics**....................................29

Why Query? 30

What Every Basic Query Letter Has................... 30

The Opening..*31*

The First Sentence Hook *31*

The Pitch *32*

The Content *33*

Your Experience *34*

The Book Title *35*

The Competition *35*

The Close *36*

Your Contact Info *37*

Personalizing Your Query 37

Research a Name *37*

Confirm the Name *39*

Get a Second Opinion *39*

On Your Mark, Get Set … 40

Query Letter "Don'ts" 40

4   The E-Mail Query Letter 43

First (Cyber) Impressions Count 43

A Subject Line That Sings 44

Keep It Professional 47

Use a Professional E-Mail Address *47*

Submit to One Agent or Editor with Each E-Mail *48*

Address the Correct Person *48*

Content Savvy 49

E-Mail Query Do's and Don'ts 52

Typos and Grammatical Errors *53*

Consistency Is Key *53*

Follow the Guidelines *54*

Be Truthful *54*

5   The "Snail Mail" Query Letter 57

The Snail Mail Advantage 57

Formatting Your Letter 58

Rules of the Paper Trail 59

All About the Content 60

Beyond Formatting 66

All Stamps Are Not Alike *66*

A Basic Font *66*

Personalize Your Stationery *67*

6   The Nonfiction Query Letter..........................**69**

First Things First...69

Query Letter Highlights 70

What's Your Nonfiction Category? 71

    The Memoir Query..71

    The Cookbook Query..74

    The Biography or History Book Query...............76

    The Travel Book Query.....................................78

    The "How-To" or "Self-Help" Book Query......... 79

    The Coffee Table Book Query............................83

    The Current Event or True Crime Query............85

7   The Fiction Query Letter **89**

Elements of Fiction 90

Query Letter Basics 91

    Keep It Short...91

    Do Your Research...91

    Get the Name Right... 92

    Establish a Connection 92

    Follow the Submission Guidelines 92

    Know Thy Recipient... 93

    Proofread Your Work....................................... 94

    Start Your Letter with a "Hook" 94

    Platform Still Matters.....................................95

    End Graciously 95

Ground Rules Unique to Fiction 95

    The "Hook" Can Be a Short Excerpt from Your Book........ 96

    Your Role as "Expert"...................................... 96

    Dedicate a Paragraph to a Short Synopsis 97

    Include a Sample from the Book........................ 97

Genre-Specific Approaches 98

    Children's Books.. 98

    Young Adult (YA) Books.................................. 98

    Romance Novels 98

    Science Fiction/Fantasy/Horror Novels.............. 99

    Historical Novels... 99

    Humor Books and Humorous Fiction................. 99

    Mysteries and Thrillers.................................. 100

The Bad, the Not-So-Bad, and the Good 100

8   **Before and After You Click "Send"** 105

Checklist: Is It a Winning Query? 105

The Waiting Game 108

Valid Reasons for Early Contact *108*

Keep Track of Your Submissions *109*

Stay Positive *110*

When to Follow Up 110

What to Say in Your Follow-Up 111

When They Offer Feedback 112

Part 3: The Book Proposal **115**

9   **Book Proposal Basics** 117

Why Have a Book Proposal? 117

Developing Your Proposal 118

Partners in Writing 120

Co-Writer *120*

Ghostwriter *121*

Freelance Writer or Editor *122*

The Collaboration Agreement 122

Advances and Royalty Splits *122*

Literary Agent Commission *123*

Writers' Credit *123*

The Parts of a Proposal 124

Getting Started 126

Cover Letter *126*

Title Page *127*

Proposal Table of Contents *128*

Don't Forget the Guidelines 129

10   **Pre-Proposal Marketing** 131

Researching the Competition 132

Online Opportunities *132*

Online Extras *134*

Other Venues 134

Your Local Bookstore *135*

The Big Book Retailers *135*

The Book Review Section of the Newspaper *135*

Professional Magazines *136*

Books in Print *136*

Is the Medium the Message?..................................137
Competition Is Welcome...............................137
Become the Resident Expert 137
Before You Write the First Word.........................139

Part 4: The Nonfiction Proposal 141

11 The Book Proposal Overview 143
Introducing the Overview 143
The Quick Hook..................................... 144
The Longer Hook......................................146
Your Credentials and Platform 146
Potential Markets 147
A Discussion of the Competition 148
The Book's Structure 149
Delivery Dates..150
Other Information 150
Enthusiasm! 150
Do's and Don'ts of a Successful Overview.............151
A Winning Overview.......................................152

12 About the Author 153
Let Me Introduce Myself ... .153
Start with a Resumé..................................154
Putting Together Your Bio 155
What Belongs in Your Bio? 155
Calling Attention to Yourself.............................157
Career 157
Education 158
Relevant Hobby......................................159
Publications...159
Personal Appearances 160
Prizes and Awards....................................160
Research 161
Personal Experience 161
Geography..161
Playing to Your Strengths 162
Business 162
Health and Nutrition 162
Pop Culture 163

Parenting..*163*
Cooking, Lifestyle, and Crafts..*163*
History and Science..*164*
Fiction *164*
Children's Books..*165*
An About the Author Example..165

13   About the Market.. **169**
The Importance of the Market 170
Why Research Your Market? 170
Show You Know Your Subject..171
We're Here to Help...172
Assemble Your Market Research..173
Know Your Primary Market *173*
Define Your Audience *173*
Find Statistics..*175*
Must-Have Stats *176*
Secondary Markets *178*
The Competitive Review Section 179
Seeking Out the Competition *180*
Writing Your Competitive Review *181*
Competitive Review: Two Versions *184*
Think Positive! 187

14   The Platform Marketing Section **189**
Platform Makes Perfect 189
A Platform's Six "Planks"..190
Media Experience *190*
Social Media Marketing *191*
Previous Publications *192*
Speaking Engagements..*192*
Product Tie-Ins..*192*
Continuous Exposure *193*
Assembling Your Platform..193
Putting It in Perspective..197
It's All About Marketing Yourself......................................198
Ideas to Get Your Platform Going.................................... 200
Sell It Yourself *200*
Create Your Own Website.. *200*
Start Blogging.. *201*

Become a Contributor 202

Speak on Your Subject.. 202

Teach 203

Use Social Networking Sites.. 203

Expand Your E-Mail Address Book 204

Get Quotes.. 205

Brand Yourself... 205

More Food for Thought... 206

A Platform Marketing Section That Sells 207

15   The Expanded Table of Contents 213

The Big Reveal 214

Creating the Expanded Table of Contents.....................215

Organizing the Book into Parts 218

Writing Your Chapter Descriptions 219

Using Bullets to Expand on Narrative Content.............219

Expanded Table of Contents Examples 220

Special Cases, Special Sections 226

16   The Nonfiction Writing Sample 229

The Writing Sample Is Key 230

Putting Together Your Nonfiction Writing Sample 231

Getting Specific..234

A Closer Look at Writing Samples 235

Part 5:   Fiction Tips and the Process............................241

17   The Fiction Writing Sample 243

Write About What You Know and Love 244

Hit the Shelves 244

Genre Mastery.. 246

Romance 246

Historical Fiction..247

Sci-Fi, Fantasy, and Horror 247

Mysteries and Thrillers.. 248

Western 249

Presenting Your Story in Three Documents 250

Short Synopsis..251

Cast of Characters...251

Expanded Synopsis..252

Polishing Your Work...254
   Be Your Own Critic..254
   Now What? 255
What to Send to the Agent.....................................256

18 Using an Agent or Not **259**
Do You Really Need an Agent?...........................260
What an Agent Can Offer 261
How to Find an Agent...263
Making a Good Match...264
Going It Alone...265
If You Opt for Self-Publishing 266

19 While You Are Waiting to Hear.................**269**
The Publishing Timeline 269
What to Do While You're Waiting 272
   Fiction 272
   Nonfiction...273
Keep Building Your Platform...............................273
You're On Your Way 274

Appendixes

A Glossary **275**
B Online Resources for Writers **289**
   Index **293**

Introduction

Getting your nonfiction or fiction book published can be a complicated and confusing process. Every year, hundreds of thousands of writers vie for the attention of the decision-makers in the publishing business. For many, especially first-time writers, it can be an overwhelming experience. *The Complete Idiot's Guide to Book Proposals & Query Letters* is designed to demystify the steps involved, help you get organized, and give you your best chance at success. We'll show you how to prepare the materials that will put your book idea in the best light, and give you tips for making your writing stand out and your marketing platform sparkle. We'll explain all of the steps and pieces needed to pitch your work effectively to get the interest of a publishing professional, and we'll share many examples along the way. This book will help get your work noticed—and have literary agents and editors asking for more.

How This Book Is Organized

Part 1, Before You Start Writing, explains everything you need to know to see if your idea has what it takes to go all the way from concept to full-length book, and how to test-run it to see whether, if you write it, there will be an audience waiting to read it.

Part 2, The Query Letter, gives you the tools and savvy you need to get your foot in the publishing door by acing the first step: getting an agent or editor to ask for more about your book.

Part 3, The Book Proposal, lays out the basics on writing a successful proposal, from the cover letter to the writing sample.

Part 4, The Nonfiction Proposal, takes you through the process, helping you clearly outline your book, define your market, position yourself as a marketable author, evaluate the competition, and choose the best sample text to represent your book.

Part 5, Fiction Tips and the Process, covers the secrets of writing a great fiction proposal. We also discuss how to decide if you need an agent, how to approach a publisher directly, considerations for if you want to self-publish your book, and how you can make yourself and your book more marketable while you're playing the waiting game.

Extras

Keep an eye out for these special sidebars throughout the book. They'll give you the inside scoop, from knowing publishing's special lingo so you can sound like a seasoned pro to what you must do—and must never do!—if you really want to get your book published.

> **DEFINITION**
>
> Check these sidebars for terms you need to know to understand and navigate the publishing world.

> **AGENTS' ADVICE**
>
> These tips from our professional experience and our agency business give you an insider's take on what you need to know, say, and do to get your book published.

> **PUBLISHING PITFALLS**
>
> These sidebars alert you to common mistakes writers make and tell you how to avoid them.

> **HOT OFF THE PRESS**
>
> These sidebars offer insights that will help you understand the expectations of publishing companies, as well as information related to the discussion.

Acknowledgments

From Marilyn Allen:

To my wonderful husband, Bill Liberis, and my lovely daughter, Erin Liberis—I thank you for being my world and for being proud of everything I do. For Emily and Will Liberis, my other children—your love and support made me remove the "step" part long ago. To my parents, Joy and George Mara, for helping me get my first job in the Worcester Public Library and for raising me to love books. (Mom, writing a book has been on my bucket list for years!) To my sisters and brothers (and their families), Carolyn, George Jr., Michael, Patrick, and Colleen—I love you and thank you for making our childhood so much fun. Especially, I would like to thank Coleen O'Shea, my partner in our literary agency business and in this book, for all her hard work and publishing smarts.

From Coleen O'Shea:

Thanks to all the talented and passionate writers who challenge us with new ideas and offer exciting opportunities to create meaningful new books. I am grateful for the many authors and clients I've worked with throughout my career both as an editor and a literary agent. Most special thanks to my parents, Ruth and Francis O'Shea, who always encouraged and inspired me. One summer holiday, my father became so engrossed in *Catch-22* by Joseph Heller that he seemed unaware of four young children racing around him, and I realized how transporting and magical a good book can be. I am especially grateful for that meaningful lesson. To my wonderful husband, David Anderson, and our amazing sons, Nicholas, Timothy, and Graham, who make my life joyous in every way. And to Marilyn Allen, the ideal business partner, who helps make our work fruitful and fun, in equal measure.

From Marilyn and Coleen:

We owe thanks to Ellen Phillips and Karla Dougherty for their research and help. A heartfelt thanks to Tom Stevens for the chance to write this book and for being a fantastic editor on this book and on the many, many others we have worked on together. To Lynn Northrup, for her wise advice. And to our clients and writers everywhere, thanks for giving us great books to read and to work on. Keep writing!

Trademarks

All terms mentioned in this book that are known to be or are suspected of being trademarks or service marks have been appropriately capitalized. Alpha Books and Penguin Group (USA) Inc. cannot attest to the accuracy of this information. Use of a term in this book should not be regarded as affecting the validity of any trademark or service mark.

Before You Start Writing

So, you want to write a book—or maybe you've already written one. But taking your book idea or manuscript from concept to book deal isn't as straightforward as you might think. In this part, you learn if you really do have a viable book idea—and if you have what it takes to carry the concept through hundreds of pages. You also learn how to find writers' groups and other venues where you can preview your project and get helpful suggestions and feedback before you submit it to an agent or editor for publication.

Does Your Book Project Have What It Takes?

In This Chapter

- The reality of writing and publishing a book
- Pre-query "musts" for fiction and nonfiction
- Originality, credibility, and finding an audience
- Book proposal elements in brief
- The crucial author platform
- The importance of a catchy title

Tell anyone at a cocktail party, a wedding, a family dinner, or even the break room in your workplace that you are a writer and you will find, at one time or another, someone who wants to share his or her idea about writing a book:

> "I have a great idea for a novel!"

> "I got a thousand hits on YouTube!"

> "I always wrote great papers in high school!"

> "I always wanted to be a writer!"

> "Everyone tells me I should write a book!"

Most people think it's easy to write a book. People do not usually assume becoming a sculptor or a painter is easy. They know it takes talent and hard work, not to mention expensive equipment and training. But writing? Everyone writes, whether it is a "to do" list or a thank-you note. All you need is a laptop or pen and paper. But once you begin writing a book, you're likely to discover that it's anything but easy.

Making Your Dream a Reality

Do you have a burning passion to take your stories from real life and turn them into a novel? Are you keeping notes in a journal in the hopes of one day turning your insights into the next Great American Novel? Perhaps you want to share with readers why your online business is booming, or you've always wanted to write about your hobby, or you are doing groundbreaking research that needs to find a wider audience, or you want to write about the memorable year when your family lived in a foreign country. Maybe you've always dreamed of becoming a writer, and are brimming with talent and creativity that needs to come out, but never knew how to begin.

Here's the reality: it's difficult to write a book from start to finish—especially if you are working or parenting full time. Writing a book takes an enormous amount of work and time. Publishing is an extremely competitive business, as agents and publishers receive a tremendous number of submissions. From the beginning, it's essential that you critically assess your idea, evaluate the marketability and publishability of your idea, and develop a valuable marketing presence so you can enhance your chances of making your writing dream a reality.

Many would-be writers don't take the steps necessary to pull their project together in a well-thought-out way. We see too many writers rushing to find an agent or pitching to publishers before their idea is fully fleshed out. There's early work you can do to help shape your idea and make you a marketable author. Think of this chapter as the research and development stage of making your writing dreams come true. Be flexible and open-minded at this stage, and get ready to shape your idea into a fully developed and market-ready book.

AGENTS' ADVICE

In the business world, there is something called the "elevator ride" test. If you cannot articulate your million-dollar idea in the time it takes to go from your floor to the lobby, then it's not going to work. This test holds true for book ideas as well. If you cannot explain why your idea is a good one in that 30-second to 1-minute ride, then you need to rethink how you are presenting it.

When you have clarity about your book idea, you're sure that you want to write, and you're ready to take the leap into the publishing world, you will find that there are different materials needed to achieve this. In the case of nonfiction, you may find that you don't need an entire manuscript to start working on your proposal. In fact, agents and editors don't want to see your entire manuscript. They want, first and foremost, a quick take on your book idea and your authority to write it. If they are interested, they will ask to see more detail about you, your book, and your writing style—but almost never the whole manuscript. In other words, there's a lot you can to do to get your book presentation ready without writing the entire book. Be aware, though, that in the case of fiction or memoirs, you'll need a sizable portion—if not all of the book—completed.

Getting the attention of the publishing world is accomplished with two things: the query letter and the proposal. We'll get into much more detail about how the publishing process works in later chapters, but for now, here's an overview.

It Starts with a Query

You are ultimately going to present your work in a succinct and intriguing *query letter* that you will send to targeted agents or editors to invite their interest in your book concept. But writing a query letter is best done from a complete proposal in order to boost your chances of getting the positive response you want. We'll tell you how to craft a query letter in Chapter 3 and get into much more detail there about the process. But here is some preliminary information you need to know.

DEFINITION

A **query letter** is a brief presentation of your book concept that invites the interest of an agent or editor in seeing more material, with the ultimate goal of introducing your book to the publishing community.

By its very nature, a query letter is short. But therein lies the challenge: within a few paragraphs, you have to sell your idea, sell your experience to write it, and sell your book's potential popularity.

Challenging, yes. But impossible? No.

Pre-Query "Musts" for Fiction

A good query letter presents all of the key points in a compelling way. The query letter itself may be short, but the work that goes into it is considerably longer and involved. Let's get started with the basic element of all query letters, proposals, and books: the writing style.

Good writing is the linchpin of the publishing business. Strong writing is particularly essential in fiction. In Chapters 7 and 17, you'll read more about writing fiction and some of the steps you can take to improve your writing. What's important to keep in mind now is that writing is a skill that can constantly be improved, so you should write, rewrite, and write again. Don't rush the process. Don't submit your work before the writing is as sharp, clean, and fresh as you can make it.

Fiction requires what we call the three C's:

- **Commitment.** Writing a novel takes passion and discipline. It may take years to achieve, multiple drafts, and tremendous effort to complete the work.

- **Compassion.** You have to dive in to the work and the world you create with passion so that your reader will want to take this journey with you.

- **Content.** Every novel is different. It may be the plot, characters, setting, or genre that drives the book forward, making the reader turn the page and satisfying the audience. Your job as the author is to achieve that compelling and textured work.

Pre-Query "Musts" for Nonfiction

In nonfiction, the rules are a bit different. Sometimes writing talent has less to do with getting a book published than originality of concept, the author's experience, and marketability. In nonfiction, content is the prevailing component.

Of course, the writing is also important in nonfiction, but there is an added opportunity of bringing in someone to help improve your writing style in nonfiction. Publishing houses and agents are adept at finding a *ghostwriter*, professional editor, "book doctor," or collaborator to write or polish books for an expert author whose writing style is weak (we'll discuss this in Chapter 9). But briefly, a collaborator or co-author is sometimes hired to work with an expert for credit, which may include cover credit, copyright credit, and shared remuneration. Each case is different, and it's your agent or editor's job to help assemble a writing team if required. If you are starting out in the process and think you need help with the writing, organization, and structure, look for a writing partner at the outset.

But if you do have talent—if your style "sings"—it's even better. You can use your talent to write a riveting query letter or book proposal, and eventually a book.

DEFINITION

A **ghostwriter** is usually a "writer for hire" who will anonymously work with an expert to write a readable book. Unlike a co-author or collaborator, the ghostwriter's name is not credited on the cover or in the book, so he or she is invisible—thus the name *ghost*writer. Typically, the payment for the ghostwriter is calculated as part of the author's advance, so the publisher pays the ghostwriter and it doesn't come out of the author's pocket, but it does ultimately reduce the author's profits from the book. However, it's well worth it, since the book might not even be publishable without the ghostwriter's help!

Originality Is Key

First and foremost, your book idea has to have something about it that packs a punch, something that separates it from the rest. Ask yourself these questions: "What is it about my book that makes it special?" "Do I have something new to say?" "Do I have a fresh story to tell?" "Is this a new look at an old idea?" In order to answer these questions correctly, you have to do your homework. Each year millions of books hit the marketplace. Does your idea have what it needs to stand out from the crowd?

Nothing grows in a vacuum, and that includes ideas. The only way to determine if your concept is worthy of a book is to do exhaustive research to make the case for it. Spend time at the bookstore looking at other books in your genre. Browse Amazon.com and barnesandnoble.com to see if there are books that are similar to yours. Search for keywords that are in your idea to see if there is anything else available.

Even if a web search or a trip to the bookstore shows a lot of books on the same subject, don't be discouraged. In many ways the marketplace is always looking for new, smart projects. There are hot trends, new research, and eager readers all poised to buy new books. New books are published every year, many on your very same subject. Your task is to develop and present a unique approach in an exciting way.

Keep in mind that originality is vital in selling your book, but not at the expense of an audience. Direct competition for your book idea is obviously not a good sign in selling yours, but *no* competition can mean that nobody's interested in the idea or topic. Maybe there hasn't been a book about the subject because there isn't a market for it, or possibly previously published books in the topic didn't sell well. But your own research will give you a good idea about recent media interest that might provide ammunition for your concept's marketability. How many people visit websites or blogs on the topic? How many websites and blogs cover it? Is it frequently discussed on TV and in magazines and newspapers? You get the idea—it's not just what's happening in the bookstore that will influence market interest in your topic. Activity in other media can also generate publisher interest in a topic.

The fact is, originality is not just about subject matter. One or both of the following ideas can make your idea unique:

- **The concept.** Whatever your idea is, your research should show that it's different and unusual. There have been many books on baking cakes, but suppose you've invented a way to make delicious gluten-free layer cakes. Nothing is going to undermine your credibility more than saying your idea is original when, in reality, there are at least 20 books on the same subject. Research isn't just an extra effort; it's a necessity. Don't be discouraged. It's better to find out if your idea is truly fresh than to spend the next few years developing a project that won't invite publisher interest.

- **Your experience.** Even if your idea is a familiar one, if you're well known or a celebrity expert in your field, an agent or editor may be interested in seeing a proposal. For example, there are a lot of books about makeup in bookstores, but Lauren Luke grew such a large following from her YouTube "how to apply" videos that she now has a book deal.

Credibility Makes a Difference

Credibility goes hand-in-hand with originality. Your experience in the field not only makes you an individual who stands out from the crowd, but also makes you believable in the eyes of readers. They will listen to you because you have experience. You are an authority.

Credibility, like originality, can come from many sources:

- **Degrees enhance your work.** Advanced degrees and accomplishments in your field give instant credibility. Publishers look for this professional weight to enhance their efforts in sales and marketing. One of our clients is a successful psychoanalyst who has written a book about happy relationships. Her eight-step plan is an original one, but without her Ph.D., a publisher wouldn't touch her. If your topic is such that credibility of the project is enhanced by the involvement of a credentialed authority, and you don't have the credentials yourself, it might make sense for you to find such a professional who will work with you on the manuscript or contribute content (such as a foreword or introduction) to your work.

- **Contacts count.** Feature your professional and personal alliances to enhance your credibility. If you teach at a prestigious university, are affiliated with a major organization, or have an association with a government office that adds recognized credibility in your field, use those relationships to your benefit.

To Market, to Market

Remember, a book won't sell if nobody wants to read it, and a publisher is in the business of contracting for books that will sell. Quite simply, your book will need to find an audience. Does your book fill a need in the market? Will it find a readership or fan base, or satisfy a devoted niche audience? This may be a compelling reason for an agent or editor to consider your book.

The keywords are "filling a need." You might have a market for your book, but if there's a lot of competition on the same subject, why should an editor publish yours? What makes your book stand out? For example, there are a lot of books about building a home-based business, but perhaps your idea goes one step further, and rather than simply relating how to get a business up and running, you show how to franchise it. Your book is about directing people how to do that—and the fact that you happen to be a successful founder of a franchised chain gives you the necessary clout to gain agent and publisher interest. The pieces—originality, credibility, confidence, and audience—are lined up and are part of your arsenal.

One way to illustrate potential audience is with the use of supporting statistics. Statistics can help build a case for a market for your book, but they have to be specific. It isn't enough to say your book is for the 9.5 million people who love tennis. Just because your book is on a popular subject doesn't make the case for why your particular book should be published. But if your market is for the 1 million seniors who take up tennis every year, you're getting closer to pinpointing a distinct audience. Your presentation is further advanced if your research shows that you know how to reach your audience through blogs, websites, organizations, mailing lists, or programs.

Base your book on your unique and popular "serving seniors tennis program" and your experience as a tennis coach, and you might just pique the interest of the agent.

AGENTS' ADVICE

Bring your laptop or a notebook to the bookstore and write down the names of the books that may be competition for your book. Flip through those books to ensure you can argue why your idea is different. This will not only help you shape your idea, but it will also assist you in preparing the Competitive Review section of your proposal (see Chapter 13).

The Next Step: The Book Proposal

Now that you've been introduced to the query letter, the second part of the process that you will need to master is the *book proposal*, a selling document that presents your concept, you as the author, your marketing opportunities, and samples of your writing. If an agent or editor responds favorably to your query letter, the next step would then be to submit the book proposal. Think of a proposal as an extended presentation of your topic that your query letter only touched on. It is used to solicit a relationship with an agent to represent your work. She will help you take your project into the publishing marketplace with the goal of generating a contract for your book. Keep in mind that the publisher, not an agent, pays the author for the right to publish the work. The agent will receive a commission for her role in getting the contract for you, the author.

DEFINITION

A **book proposal** is the fleshed-out presentation of a book in development. Components of a book proposal include a cover letter, title page, overview, About the Author section, platform and promotion plans, review of the market and audience for the book, overview of the competition, Table of Contents and Expanded Table of Contents, and sample text.

Writing the proposal is often harder than the book itself because you have to conceive of the entire project and communicate the content and your expertise in writing the work in a short and compelling manner. We discuss book proposal elements in detail in Part 4, but here's an overview of the crucial sections that any strong proposal should include:

- **Overview.** This is a snapshot of what the book is about; if it's original and marketable; and if you, the author, are marketable (see Chapter 11).

- **About the Author.** Here's your opportunity to prove that you're the best person to write the book by showing your credentials (see Chapter 12).

- **About the Market.** This section provides plenty of credible stats to prove to a publisher there's a ready-made audience for your book, reviews the competition, and discusses relevant market trends (see Chapter 13).

- **Platform marketing.** A strong platform shows a publisher that you can help sell your book through media contacts, public appearances, media opportunities, a popular website and/or blog, seminars and lectures, a client base, and so on (see Chapter 14).

- **Expanded Table of Contents.** This gives an overview of the logic, flow, and content of the book, with brief descriptive paragraphs presenting the content of each part and chapter title of the work (see Chapter 15).

- **The writing sample.** Finally, here is the proof of the pudding, when you show agents and editors that you can really write (see Chapter 16 for nonfiction and Chapter 17 for fiction).

As you research your book idea and project, you will want to keep all of these proposal categories in mind. You may want to establish folders for each section where you can keep and collate relevant documents, notes, and ideas. Investigate what other writers in your category are up to and keep an eye on relevant current events.

Creating a Platform

The biggest hurdle for many authors is developing a winning platform. One of the biggest buzzwords in publishing over the past few years is "platform." Every time an agent or editor picks up a query letter or proposal, she is thinking about its platform. Platform is, in reality, a way of "branding" yourself. It's your credibility, originality, potential audience, and marketability combined into one dynamic package. This becomes your ability to reach readers and sell books.

We first heard the word "platform" when we worked inside major publishing houses. Editors bring projects to the editorial or publication board meetings, where decisions are made about acquiring or passing on a project. Authors of projects that have an established platform might include a syndication placement in a newspaper or magazine, a regular slot on a TV or radio show, a speaking or seminar business, a large or busy website or blog, or a sizable following on Facebook or Twitter. The publisher is looking for the author's ability to reach his specific market to help him sell books. It makes the publisher's job easier and the potential for success more likely.

Your platform comes from your visibility in the marketplace. Does your name go on for pages on Google? Do you have the respect of your peers? Do you have a list of supporting quotes from related experts in your field? Have you been on TV or the radio talking about your topic?

You need to focus on creating and developing your platform while you work on your proposal. Generating a name for yourself and building your audience will help sell the book idea to an agent or editor.

Here are some things you can do right now to start building your platform:

- **Build a following.** In today's world, you don't have to have a hit TV show to help you achieve recognition. Social media marketing represents an opportunity for writers to build a community around their topic as they work on their book. A website, a Facebook fan page, a popular blog—any of these can build credibility and an audience one click at a time.

- **Create a website.** This can be a site devoted to your topic, or a website all about you. Or you can write for another successful website and build a profile that way. Start a blog, Tweet, join social networks, and observe successful web activity in your area. You'll be set up to promote your book when it is published and to generate an audience for your topic—and yourself.

- **Make a media list.** The famous late Hollywood producer David O. Selznick once said that "there is no such thing as bad publicity." For your proposal, you are going to need specific publicity opportunities. Observe which magazines, newspapers, blogs, websites, radio programs, and TV shows cover or deal with your topic. Keep a list of publicity opportunities and build media contacts.

- **Establish relevant relationships.** The next time you go to your local bookstore, introduce yourself to the manager. Let her know that you are writing a book. Become friendly with the staff. They are at the forefront of the market. Ask them what is selling and why it sells. Ask about trends and what customers ask about. You might learn something that will inform your own project. Join appropriate local organizations or professional organizations that may help you expand your contact list.

HOT OFF THE PRESS

One of the most famous examples of credibility in the making is Julie Powell, who began a blog in 2002 about her experiences creating each of the recipes in *Mastering the Art of French Cooking* by Julia Child, Louisette Bertholle, and Simone Beck. Powell's blogs later became a bestselling book, *Julie & Julia,* even before she became famous in Nora Ephron's award-winning movie of the same name.

A book proposal takes effort. But publishing is a business. Think about it from a different perspective: you are asking a publisher to invest time and money in you and your work, for money, to write your book. What is it about you and your concept that will invite such an investment?

We're sometimes amazed at the number of prospective clients who overlook their experience when they try to sell themselves and their idea. They haven't spent enough time in the research stage of preparing their pitch and ignore some relevant points of their experience that might impress us. Maybe they have a website that receives thousands of hits. Maybe they've given lectures at universities around the world or headline conferences on their subject. Maybe they've published articles in national publications. You'd be surprised at the things you think are not important that can help sell you and your book. You must examine and list all of your pertinent experience. But be prepared to be honest and critical about your focus.

What's in a Name?

One word: *Jaws.* You might not remember the author (it was Peter Benchley), but you'll never forget the title of his book, which went on to become a blockbuster movie series. Even teenagers who weren't born when the book came out know *Jaws* is about a great white shark. That's the power of a good title. It positions your project and draws in the reader, and it sends a message to an agent and editor about the book's category and potential readership.

Good titles can be difficult to come up with and take a great deal of thought. Here are some real attention-grabbing titles:

- *Making Peace with Your Past* by H. Norman Wright
- *Blink* by Malcolm Gladwell
- *Freakonomics* by Steven D. Levitt and Stephen J. Dubner
- *Skinny Bitch* by Rory Freedman and Kim Barnouin
- *The Fat Flush Plan* by Ann Louise Gittleman
- *Marley and Me* by John Grogan

Finding a good title is worth the effort. You can use the title to brand yourself and your book. Even if the title changes between when you send your initial query letter to when you publish the book, it's important to start with a punchy title that will get you noticed and make an agent or editor want to read more.

HOT OFF THE PRESS

You love your title, and you want your platform to grow, so do some research. You cannot copyright a title, but you can check sites such as www.amazon.com, www.barnesandnoble.com, and www.borders.com to see if the title is already in use. If the title hasn't been used, think about starting a website. Today, every smart author maintains a website. If you are not yet ready to start setting up your website, you can still make sure no one steals the name of your book. Sites such as www.gotomydomain. com will give you legal license to make the name yours online, as in www. titleofmybook.com. It costs very little, but you have to make sure you keep renewing the name to protect your site.

Using a Subtitle

A book has to send a clear message to the potential audience. Keep in mind that agents and editors are bombarded with submissions. Make it easy for them to remember your book and correspondence. If you are writing a book about marriage but title your book *Blueprints for Success*, at a quick glance it may be mistaken for a book on architecture instead of personal relationships. A subtitle adds some clarity: *Blueprints for Success: Stories from Successful Marriages.* Subtitles give you the opportunity to provide more top-line information about the book's content.

You don't usually see subtitles on novels, except for perhaps *A Novel.* But most nonfiction books have subtitles that clarify and expand on the central concept. A good subtitle might keep the browser from putting the book back on the shelf.

Invest the time to think of a powerful and catchy title and subtitle, but be flexible along the way. With your input, the publisher will retain the right to set the final title of a book.

Keep It Easy to Find with Keywords

This point applies primarily to nonfiction. With the millions of books in print in all formats, you want to make it easy for your audience to find your title in an electronic search. A computer can go through thousands of files every second, but it cannot think for you. From Amazon.com to your local library's online site, the way to find a book is through a keyword: an author's name, a title, or a genre. If your name is not exactly a household name and a reader is not sure of the exact title, the only way to find you is through keywords. Do a trial run of titles on Amazon.com and other online booksellers to see how successful author, title, and keyword searches help potential readers in finding the book they want.

The Least You Need to Know

- Research your idea to make sure it's original and marketable.
- Know your competition, and be ready to support the reasons why your book idea is different—and better.
- The first step to getting your work published is understanding the query letter and book proposal components.

- It's never too early to start building your media platform. Start building name and content recognition with a website or a blog, newspaper column, or speaking engagements to enhance your experience and expertise in a specific area.

- A great title is also a great sales tool: it will jump off the page as an agent or editor reads your query letter and proposal.

Test-Run Your Project

In This Chapter

- Why feedback is important
- Joining a writers' group
- Finding a writers' conference

A truism: Your friends and family are predisposed to love your idea. Another truism: They might not be right.

Let's face it, people who love you will probably love your idea. However, family, friends, or even business colleagues may not be in the position to give you an accurate and honest appraisal of your work. The goal is to improve your work—both your writing and your submission materials. You need to get your material as smart and polished as possible to get the attention of busy publishing professionals. And don't forget, there are hundreds—and maybe more—writers who are your competition, all trying to get in that same door.

In short, you need to get feedback elsewhere.

Why Waste Time on Feedback?

If a doctor wanted to do surgery on your back, you would most likely get a second opinion from another doctor. After all, you want to make sure you're doing the right thing.

The same goes for your book idea. Your instincts might tell you it's a good one, but you need to get a second opinion before you send out that all-important query letter.

PUBLISHING PITFALLS

There is no such thing as a B+ in publishing, or even an A-. You have to get an A+ the first time out. The worst thing you can say is, "I know my idea needs work, but I wanted you to see it right away." Agents and editors don't have time to read material that is second best.

Get Thee to a Writers' Group

The benefits of a writers' group have been bandied about for years. Some authors swear by them; others consider them buzz kill. Which is right? Neither—as long as you join a writers' group that works for you. Many of our authors tell us that they'd never have finished their books if it hadn't been for the support and feedback they received from their writers' group. We believe they can be a good source for feedback, but only if you like and respect the other members.

Let's take a closer look at some of the elements to keep in mind.

Clear Goals and Procedures

A good writer's group has clearly defined goals that all members need to reach in order to stay in the group. This can be anything from presenting a new chapter at every meeting to providing only feedback that's constructive. A crucial part of the group's procedure is to ensure that each person gets a chance to speak about her work or critique another person's work. It is not the place to talk about what you want to write "someday."

A Compatible Culture

Yes, writing is writing, but there are many different styles. A scientist involved in cutting-edge research is not going to write the same way as a psychologist who has a six-week program for couples therapy. A mystery writer will focus on different elements than an early-reader picture book writer. A Christian fiction writer has concerns that are different than a Danielle Steel wannabe. In other words, there are different writing styles all with the same goal of getting published.

Make sure the group you decide to join is made up of members who are writing in the same genre or category. It can save you a lot of painful criticism from writers who don't know your genre—as well as ensure you are getting the right feedback.

Work, Not Play

It is one thing to chat for a few minutes before starting a meeting, but it is quite another to spend half the allotted time discussing the obscene advance a celebrity author received, or, for that matter, the teachers in your town's middle school. Within 10 minutes, everyone should be settled in their seats, their minds and notebooks open, and ready to begin.

Location, Location, Location

Your writers' group might stimulate you, motivate you, and make you feel great after your session, but try to find one in a convenient location so the task of getting there and back is minimized.

Almost every city or town has a writers' group. There is bound to be a group that, if not right around the corner, is close enough so you can conveniently attend:

- Check with your local library or community center.

- Ask people at your local bookstore.

- Check the local papers and community websites.

- Research Craigslist and other online service organizations. Use an online search engine to find information on local writers' groups; it's a big plus if they also give reviews.

- Get a local college or university catalogue and see if they have writers' groups for noncredit.

PUBLISHING PITFALLS

Online writing classes and groups are another way to go, but beware. Because they are online, it can be more difficult to determine if someone is a loose cannon, sending you negative feedback just to be mean. It's also more difficult to relay critiques in a clear, concise way and they may be misunderstood.

Rules to Criticize By

One of our authors felt so raw from her writers' group critique that she didn't put pen to paper for two years. Don't let that happen to you. At the first meeting, you should get a pretty good idea of the lay of the writer land. Is there a member who makes nasty comments? Is there someone who tries to sabotage another member to get rid of the "competition"? Is there someone whom your instincts tell you not to trust? If so, politely say good-bye and don't look back.

Critiques are, of course, the lifeblood of any writers' group. You are there to get feedback on your work from fellow writers working in the same genre. A good way to measure: during your first meeting, be an observer. See if critiques are controlled and provide valuable insights. Here are some rules to follow:

- Critiques are only given to the work at hand. It is not about you; it's about your work.

- The critiques must be constructive and provide insight. A good critique might be a suggestion to add more statistics or to make a paragraph clearer. A bad critique gives a judgment rather than providing helpful suggestions. If you see an emotional reaction or a condemnation of your book instead of content- or logic-driven commentary, you're almost certainly looking at a bad critique. A bad critique may start with "I don't like …", "I don't know why …", or "It just doesn't speak to me …."

- Critiques should last no more than 10 to 15 minutes, depending on the size of the group. Any more than that, and it's likely that some members won't be able to give you some valuable feedback—or that you won't be able to provide feedback to them. Ideally, every member should be able to give a critique, and no members should be allowed to monopolize the session.

There are ground rules for you, the critique-ee, too. Don't be defensive when a member discusses your work. Listen. He may be making a valuable point. And always remember that you joined this group for exactly that kind of criticism to make your work better. If you are overly sensitive to the remarks made by someone, stay focused on the fact that the member took the time to read your piece, take notes, and offer to help.

AGENTS' ADVICE

A writers' group is a professional support group, and friendship is more a benefit than a rule. On the other hand, it is important to like the people in your group. You'll feel more comfortable and do better work.

When It's Not Working

If you decide for whatever reason that you're not getting what you want from participating in a group, don't prolong the agony: let your feet do the talking and find another group. Keep the warning signs (disorganization, negativity, a few people monopolizing the session, and so on) in mind as you evaluate each group. Remember, the goal is to improve your writing and your book.

Writers' Conferences: Writing with Benefits

While you are writing your novel, developing your proposal, or testing your ideas with other writers, consider attending a writers' conference. It can be enjoyable and keep you in the writer groove.

There are many benefits in going to a writers' conference, besides the obvious benefit of being away, on your own, and having all day and night to write without interruption. These include the following:

- **Networking.** Writers' conferences are great ways to meet fellow writers, literary agents, editors, and publishers. These names can be very helpful when it comes time to try to sell your book. You might even be able to get into a conversation with an agent or editor about your idea—a verbal query!

- **Honing your writing skills.** Many conferences have visiting faculty who conduct lectures on writing.

- **Getting the feedback you need.** For one to two weeks, you will eat, drink, and sleep writing. You will be among people who all want the same thing: improving your writing and getting published. A writers' conference is a great way to start an impromptu writers' group anytime, anywhere—from stretched out on a lush summer lawn to sitting next to the large stone fireplace in the main building.

If you go the writers' conference route, try to attend as many sessions as possible with established authors and industry experts. Some conferences give you a once-in-a-lifetime opportunity to go over your work one on one with an established author or publishing professional. It can be an excellent opportunity to polish your pitch and learn about both the strengths and weaknesses of your material.

Rules of Engagement

Writers' conferences aren't cheap. The cost of room and board, three meals a day, and an excellent faculty all add up. The good news is that many conferences have grants to help defray some of the costs. They also have working scholarships for people who can't afford to pay full price. Writers who receive a scholarship usually do 20 hours a week of waiting tables or cleaning.

And, just like college, you have to apply and be accepted in order to go to a writers' conference. More times than not, submissions include a story or 15 pages of a novel, memoir, or nonfiction piece, as well as two or three references. (These can include creative writing teachers, journalists you've worked with, employers, or anyone else who can attest to your writing ability.)

HOT OFF THE PRESS

A writers' colony is different from a conference. A conference lasts for a weekend up to two weeks and it's an intense time for learning, meeting and greeting, and gaining feedback. A writers' colony, on the other hand, usually has spots for one to three months, time in which writers can work in solitude when they want, or time to talk to other writers about their work. Some examples include MacDowell in New England and Yaddo in upstate New York. See Appendix B for more information.

Finding the Best Writers' Conference

Just like choosing a college, choosing a writers' conference is part reputation, part monetary, part quality of visiting faculty, and part talent of fellow participants.

There are hundreds of conferences throughout the United States and in Europe that cater to specific genres. There are travel-specific conferences. Memoir-writing conferences. Romance-novel-writing conferences. Mystery- , young adult- , and nonfiction-writing conferences. The obvious choice for you would be a conference in the genre you are writing. Be smart: narrow the field.

Money, too, is part of the equation. There might be a terrific conference in Hawaii next summer, but the cost of the conference, plus travel, is too exorbitant.

Finally, the perfect writers' conference for you should have a faculty you are familiar with; its members should be respected experts in their field. This will help ensure that the feedback you receive is sound.

Researching the Right Writers' Conference

Several online resources can help guide you to the perfect writers' conference for you:

- Professional organizations, such as the Author's Guild or the American Medical Writers Association, usually have a list of conferences that have been helpful for their members.

- Trade magazines and associations, such as *Poets & Writers* and *The Writer's Digest*, also have lists of conferences, as well as classified ads for them. *Poets & Writers* also has a database of writers' conferences and centers.

- Google and other search engines will open several pages when you type in "Writers' Conferences." You can check them out online and ask to see a catalogue.

The Least You Need to Know

- Friends and family can make you feel great about your work, but you need to temper their enthusiasm with feedback from objective third-party individuals.

- Feedback is not designed to discourage you. Rather, good feedback will provide the insight you need to make your query letter, proposal, and ultimately your book the best it can be.

- Make sure a writers' group culture matches your own.

- Make sure the conferences you attend are relevant to your book's topic.

The Query Letter

What exactly is a query letter—and why is it so important? Easy: it's the first impression an agent or editor has of you and your work. This part gives you everything you need to write a query letter that gets noticed—from grabbing the attention of an editor or agent from the very first sentence to seamlessly adding facts or statistics, from clearly and concisely showing the need for this book to showcasing your marketability as an author and expert. We even give you a checklist to make sure you have all the right elements in your letter before you press Send!

Query Letter Basics

In This Chapter

- Why you need a query letter
- The elements of an effective query letter
- Customizing your query letter
- If you get a positive response
- What to avoid in your query letter

So you want to write a book and get it published. You have a fantastic idea, a one-in-a-million topic that you know will sell. Congratulations! But how do you get an agent or editor to agree with you and want to work with you? How do you convey your concept and passion to publishing professionals so that your project is one they believe in, too?

That's where a query letter comes in. This letter gives you an opportunity to successfully present your project so that an agent will want to represent it and help sell it to a publisher. Or, if you're sending your query directly to a publishing house, it must convince an acquiring editor to champion your book for acquisition. This is the first view a publishing professional sees of you and the work, so it has to be perfect.

Why Query?

A query letter is the first impression of your work. It has to accurately yet persuasively present you and your project. Your ultimate goal is to get the recipient to request more material. If your work is fiction, good writing is the key. You want the agent to be eager to read more, so say up front that you have a finished manuscript. If your work is nonfiction, you have to sell your concept, hook the recipient, and state that your proposal and sample chapters are available. You'll still need to do some work once you're in (that's when you'll need a book proposal, which we'll cover in Parts 3 and 4).

An agent or editor receives hundreds of e-mails and letters a week, and more times than not, your query letter will be given a quick scan—not a full read. In order to pique an agent's or editor's interest, you need to give them something that intrigues them or, as an editor once told us, "stops me in my tracks as I begin to read."

A query letter is that element of surprise, the object of intrigue, which will either get their attention from the start—or give them a chance to practice their backhand as they aim for the wastebasket. In other words, a query letter has to be concise, to the point, and exciting. You don't get a second chance with that editor or agent.

HOT OFF THE PRESS

Query letters are not just a one-sided affair. Writing a query letter saves *you* time. If an agent isn't interested in your project, you can cross the name off your list and move on. Even if the agent turns you down, you might be given some useful feedback that could help you refine future submissions.

What Every Basic Query Letter Has

You're probably getting the idea by now that writing a query letter isn't as easy as dashing off an e-mail, and you'll almost certainly write several versions before you settle on the best. But it's time well spent, because it makes you really focus on your book, which will help you at every stage of the process. And, of course, the query letter is your only chance to hook an agent or editor into wanting to see more.

There are nine essential elements to a good query letter. They hold true for fiction as well as nonfiction queries, so read them closely.

The Opening

"Dear sir or madam," "Dear agent," "Dear Random House," "To whom it may concern," and other generic openings are good ways to send your unread query letter straight into the recycling bin. It's every bit as important to do research on addressing your query to the person you want to read it as it is to research the topic of your book, the competition, and the market. The agents or editors who see your query letter should know that you cared enough to look them up by name before you wrote. If not, they might assume you're not as knowledgeable about the publishing process as you should be, or that you're not making every effort to present yourself as the best candidate for a project as detail-oriented and time-consuming as writing a book. (You'll find more on researching a name later in this chapter, and on choosing the right agent in Chapter 18.)

The First Sentence Hook

Imagine yourself an agent who's just come into the office for the day. You go through your mail, browsing quickly through each letter until—wham!—you read a first sentence that grabs your attention. Instead of tossing or deleting this letter, you read on. This first sentence is the all-important hook. You can support the hook with another sentence or two, as in some of the examples that follow, but you'll lose your reader's interest if the first sentence doesn't grab their attention.

There are four ways to "reel in the reader":

- **Fascinating fact or cutting-edge information.** In this type of hook, you quote a statistic or state a provocative fact that sets the premise of your book:

Over 15 million Americans suffer from depression or bipolar disorder—but only 1.5 million of them seek out help.

- **Question.** This hook is a variation in how to present your information:

  Did you know that over 15 million Americans suffer from depression or bipolar disorder—but only 1.5 million of them seek out help?

- **Story.** An anecdote can be a good way to grab attention, if it is provocative enough:

  There I was with two choices: pretend there was nothing mentally wrong with me or destroy my marriage. I chose the former.

- **Platform-based opening line.** A good hook can be your credentials, which demonstrate your marketability:

  For 20 years in my role as a professor of psychiatry at Harvard University, I have given over 1,000 presentations and written extensively in major journals about mental illness. I am considered one of the world's authorities on genetic causes of mental illness. This is the first time I've admitted I suffer from bipolar disease.

PUBLISHING PITFALLS

Just as there are hooks that work, there are also those that do not work. The point is to grab attention, so avoid starting with weak personal introductions or superfluous pleasantries. Avoid generic pitches. Your idea and your writing are essential. (But we'll say it: if you are famous, you can start with your name and it's likely you'll jump to the head of the list.)

The Pitch

After an effective opening comes the pitch, the "selling" sentence or sentences that describes your project:

- **Perfect pitch.** A pitch that works is one that sets up the rationale of your book and the need for it in the marketplace:

There are millions of Americans out there like me, so afraid of the stigma of mental illness that they live in shadow, realizing less than half of their potential. It is my hope that my memoir will inspire them to seek the help they need.

- **Too pitchy.** A pitch that doesn't work is one that exaggerates or makes the hook miss the water:

    What's wrong with these people! Why are they letting social stigma stand in their way? My book will enable these people to get the help they need.

- **Not enough pitch.** If even the pitch is boring, what will the book be like? A weak pitch misses the mark and will cause an agent or editor to lose interest in you:

    Mental illness is everywhere. I should know, I suffer from it myself. This is my story.

The Content

This is the substance of your query. Here you will offer how you'll answer the premise stated in your introductory sentences. Think of this as a short synopsis of the content:

- **Successful content.** A couple of solid informative sentences delve deeper into the need for this book:

    We're good at hiding our secrets. We misconstrue strength with stoicism. The bravest thing I ever did was admit I was mentally ill. This admission made me strong, but I had to hit rock bottom first.

- **Content overload.** Poor content can be either too lengthy or too off-course:

    Alzheimer's disease is a real problem today as baby boomers age. Many people with bipolar disorder find themselves in the role of caretaker for their elderly mothers or fathers.

Your Experience

Now it's time to show the editor or agent what you've got. You need to spell out why you are the person to write this book. If you haven't begun your query with your platform, now is the time to hammer it home. This can be done in two ways:

- **Your credentials.** State who you are and your special qualifications to write this book:

   I am a tenured professor of psychiatry at Harvard University and the academic community knows my name. I was the keynote speaker at the 2009 American Psychiatric Association Annual Conference. I have also been published in numerous psychiatric journals, including *Affective Disorders* and *Annals of Psychiatry.* What they don't know about me are details about my illness, which I have been blogging about. My blog, mysecretbipolarlife, is followed by 10,000 people each month. Readers have written how I inspire them and how I've helped them cope with their own illness, in the workplace and with family and friends.

- **Your experience.** Here, your experience is subtly sprinkled in with your book idea:

   As both a professor of psychiatry at Harvard University steeped in the clinical aspects of mental illness as well as a member of an online community made up of everyday people with bipolar disorder, I know firsthand the power of standing up to stigma. There is the tremendous need for a book that provides hope along with real-world help.

PUBLISHING PITFALLS

There is a fine line between stating your expertise and being grandiose about what you've accomplished. Be honest and realistic. Remember, with online research any agent can easily check your claims. Integrate your experience and avoid statements like "I am the greatest!" (unless, of course, you are Muhammad Ali).

The Book Title

You not only have the agent's attention, but you've outlined the need for your book. You've also shown why you are the best person to write it. If you haven't mentioned it earlier, now is the time to "open the curtain" and announce the book title:

- **The title says it all.** Whet the agent's appetite with a provocative title. Here's an example of good title placement:

    I realized that with my book, *Surviving Stigma: When to Know That You Need Help*, I could reach the millions of Americans living unhappy half-lives because of their fear of mental illness.

- **The flat title.** A weak announcement of your title can undo all the good you've done in your query, turning the question, "What?" into "So what?" This title is weak and poorly placed:

    My book is called *Surviving Stigma*, and I wrote it to address people with mental disease.

The Competition

A query letter may not require you to add details of the competition to your book, but acknowledging that there is competition shows two things:

- You know your audience.

- You are able to demonstrate how your book is different.

Writing about the competition needs to be done with clarity and without exaggeration. Sometimes a groundbreaking book in the marketplace or a hot trend should be cited to demonstrate that there is the potential of a sizeable readership for the topic. (Details about competitive works come in the proposal. For more on researching and presenting the competition, see Chapters 10 and 13.)

Here's an example of good competition recognition:

> Few books combine breadth of clinical experience with real-life trauma. I offer a unique perspective of help and hope. The category bestseller, *Bipolar Wisdom* by Anne Smith, M.D., lacks a patient's viewpoint.

This example is good because it mentions that the book the author gives as competition is the category bestseller, then goes on to give a specific benefit the author's proposed book offers that the bestseller lacks.

And here's an example of bad competition recognition:

> Some other books out there include *Mental Illness and Me*, *Mental Illness Clinical Trials*, *Am I Crazy?*, and countless more. But my book is different!

This example is bad because the competitive books appear to be picked at random, with no regard to how well they did in the market, and the author doesn't address how his or her book will be different and better.

The takeaway point? Vagueness is bad, and specifics are good—but make those specifics count! This isn't the place for overwhelming the agent or editor with details about the competition. A comprehensive competitive analysis will be included in your book proposal, as we discuss in Chapter 13.

The Close

Because the goal is to have the agent request to see more material, be sure to state details about your progress. Is the novel complete? Do you have a proposal and sample chapters available for review? Let the agent know.

Remember your manners: always end your query letter by thanking the agent for her time. It doesn't hurt to add, "I look forward to hearing from you," but make sure the "thank you" is the last sentence in your letter followed by your name and signature.

Your Contact Info

The hard work is done. All that's left in your query letter is the all-important contact information. Place it apart from the rest of your letter and state it clearly, concisely, and completely. Make sure to include the following:

- Main address, either home or office
- Main phone number
- Secondary phone number (provide your cell if it's not your main contact number)
- E-mail address
- Website address, if applicable (make sure the links work)
- LinkedIn information, if applicable, especially if your entry contains media information and/or other accomplishments
- Fax number, if applicable

Personalizing Your Query

Once your query letter is written, you can use it over and over again. Simply change the name and address of the person you're sending it to. There is an important caveat: if your query letter doesn't elicit a positive response, perhaps it is flawed. You will have to be objective and consider that your letter should be reworked.

Submitting your query may sound easy. Just get the name and address and you're all set. But there is an art to personalizing your query, too.

Research a Name

In order to ensure your query letter gets into the right hands, you need to get a name. Research is easy today, thanks to the Internet; almost every agent and publishing house has a website.

Research your publishing contact so you put together an appropriate list to approach. Agents will usually spell out the types of genres and categories they focus on. Be prepared to refine your query. Using our example of the bipolar professor, if an agency has a particular interest in health topics, you might feature that point in your letter. Another agency might specialize in memoirs, and a query that highlights the "real-life" story in the book will be better received.

If you are querying directly to a publishing house, it's more difficult to identify the appropriate editor. Most websites list books but not editors. But all is not lost: look for a fiction or nonfiction book on the site that is close to your area of interest or genre. Jot down the titles, go to your local library or bookstore, take the book off the shelf, and read the acknowledgments. Most authors thank their editors for their help.

If you don't know from the name whether the person you are writing to is male or female, try these tips:

- Call the publishing house and ask the switchboard operator. The operator will know, and you can avoid the embarrassment of addressing Mr. Pat Jones as "Ms."

- Go to the agent's website. The "About Us" or "Agent Bio" section should have a couple of "he's" or "she's" sprinkled in the text, cluing you in to the agent's gender.

- If all else fails, go for "Dear Editor." It's not the best way to personalize your letter, but it's far better than "To Whom It May Concern."

AGENTS' ADVICE

As agents, we pay attention to personal connections. If you know one of our authors, met us at a conference, or know one of our friends, mention this up front. We respond to this information.

Offline, there's always the library. Reference books such as the *Literary Marketplace* will give you the names and addresses of editors and agents.

Confirm the Name

Once you have a name of an editor or agent, you need to confirm it. People move around a lot and an editor might have recently moved to another firm. Similarly, an agent at a bigger agency might have set up his own agency.

How to confirm a name? Simply call the publisher or agency and ask. The operator will let you know if the person is still there; you can also ask for the exact title of the person. What about editors who do not work in the physical office? Although an operator may not know the answer, an administrator might. Ask to be connected to the editorial department. When you get a live person, ask if the editor in question works off-site and, if so, how she prefers to get submissions. (Resist the urge to verbally pitch your book on the phone.)

Get a Second Opinion

After you've written several versions of your query letter and have one you think will garner interest, it's time for a reality check. Before you send it off, show it around. If you know people who work in publishing, ask them to look it over and give you an honest opinion. If you know published authors, ask them to read your query letter and give you some feedback on how you can improve it. If you're in a writers' group (see Chapter 2), show the group your letter and ask for input.

Don't limit your review to writers. Your query letter is a marketing tool. If friends or family members are in sales, advertising, copywriting, or marketing, show them your letter and ask them if it sells you and your book effectively. They may have helpful suggestions to offer.

Even if you don't know writers or marketers, you still need to get a trusted second opinion before sending your query letter out into the world. Show it to friends, colleagues, or family members whose advice you respect. They may not know much about publishing, but they may be able to spot weaknesses in your letter.

On Your Mark, Get Set ...

Haste might make waste, but not when it comes to query letters. If you get a "yes, we'd like to see more" from an editor or agent, send your book proposal out immediately. Don't wait for her to forget about you or lose enthusiasm. "Strike when the iron is hot" is another cliché, but it is apt. It's important to label everything clearly. Always use the same subject line in follow-up correspondence with an agent or editor, including e-mails about your query, proposal, and manuscript. The subject line should include both your name and the book's title—another reason why a catchy title is important! You should use the phrase "requested material" in subsequent communications.

It's a good idea to keep a logbook of all your submissions. Note who received it, the date sent, and the query letter and/or other material sent to them. Record any follow-up.

> **AGENTS' ADVICE**
>
> This might sound like a no-brainer, but don't send out a query letter before you have written your book proposal. The query letter might go to the agent or editor first, but you need to have the proposal ready to be sent out as soon as possible when requested. Keep in mind, too, that the query letter might look easy because it's a short document, but in fact it can be the hardest piece to write.

Query Letter "Don'ts"

Some of the things to avoid in your query letter are obvious, but others are not. Here is a list of what to avoid:

- **Don't be self-effacing.** It might be charming in person, but your query letter has to show confidence. If you aren't sure about your experience or book idea, why should an agent or editor be?

- **Don't mention who has already received and rejected your work.** No one has to know who rejected you. It'll just make this editor or agent think twice about rejecting you, too.

- **Don't ask about money and deal terms.** There is a time and place for everything, and money discussions are *never* mentioned until you are in contract discussions with a publisher.

- **Don't request advice.** An editor or agent has to offer enough comments and changes to his signed authors. There is little time for giving suggestions to a stranger who has just written a query letter. On the other hand, if an editor or agent thinks your idea has promise, he might voluntarily offer you advice.

- **Don't tell your life story unless that experience relates directly to the book.** Yes, an editor or agent needs to know the reasons why you are an expert on your subject, but she does not need to know about your difficult children, financial woes, or mental state.

- **Don't mention how happy you would be to be published.** Yes, you would. And yes, an agent or editor knows that very, very well. No need to call it out.

- **Don't write another query letter to the same agent after you have been rejected.** A no is a no. Period. Move on to the next.

- **Don't make big promises.** You won't impress an agent or editor with "This idea is a surefire fit for *The Today Show!*", "Oprah will love this!", or "This will sell better than *The Da Vinci Code*."

- **Don't include off-color or silly remarks.** It might be all in good fun on your end, but inappropriate language can be very off-putting when it's sent to a stranger. Working with a writer is a long and involved commitment of time. Editors and agents want to know that they are working with clients who work professionally throughout the process.

If you haven't heard back from an editor or agent in over a month, you can write him again in a carefully crafted follow-up. If there have been new developments in your career or a new media development, or if you have made multiple submissions of your query letter and another agent has expressed interest, then by all means, share that information. If there is still no word, go on to the next person on your list.

The Least You Need to Know

- A query letter gives an agent or editor the first impression of your work, so make every word count and check it carefully.
- All effective query letters begin with a "hook" to grab the reader's attention and end with a closing "thank you."
- Do your homework when researching an agent or editor. Always double-check the name and where she works. Make sure she covers the genre you are working on.
- If you get a positive response, have your book proposal, sample chapters, or novel ready to send out immediately.
- Don't ask for advice, discuss money or book deals, or commit other "don'ts" in your query letter.

The E-Mail Query Letter

In This Chapter

- Make your first cyber impression count
- Creating a subject line that commands "Open!"
- Keeping it professional
- Grabbing their attention with concise, targeted content
- E-mail query letter do's and don'ts

Once upon a time, an aspiring writer sat down at a typewriter with a stack of paper and a supply of Wite-Out on the desk and laboriously banged out a query letter—which might have taken one full day or longer to produce.

No more. Although writing a "snail mail" query letter is occasionally the way to go, as we'll discuss in Chapter 5, today's publishing entry of choice is an electronic submission via e-mail. That means coming up with more than just a good grasp of grammar and a terrific idea. You need a punchy subject line, a professional style, and a "think short" mentality to make your e-mail query work.

First (Cyber) Impressions Count

Some publishing professionals estimate that only 1 percent of all queries ever result in representation. Put another way: for every 100 queries an agent reads, only *one* author has a shot at becoming a client. Yes, that means the odds are against you—but they aren't impossible. As the adage goes, "You gotta be in it to win it." Increase your chances of getting into that coveted 1 percent by following a few simple ground rules before you even keystroke the word "Dear."

We all know that first impressions matter, but with an e-mail query that's usually all you get. So that first contact has to be your best. But there is one fact that gives you an advantage: editors and agents *need* you because publishing has a pipeline that must be filled with new projects. They're not going to put their Spam Blocker on because it just might happen that one of those "deleted, do not pass go" queries is the next bestseller. Reading a stranger's e-mail query is part of their job. Therefore, you already have a built-in audience ready and willing to let their attention be grabbed.

But there is a big difference between reading a *stranger's* e-mail and reading a *strange* e-mail. Faster than you can say the word "attention," you can lose his if you write something strange or inappropriate in your query, such as "I have been a fan of yours for a long, long time," "You will love this book, I KNOW it," or "Please don't say no!" You need to be at your professional best right out of the cybergate, with a subject line that draws in the agent or editor.

HOT OFF THE PRESS

It is common for a single literary agent to receive over 100 e-mail queries each day. And that doesn't include all the other e-mails from publishers or existing clients. That means your e-mail has to be stellar to stand out among the rest.

A Subject Line That Sings

When your e-mail query arrives in an agent or editor's mailbox, one of the first things she'll notice is your subject line. This is the first opportunity for you to impress the agent or editor and start your relationship on a strong note. Your task is to create an intriguing subject line that will persuade the agent or editor to open and read your e-mail. Generic or bland subject lines don't succeed. Avoid one that simply says "Query." Also, don't skip this important point by leaving the subject line blank.

We've listed some sample subject lines next, organized per project, and rated them "good," "fair," and just plain "bad." Good subject lines will get the agent or editor to open your e-mail. (Notice in the following examples how they contain the book title.) Fair subject lines are "iffy." Although they may also contain the book title, the title may be too ambiguous or grandiose to make a good impression. And bad subject lines? These may or may not contain the book title, and be too vague and generic. They'll be deleted as quickly as those spam e-mails to make money fast by working at home.

For a memoir:

- **Good:** *Cinderella Nights, Stepmother Days.* This subject line is good because it's an attention-grabbing title that positions the book in a way that will resonate with stepmoms who struggle between their love for their spouse and their issues with their inherited families.

- **Fair:** *My Life as a Stepmom.* Okay, this says what it is. But frankly, what is compelling about your life, unless you're famous in your own right? The subject line needs more punch.

- **Bad:** *Memoir idea.* Unless you're Elizabeth Taylor, Sandra Bullock, or another famous stepmom, no agent or editor is going to get past this to see what you actually have to say. Remember the importance of the hook!

For a how-to book on quilting:

- **Good:** *Covered with Love: 20 Easy Bed Quilts for Giving and Sharing.* This subject line is sweet but also specific, and it includes not only the number of patterns but that all-important word "easy."

- **Fair:** *Original Designs for Bed Quilts.* This subject line says what the book's about—bed quilts—and "original" is a strong sell, like "easy." But it doesn't say how many projects are in the book, and it doesn't make these bed quilts stand out from the thousands of patterns already on the market.

- **Bad:** *Quilt ideas.* This sounds like the author hasn't thought through the project before submitting it. Vague and, again, there's nothing to capture an agent's or editor's interest.

For a cookbook:

- **Good:** *Moonpies Are from Mars, Scones Are from Venus: Bringing Couples Together with 150 Delicious Desserts.* This catchy subject line is a good play on a title everyone knows. It backs its cuteness with a descriptive subtitle and a specific number of recipes.

- **Fair:** *The Guy-Friendly Dessert Book.* There's nothing wrong with guy cookbooks, but that's not really what this book's about. And the title's not specific enough to draw an agent or editor in.

- **Bad:** *Desserts for Everyone.* This title is too general. No one could guess from this title what the book is really about.

For a mystery:

- **Good:** *Death Corn Five: A Culinary Mystery.* The funny pun is a winner. Nobody's going to forget this title!

- **Fair:** *The Last Picnic.* This is promising, but not as grabby as the "good" title.

- **Bad:** *Food Poisoning: A Mystery.* Who wants to read about food poisoning? Thanks but no thanks.

Once you've grabbed an agent's or editor's attention, it's important to add your own name to the subject line of all subsequent correspondence as well as the book's title—for example, "Jenna Maury, *Death Corn Five.*" From this point on, you can skip the subtitle.

AGENTS' ADVICE

As the saying goes, "There are riches in the niches." Be specific. A book on a post-pregnancy weight-loss program is more intriguing than a query simply headlined "weight loss."

Keep It Professional

E-mail has a way of feeling very informal, especially because we use it for everything from updating our Facebook status to instant-messaging a friend sitting three seats away at a concert. Even at work, we may use little smiley faces and other emoticons and abbreviations such as LOL to make sure the recipient doesn't misinterpret an ironic phrase as a nasty remark or a nanosecond rant as an angry riff.

But when it comes to e-mail queries, you have to be extra careful. Don't let the sometimes casual etiquette e-mail rules invite you into being too informal in your query pitch. You must think of your query as a business pitch. Everything about it—from the e-mail address it comes from to the name of the person to whom it's addressed—needs to be polished and set up to impress.

Use a Professional E-Mail Address

In the early days of Internet addresses, people often chose e-mail address names that added some personal characteristic, like bosoxfan2006@agg.com or 3kidsandadog@llm.com. As a professional writer, you need to set up an e-mail account that reflects your professionalism. This level of detail may seem excessive, but we know that image matters. An account that signals your devotion to butterflies, bees, Lady Gaga, or Apple may not advance your cause.

AGENTS' ADVICE

You need to rethink what you know about writing a business letter: the date, the editor/agent's address, your return address, and so on. In an e-mail, the date's right there in the recipient's mailbox. You don't have to do a thing. The e-mail address is the "to" line—and that's a one-line .com or .net address rather than a five-liner with title, company, street, city, and state. Yes, the editor or agent will need your contact information, but not up front. Unless your name is Dan Brown or Stephanie Meyer, the content of your e-mail is what matters first—followed by your contact info.

Submit to One Agent or Editor with Each E-Mail

E-mail simplifies communication. We can quickly compose a letter and send it to multiple recipients. It's as easy as cutting and pasting. That's all well and good for year-end letters, but not for getting your book published. Querying one agent or editor in each e-mail submission sends the message that you have a strong interest in working with that one person and that you admire her list of clients and books she represents. Querying multiple agents or editors simultaneously suggests that you are casting your net too wide and not submitting strategically.

An agent or editor can tell if you've sent one query to multiple people even if you send it out as a blind cc; when he gets an e-mail and the "To" and "From" are the same e-mail address, he knows it's a multiple submission. Another clear sign of a mass submission is when the address header indicates "To: Undisclosed Recipients."

A generic salutation is another dead giveaway that the writer didn't want to bother individualizing the e-mail. This is the first thing that an agent will see from you and it's important that you get off to a good start.

Address the Correct Person

This might sound like a no-brainer to you, but almost every day we receive queries addressed to "Submission Department," "Literary Agent," or "To Whom It May Concern." When sending your query letter to agents or editors, make sure you always address them by name.

It's not any better if you send your query to someone who no longer works at the agency or publishing house, misspell the name, or refer to a Mr. as a Ms. and vice versa. If you don't take the time and effort to find out the correct name of the person to whom you're sending your query, why should he take the time to look at your query?

A search engine such as Google is a good place to start your research to find an agent or editor. Almost every agency has a website, so you can continue your research online. But don't rely on that information—it may be old. Once you have a name, call the publishing house or agent to ensure that the person in question is still there.

Other ways to get this information are through LinkedIn, publisherslunch.com, or your public library's most up-to-date *Literary Marketplace*. (See Appendix B for other online resources.)

> **AGENTS' ADVICE**
>
> Remember, if you have any connection to the agent through another client or mutual acquaintance, be sure to mention that fact in your e-mail query.

Other rules for writing salutations include these:

- Avoid "To whom it may concern."
- Avoid "Sir or Madam."
- Avoid "Submissions" or "Submissions Department."
- Avoid an unprofessional greeting that could signal you are addressing multiple people simultaneously, like "Hello Agent."

Following these recommendations will make your salutation professional and appropriate.

Content Savvy

Okay, you've selected a powerful subject line, and you've identified the right person, address, and salutation. It's time now for the focal point of your message: the e-mail query content. You need to be succinct but still maintain the agent's or editor's interest. Organize your copy and avoid large, meandering blocks of type that might cause the agent to lose focus. Short, crisp paragraphs are best to hold the attention of your reader. It's a fine balance, true, but if you keep to the following suggestions, you'll be able to walk it just fine:

- Start your letter with a "hook" to get the agent's or editor's interest, and then go right into your idea.

- Keep the body of the content to one or two paragraphs (100 to 200 words total).

- End with a little bit about yourself (especially if you are presenting yourself as an expert on the subject).

- Always end with a gracious thank-you and closing.

- Add your contact information at the end.

AGENTS' ADVICE

Remember your platform. Anything that can help you promote yourself to the agent or editor you can use to your advantage in your query: a regular radio show or TV segment, a syndicated newspaper column, a huge Facebook fan page, a large following on Twitter, a successful website, or a seminar business, for example. You can use any or all of these to promote your marketability. And, if pertinent enough, it can even be your hook.

Take a look at the following query letter. It's poorly written and lacks focus and distinction:

Dear Mr. Samson:

In today's economy people are going crazy and sick with worry about their jobs and families because their savings are disappearing into thin air. You can't pick up a newspaper that doesn't mention these issues. I can help because I am a financial planner. I teach a night course at the local high school where I live with my wife and three children in New Jersey. My book will help you. I am Henry Brown and my book is *Debt Be Gone*.

My friends and neighbors tell me they like what I have to say and my tips have helped them learn how to save money. I want to share my tips with the world. I want to send my proposal to you. You can reach me at iliketojog@aom.com.

Let me hear from you.

Sincerely,

Henry Brown

In this next query letter, we've tightened the focus and added complete contact information:

Dear Mr. Samson:

In today's economy people's savings are shrinking at an alarming rate. Americans are putting off vacations, home renovations, and retirement. I am Henry Brown, CPA, whose financial planning program has been franchised through the country and adopted by over 500,000 happy customers. My book, *Debt Be Gone*, is based on my program and shows how to stop worrying about debt and develop a plan for financial recovery.

I have a newsletter e-mail list of 150,000 subscribers, and my website, www.debtbegone.com, receives 25,000 hits each month. I have a proposal ready to submit for your review.

Please contact me at HenryBrown@debtbegone.com or 914-555-1212.

I look forward to hearing of your interest. Thank you for your consideration.

Sincerely,

Henry Brown, CPA
14 Oak Drive
Smithfield, AZ 01234

Why is the second e-mail better? It's concise—under 150 words—while getting the points across. But there are other reasons, too. We've put our comments in bold and brackets to show you what makes this e-mail a winner.

Dear Mr. Samson:

In today's economy people's savings are shrinking at an alarming rate. Americans are putting off vacations, home renovation, and retirement. **[Good introduction of a universal problem.]** I am Henry Brown, CPA, whose financial planning program has been franchised through the country and adopted by over 500,000 happy customers. My book, *Debt Be Gone*, is based on my program and shows how to stop worrying about debt and develop a plan for financial recovery. **[Establishes book content and platform quickly. The professional credentials are a must and the author has them; a good targeted audience that is clearly identified.]**

I have a newsletter e-mail list of 150,000 subscribers, and my website, www.debtbegone.com, receives 25,000 hits each month. I have a proposal ready to submit for your review. **[Excellent details about platform continue; this author sounds like a professional we might like to work with.]**

Please contact me at HenryBrown@debtbegone.com or 914-555-1212.

I look forward to hearing of your interest. Thank you for your consideration. **[Note the polite tone throughout and the closing "thank you."]**

Sincerely,

Henry Brown, CPA
14 Oak Drive
Smithfield, AZ 01234 **[Top marks for providing full contact information and professional credentials.]**

E-Mail Query Do's and Don'ts

Understanding the basic structure of an e-mail query is one thing, but there are still a few tips to keep in mind to ensure that your e-mail is polished and professional—and, most important of all, gets a positive response.

Typos and Grammatical Errors

Glaring errors like typos and grammatical mistakes will get you noticed—in the wrong way. Remember, this is an industry that celebrates the written word. If you can't get the basic elements right at the start, an agent won't have confidence in your ability to write a whole book. Yes, there is spell-check function and a grammar checker, and you should use it, but we all know how mistakes slip through that program. Don't let your hard work get sidelined because of careless errors. Our advice? Proofread your query letter—and then proofread it again. Printing it out and letting it sit overnight enables you to read it with fresh eyes the next day. Or ask your part-ner, friend, or colleague to read your work. She may find typos you missed, and give you some important tips about the content of your query as well. Finally, before pushing Send, print out your query to ensure it is perfect, and then e-mail it to yourself to make sure the formatting works in transmission.

PUBLISHING PITFALLS

Don't use ALL CAPITAL LETTERS in your e-mail query; this will only an-noy your recipient. Using capitals doesn't enhance your point; rather, it distracts and is often viewed as shouting at the recipient. Using too many exclamation points won't win you any extra consideration, either.

Consistency Is Key

Your task is to make your submission straightforward, memorable, and easy for an agent to review. A surefire way of achieving this at the outset is to always be consistent in your contact information. If you go by "Timothy" professionally, don't refer to yourself some-times as "Tim." Don't use your real name and then switch to a pen name, and certainly don't use one name in your return address and provide another in your contact information. Your e-mail address and phone numbers should be easy to spot in the query and must always be the same. If you're a woman who uses both her maiden and mar-ried name, avoid any confusion by ensuring that the e-mail address and contact name are identical. Help the agent or editor stay focused on your work by making it easy for her to identify and find you.

Follow the Guidelines

Every agent has a preference for query submissions. Whether it's standard procedure at a literary agency or an individual choice, the guidelines they present must be followed. Otherwise, all your good work will be for naught as the agent in question deletes your e-mail for not following the rules. You can find these guidelines on an agency website, or in a reference book such as *Literary Marketplace* at your local library.

But wherever you find the guidelines, it's important to stick to them. For example, one agent we know likes to have a CV (curriculum vitae) or resumé embedded in every query request. If you don't follow her rules, she'll reject you without reading a word. Unless the agent you are approaching specifies that she will accept attachments, do not send them. Unsolicited attachments may scare agents because of the fear of computer viruses.

PUBLISHING PITFALLS

You are about to enter a professional relationship, so use a professional tone. Avoid anything that might sound charming to your friends but too friendly or familiar to an agent or editor. We wouldn't recommend writing "How are you?" in a query, nor should you send personal photos or anything else that you might send to a friend. You want to invite interest from an agent, not a friendship.

Agents and editors also have guidelines about what they're interested in and look to represent. Do your homework. You shouldn't send a fiction query to someone who doesn't represent fiction authors. Align your work with an agent or editor who has expertise in your genre—for example, don't send your historical novel to an agency that specializes in children's books. Always target your submission to avoid wasting time.

Be Truthful

When pitching your concept to an agent or editor, it is essential that your statements and statistics are meaningful and substantive. With the Internet, your claims can be checked. Don't embellish any sales histories, but if you have accurate numbers of any prior publishing history, online newsletter subscribers, or followers of your blog, by all means include them in your query. Don't make false assertions and say that you're a registered nurse when, in reality, you've been taking care of an aging parent.

The truth of the matter is that if you lie in a query and an agent or editor shows interest in you, sooner or later your lie will come out. Some lies are easier to uncover than others (like whether or not you've had any short stories or articles published). Others are harder (like whether or not you attended a writers' conference) but the truth will always come out. Have some faith in yourself and rely on your own real accomplishments.

PUBLISHING PITFALLS

Avoid words and phrases such as "extraordinary," "one of a kind," "guaranteed money-maker," or "groundbreaking." These phrases might sound like surefire bets to you, but they signal hyperbole and diminish credibility. An agent has probably read all these words many times before.

The Least You Need to Know

- Many publishers today prefer electronic submission via e-mail.
- A good subject line grabs an agent or editor's attention in a positive way right from the start.
- From your salutation to your closing, make sure everything about your e-mail query is polished and professional.
- Limit the content of your e-mail query to a few succinct paragraphs that maintain the agent or editor's interest.
- Maximize your chances for success by proofreading your e-mail query carefully, supplying consistent contact information, following the guidelines, and being honest about your accomplishments.

The "Snail Mail" Query Letter

In This Chapter

- When to send your query through the mail
- The preferred format
- Rules for success
- Making your query letter stand out
- The extras that get you noticed

You may think that paper mail has gone the way of the Walkman or VCR, but, in reality, some publishers and agents prefer the written word that comes in "snail mail" over an e-mail.

Keep in mind that even in today's electronic world, people who work in publishing have great affection for and interest in the written, printed word. Sometimes it's the physical properties of a proposal that are best displayed in a hardcopy. For others, it is simply office management, a way to keep query submissions separate from ongoing client and publisher files, making it easier to manage both. Check with the agency or publisher you are sending your query to for the preferred method of submission.

The Snail Mail Advantage

With a paper query, agents and editors can see, in black and white, what you are offering. They can look over your letter and think about it without forgetting about it, as they might more easily do with an e-mail query (see Chapter 4). Paper query letters are a visual reminder of what you have submitted.

For example, let's say you are an expert jewelry-maker and your work is sold online and at select high-end craft fairs. Your idea is to write a book about making jewelry from recycled products. Your work might need to be seen to sell itself best. A sampling of photographs of some of your pieces might make the most persuasive case for your book. Snail mail can be a great opportunity for you. With a paper query letter, you can take a bit more time to get to the point. You have more opportunity to impress an agent or editor.

The permanence of a paper query can also be a foil: everything you write takes on a strong significance. A typo will be glaring. The tone will be more important. The first impression will be stronger. With a snail mail query letter, there are other variables to consider.

AGENTS' ADVICE

It might be a strategic choice to send a snail mail query. If there is one key chart, photo, illustration, or diagram that makes the case for your project and may not format properly online, be too big a file for an agent to accept, and is best seen in hardcopy, you might elect to print and mail your query.

Formatting Your Letter

The format most agents prefer, and in which the majority of query letters are sent, follows a traditional format, as outlined in the following table. (However, if an agent specifies a particular format, and you want to submit your query letter to that agent, create a modified version that conforms to his requirements.)

The Standard Query Letter Format

Element	Format
Margins	1" from top/bottom/sides
Spacing	Single-spaced

Element	Format
Paragraphs	1 line between paragraphs
Font	12 pt.
Typeface	Times New Roman, Courier, and Arial are the most common
Pages	1 page is best
Return address/your address	At top: either flush left or 4" from left-hand margin
Date	Skip 1 line after return address; underneath return address
Inside address/their address	Skip 4 lines; flush left
Salutation	Skip 1 line after inside address; end with colon or comma
Body/content	Skip 1 line after salutation: 3 to 5 paragraphs; flush left
Sign-off	Skip 1 line after body; flush left
Signature	Skip 3–4 lines for handwritten name; flush left; type name
Attachments	Skip 1 line after signature; flush left; /Attach

Rules of the Paper Trail

There are several rules when it comes to writing a query by snail mail:

- Use a computer keyboard. Publishing is computer-driven, and using a typewriter—or worse, pen and ink—sends a message that you're living in another century, which could spell problems for the editor. Editors expect manuscripts to be delivered in electronic files written in Microsoft Word—in fact, many publishing contracts specify this—so you should be fluent in Word before you submit a proposal.

- Print on 8½x11" 20-pound paper. Think of the business letters you have received either at work or at home. They might have different logos and different-colored fonts, but they are all on this size and weight paper. It is standard practice.

- Save the blue or pink paper for the next baby shower invite. Query letters should be typed on neutral stationery, either white or light cream. Let the idea speak for itself. Recycled paper is not necessary, but might be clever if you are proposing a book on green living. And, of course, it's a good way to reduce your carbon footprint.

- Remember that a query is all business. Unless you know the person you are writing very well, keep your note formal. Address the agent or publisher as "Dear Mr." or "Dear Ms." Keep slang out of your content.

- Include your complete address, including street, e-mail, and phone number. Although you are querying by mail, the agent may choose to contact you by e-mail or phone. Make sure this information is included in your letter.

- Be sure to include a self-addressed, stamped envelope for a printed response—especially if the literary agency's website specifies this.

HOT OFF THE PRESS

Plain bond is a good, solid writing paper that works well in printers and faxes. The name comes from the type of paper that was originally used for government bonds.

All About the Content

You can format your letter to perfection and pick out the most expensive white paper. You can have three people read your query letter to make sure it's grammatically correct, and three more review it to make sure it's letter- and punctuation-perfect. But if you can't get the reader's attention, none of that matters.

Whether snail mail or e-mail, content is king. You need these:

- A first paragraph that grabs hold of the editor or agent, one that demonstrates why this book needs to be published

- An idea explained clearly and provocatively, combined with the reasons why this book must be written

- A platform that highlights your career or expertise in the subject and also shows that you know your audience

- A sentence or two about the competition and potential audience

- Easily found contact information

Here is an example of a bad snail mail query letter, from its format to its content:

May 10, 2010

Joan Smith

100 Tarry Road
New Brunswick, NJ 07000

Ms. Patricia Jones
Jones & Jones Literary Agency
1111 Side Street
New York, NY 10000

Hi Patty!

One of the most overused four-letter words in the English language is diet—but not in the "lose weight now" way you think. (Bet you thought I was thinking of something else!) From soybeans to soy ice cream, free-range chickens to free-range eggs, most of us know what is good for us and what is bad. Unfortunately, we've taken the joy of eating out of the equation. Food has become a national obsession and many Americans have sworn off everything from pasta to just about anything cooked. Think raw, raw, raw!!

I'm not saying we shouldn't eat healthy, but I do believe in the Greeks ancient motto: "Moderation in all things." As a nutritionist—and gourmet cook—I've learned to create a balance between food bliss and food blah. The result is Food Bliss, an amazing program for my patients who are sick. It really works!!

It is time for me to share Food Bliss with the world. As a cook and my family's rising star, I guarantee it will make a lot of money!

Please let me know if you are interested in Food Bliss as soon as you can.

Call me?

Joan

From the inappropriate intimacy to the exaggeration, from the absence of a platform to an inconsistent format, this letter is a mess. Here is how to make it better:

> Joan Smith
> 100 Tarry Road
> New Brunswick, NJ 07000
> www.foodbliss.com
> joansmith@foodbliss.com
> 999-555-1234
>
> May 10, 2010

Or:

Joan Smith
100 Tarry Road
New Brunswick, NJ 07000
www.foodbliss.com
joansmith@foodbliss.com
999-555-1234

May 10, 2010

Ms. Patricia Jones
Jones & Jones Literary Agency
1111 Side Street
New York, NY 10000

Dear Ms. Jones: (or Dear Ms. Jones,)

One of the most overused four-letter words in the English language is diet, but not in the "lose weight now" way you think. From soybeans to soy ice cream, free-range chickens to free-range eggs, most of us know what is good for us and what is bad. Food has become a national obsession and trends abound. Americans have sworn off everything from pasta to cooked food. We have lost the joy of food.

I'm not saying we shouldn't eat healthy, but I do believe in the Greeks' ancient motto: "Moderation in all things." As a registered dietician and a graduate of the American Culinary Institute, my work has appeared in several national magazines including *Food & Wine*, *Good Housekeeping*, and *Woman's Day*. I have developed a loyal following on Facebook and I share my program that creates a balance between food bliss and food blah on my website, www.foodbliss.com.

Now I plan to write a book on the program called *Food Bliss: Gourmet Meals for Health and Happiness*. Hundreds of my patients have been on my program and improved their health concerns and lost weight. *Food Bliss* has succeeded with my patients, and I want to share the program and recipes with other people who need to eat well and wisely. I have done an exhaustive search of available titles in the healthy-cooking category, and only one is authored by a classically trained chef such as myself.

My proposal, including a strong marketing plan for *Food Bliss*, is available for review and I would like to send it to you.

You can reach me at the above address, at 999-555-1234, or at joansmith@foodbliss.com.

Thank you for your consideration.

All best,

Joan Smith

Joan Smith

Why is this query letter better? The obvious reason is the clear and concise formatting. But there are other reasons. We've annotated the letter below so that you can see the subtle and not-so-subtle reasons this is heads above the other example:

Joan Smith
100 Tarry Road
New Brunswick, NJ 07000
www.foodbliss.com
joansmith@foodbliss.com
999-555-1234

May 10, 2010

Or: [Either return address and date format is correct.]

Joan Smith
100 Tarry Road
New Brunswick, NJ 07000
www.foodbliss.com
joansmith@foodbliss.com
999-555-1234

[Skip 1 line]

May 10, 2010

[Skip 1 line]

Ms. Patricia Jones
Jones & Jones Literary Agency
1111 Side Street
New York, NY 10000

[Skip 1 line]

Dear Ms. Jones: (or Dear Ms. Jones,) **[In today's world, using a comma doesn't diminish a letter's formality.]**

One of the most overused four-letter words in the English language is diet, but not in the "lose weight now" way you think. From soybeans to soy ice cream, free-range chickens to free-range eggs, most of us know what is good for us and what is bad. Food has become a national obsession and trends abound.

Americans have sworn off everything from pasta to cooked food. We have lost the joy of food. [**This is a provocative opening paragraph.**]

I'm not saying we shouldn't eat healthy, but I do believe in the Greeks' ancient motto: "Moderation in all things." As a registered dietician and a graduate of the American Culinary Institute [**Now introducing the all-important platform ...**], my work has appeared in several national magazines including *Food & Wine, Good Housekeeping,* and *Woman's Day.* [**The author has a lot of experience and visibility!**] I have developed a loyal following on Facebook and I share my program that creates a balance between food bliss and food blah on my website, www.foodbliss.com. [**This paragraph gets to the point—leading up to the book idea.**]

Now I plan to write a book on the program called *Food Bliss: Gourmet Meals for Health and Happiness.* Hundreds of my patients have been on my program and improved their health concerns and lost weight. *Food Bliss* has succeeded with my patients, and I want to share the program and recipes with other people who need to eat well and wisely. [**Here, the author gives the agent or publisher another taste of her expertise.**] I have done an exhaustive search of available titles in the healthy-cooking category, and only one is authored by a classically trained chef such as myself. [**The author shows she has done her homework in addressing the competition. She also shows that there is very little competition for her book out there.**]

My proposal, including a strong marketing plan for *Food Bliss,* is available for review [**The author reiterates that she has a thought-out platform to boot.**] and I would like to send it to you.

You can reach me at the above address, at 999-555-1234, or at joansmith@foodbliss.com. [**Contact information is critical.**]

Thank you for your consideration. [**Always close with "Thank you."**]

All best,

Joan Smith

Joan Smith [**This letter leaves enough room for the signature to be handwritten, too.**]

Beyond Formatting

Understanding the structure of a snail mail query letter gives you the professional edge you need when writing to a stranger. But adding a few extras to the presentation can make your letter stand out from the rest.

All Stamps Are Not Alike

It's important to remember that this is a business correspondence and standard-issue postage stamps are best. This isn't the time to showcase your personally designed stamp featuring your puppy.

A Basic Font

There are hundreds of different fonts and point sizes you can use, but for a query letter, stick with the neutral basics. Here are several of the most popular fonts we've seen in query letters and proposals:

- Times New Roman
- Courier
- Arial
- Tahoma
- Microsoft Sans Serif
- Verdana

- Trebuchet MS
- Georgia

Personalize Your Stationery

The days of going to a stationery store to get individualized paper and envelopes still exist, but more and more people are creating their own *letterhead* at home on the computer. Not only does your Word program have templates you can use, but there are companies that can help you create the look you want. Do a search online for customized stationery and at least five pages of links show up.

DEFINITION

Letterhead is the printed or engraved address, which also may include e-mail address and website, at the top of a letter. Business letterhead will usually have a logo design along with the address.

One caveat is this: like everything else in a query letter, your stationery needs to look business-friendly. Avoid hearts, cartoon characters, "From the desk of ..." taglines, and gold leaf. Pick out a neutral color and create a letterhead template you can use over and over again.

To make your query letter less "snail" and more "mail," save your stationery template on your computer. Save the composed query letter on your computer, too. This way, you can cut and paste with each new letter—but don't forget to change the date and the name and address of each recipient.

Keep in mind that the envelope you mail to the agent is part of the presentation. Don't use your holiday labels, write with a marker, or tape printed labels on the face of the envelope. Keep it clean and professional. Use legal-size envelopes, and match them to the paper you've used for the letter: white with white or cream with cream.

The Least You Need to Know

- Using a snail mail query letter gives you the opportunity to include a critical visual element to help explain your work.
- Use a business letter format when composing your query that includes a commonly used typeface, a 12-pt. font, 1-inch margins, and single spacing.
- Always use a computer to type your query letter; never hand-write it or type it on a typewriter.
- Focus on the content, starting with a paragraph that grabs the reader's attention, and ending with your contact information and a "thank you."
- Pay attention to details: choose the right stamp and envelope, and create a professional-looking letterhead.

The Nonfiction Query Letter

In This Chapter

- Learning the fundamentals of nonfiction queries
- Highlights of good query writing
- Sample query letters for different categories

Nonfiction is a broad term. Its literal definition is anything that isn't fiction, which means it's based on fact. This encompasses a lot of territory, from cookbooks to true crime, memoirs to travel, and history to test prep … any fact-based books. The best way to start to write a successful nonfiction query letter is to know what subcategory best describes your nonfiction work.

First Things First

The fundamentals for all query letters stay pretty much the same, despite the category. Your nonfiction proposal should be ready before you start querying agents. A good technique is to read your proposal, pull out the three to five most persuasive points, and make them the core of your query presentation. You need to start with a "hook" to grab the agent or editor's attention, work in the reasons for your book and why you should write it, and, ultimately, leave him asking for more.

Query Letter Highlights

Before we go into category-specific query letters, let's briefly go over the highlights for good query letter writing. (Review Chapter 3 for query letter basics, Chapter 4 for sending an e-mail query, and Chapter 5 for sending a "snail mail" query.)

- Aim for a one-page query letter or about 150 words if using e-mail.

- Do your research. Become knowledgeable about your category. Find out what books are selling and why. Understand how your project fits in the category. Make sure you can answer the question: "Why does the world need my book?"

- Grab their attention right from the start. Pull out a key fact, statistic, or trend from your proposal, one that will stop the agent in her tracks and demonstrate both the audience and the need for the book.

- Think about your personal or work history, your resumé or experience, and be prepared to detail how it supports the content of the work. Remember your expertise must align with the area you are writing about. If you are a cookbook writer, you might be a caterer; own a restaurant or take-out shop; blog about food, cooking, or restaurants; or appear on a cooking program. For example, one of our medical authors is a successful surgeon at a major hospital. He also writes a wine column in a major publication. This unique biographical detail would be the key line in the query letter that pitches his interest in writing a book about American wineries—not the fact that he's a surgeon.

- Build your marketing platform. You should have worked hard at developing your platform before thinking it's time to write a book. Experience usually equals expertise, and leads to visibility and marketability. This is what publishers are demanding, so editors and agents are looking for that information in your query. We'll discuss how to present your platform in Chapter 14, but for now, start by asking yourself these questions:

- Do I have a website?

- Do I have a Facebook fan page?

- Am I capturing e-mail names from visitors to my website?

- Do I have a magazine or online column?

- Do I make TV appearances, or am I a guest on radio shows?

- Do I have regular seminars and speaking engagements?

- Do I have a list of credentialed authorities in the field who will offer quotes and endorsements to support my work?

- Does my work offer a special relationship with an organization or corporation that would likely buy bulk copies of my work at publication or promote my book on its website?

- Provide full contact information. If you don't provide your contact information, including a working phone number and e-mail address, the agent or editor will never be able to contact you with any potential good news.

- Always be prepared. Have your book proposal ready to send out as soon as you get a positive response.

What's Your Nonfiction Category?

We've received hundreds of nonfiction query letters on hundreds of different topics over the years. But every one of these letters fits in a certain nonfiction subcategory, each with its unique "take" on the general query. Let's go over the most popular nonfiction categories to see where you fit in. For each category, we've included annotated examples of poor and good query letters.

The Memoir Query

A *memoir* is a narrative that focuses on a personal time, experiences, or people in your life. The story may be all about you, but it has to be universal enough to interest other people besides your wife, your husband, or your Uncle Bob. (Think *A Year in Provence* by Peter Mayles.) Don't confuse a memoir with an *autobiography*, which is a history of a person's whole life, such as the life story of a president or head of a major corporation. Autobiographies are pitched and sold differently than memoirs. An autobiography of a famous person is dependent on the profile of the subject; the memoir is often driven by the broad appeal of the story and the writing.

> **HOT OFF THE PRESS**
>
> Memoirs can be tricky. Many editors and agents consider them a hybrid of fiction and nonfiction, but a key point for a memoir is the quality of the writing. Some publishing professionals may want to see the entire manuscript before saying "yes." Before you send off your memoir query, make sure you have at least half of it written; a proposal may not be enough.

In a memoir query, you need to get right into the elements of the story that demonstrate why your experience would be compelling to an audience. The writing must make the reader care.

Here is an annotated example of a bad memoir query letter, followed by a good one:

Dear Mr. Little,

I've just finished writing about my life, a story of sex, drugs, and greed that everyone will find inspiring. **[Another one? What makes this one more than just another cliché?]** Several people I know have read it and think it's really good. **[Of course they did—they know you.]**

Please let me know if you'd like to read it. I'm almost done with the writing! **[Too little information about your life, what you are doing now, and what the book is about.]** You can reach me at carlrichards@downonthefarm.com.

Thanks! **[The exclamation mark is unnecessary.]**

Carl Richards

Dear Mr. Little,

There are hundreds of stories about overcoming addiction, but mine is a little different: I spent 20 years as head of a Fortune 500 company without anyone noticing my problem. **[An interesting twist!]**

I am no longer at the company. I've found peace in a quiet life in the country, running a small B&B and an organic farm where our guests work in the field during the day, learning about raising their food. We have received national awards and media coverage, drawing visitors from around the nation. My memoir, called *Down on the Farm: From Crackhead CEO to Contented Country Life*, not only details how I hid my addiction while in a high-pressure job, but also what my guests are like—and how I handle them—at the B&B and farm. I am in discussion with a film company that will produce a documentary about our work. **[A second good twist. It could create some good subplots. And an exciting marketing and publicity opportunity if the documentary is done.]** I've included a photograph of last week's guests and harvest. **[The visual will add authenticity and help the query stand out in the agent's or publisher's mind.]**

I've written three quarters of the book and a detailed outline of the remaining chapters. **[That should be enough to make a decision.]**

You can reach me at carlrichards@downonthefarm.com or at 999-555-1234. **[Two choices are better than one!]**

I hope you'll want to see my work, and thank you for your consideration.

Sincerely,

Carl Richards

The Cookbook Query

Part of the challenge with a cookbook query is getting the agent or editor to envision your delicious food without seeing or tasting it. But with enough tantalizingly named dishes, and information about your experience, you may hear back faster than you can say, "Bon appétit!"

Here is an annotated example of a bad cookbook query, followed by a good one:

Dear Ms. Big,

I'm writing you because you published Julia Childs' cookbooks. **[Kudos to the editor, but she or he already knows that. Just because you've done your homework doesn't mean you get an automatic read. And misspelling Julia's name (it's Julia Child, not Childs) is certainly not going to impress the editor.]**

My cookbook, *God Bless* is all about Thanksgiving, soup to nuts. I have a delicious turkey recipes, desserts like apple crisp, and even appetizers that go perfectly with a traditional Thanksgiving feast. **[Nothing in this paragraph is mouthwatering or different; it doesn't say anything unexpected. It doesn't offer any platform. And the grammar is poor, to boot.]**

All the recipes in *God Bless* have been tested in hundreds of family dinners through the years. **[By whom? And what are your credentials? What makes your book stand out from the competition?]** Please let me know if you'd like a "taste"! **[Too cute for a formal business letter.]**

You can reach me at blessme@ilovebonbons.com. I look forward to your sitting down at my table! **[Too cute, and the e-mail address is unprofessional.]**

Thankfully yours, **[Once again, too cute.]**

Sally Lee

Dear Ms. Big,

Turkey may be the centerpiece of a Thanksgiving dinner, but what everybody waits for is dessert. I specialize in home-style pies that I sell year 'round in my bakeshop. My pies are featured in four well-known food catalogs, including Williams-Sonoma and Stonewall Kitchen, as well as the King Arthur Flour Company and Vermont Country Store websites. We sell over 100 kinds of pies, and create new ones regularly; we sell over 2,000 pies each week. For Thanksgiving, our business swells to over 15,000 pies a week. **[An example of finding uniqueness in a niche, and the sales numbers impress, too.]**

My cookbook, *God Bless Pies*, is all about classic Thanksgiving favorites with many wonderful twists, such as Bourbon Pecan Pie, Golden Apple Tart, Nutty Pumpkin Pie, and many more. All are easy to make and guaranteed to please. **[The author highlights some different-sounding recipes and also mentions how easy they are to prepare.]**

Based on the recipes I've perfected over the years, the awards I've won, and my clientele—including several A-list celebrities, such as Sarah Jessica Parker and Carrie Underwood, who have told me they would endorse my book **[Here's the expertise—and a great platform!]** *God Bless Pies* can help the home baker bring a delicious and more unusual addition to any Thanksgiving table. **[Yes, this book is likely to stand out from the competition. In reality, a Thanksgiving-focused cookbook would probably win a publisher and audience, since it's specific and that's what publishers are looking for. But a Thanksgiving pie–focused cookbook would be even more appealing, since you're tightening the focus. The real sell here is the celebrity angle with the pies, their popularity, and their creator's awards.]**

Please let me know if you'd like to see my proposal as well as accompanying full-color photographs of the completed dish. **[Adding the fact that she has photos is an unexpected plus.]** You can reach me at sally@godblesspies.com or 212-555-1234.

Thank you so much for your consideration.

Sally Lee

The Biography or History Book Query

In order to write a successful biography or history book, you have to be passionate and knowledgeable about your subject. It has to be about someone or some period that you've already studied and researched, with access to many primary or rare sources. And, as any good journalist will tell you, those sources must be checked and double-checked before you use them.

AGENTS' ADVICE

When writing a query letter for a biography or history book, it's important to have a new perspective on a topic, new things to say, or new insights to share. There have been many books on Abraham Lincoln, for example, but one that considers his early education based on material found at the Illinois Historical Society might make a compelling book.

Here are the key elements in a good biography and history query:

- Detail the primary and/or unusual sources you've used.
- Demonstrate why your book would have an audience.
- Provide your scholarly experience.

Here are annotated examples of a bad biography query, followed by a good one:

Dear Ms. Apple,

Helen of Troy lived a long time ago, but the myth of her beauty lives on. **[Does it? The author needs to add more detail.]** I have read so much about her that I feel she speaks to me! **[Uh-oh, weirdo alert?]**

My book, *The Most Beautiful Woman in the World*, is the result of my research into the life and times of Helen of Troy. I know people will want to read this biography and I'd like to send you my proposal. **[Where's the proof that people will want to read this book? What kind of research has the author done? What are the author's credentials?]**

Thank you so much. [**The thank-you is great, but the author forgot her contact information!**]

Mary Prince

Dear Ms. Apple,

Helen of Troy was more than the "face that launched a thousand ships." She was a real person caught up in a political war that lasted for generations. She was also a woman who risked everything for the man she loved. [**The author has given a reason for his or her interest, as well as made the subject timely—all in the first paragraph!**]

I've been fascinated by Helen of Troy's story since I was in college. My archeological degree gave me opportunities to explore the land where Troy was built, and my Master's in ancient languages gave me the ability to read rare documents from that time. [**The author's credentials are solid, and the access to rare research is a real plus. We hear good platform!**]

The result of my research is *The Most Beautiful Woman in the World*, a book filled with the passion, lust, war, and Byzantine-like politics that would make this biography a blockbuster. [**Reinforced the reasons why this biography is timely.**]

I hope you will be interested in seeing more of my proposal for my biography of Helen of Troy. The manuscript is complete. You can reach me at maryprince@loa.com or 415-555-1234. [**Contact information is included.**]

Thank you for your consideration. [**Polite closing.**]

Mary Prince

PUBLISHING PITFALLS

If an editor or agent's submission guidelines request a query letter, don't decide to send along the book proposal, too. It's a real turn-off when a would-be author flouts the rules.

The Travel Book Query

There are travel guides and travel memoirs. The armchair traveler is the reader who travels along with you on your adventures. The book must be able to transport the reader to Paris or Thailand or whatever country or city you are describing; you need to make the reader feel as if she has been there.

Travel guides are used before and during actual trips for planning and sightseeing purposes. The greatest challenge for a query letter in this genre is to get that feeling of "being there" in four paragraphs or less.

Here's an annotated example of a travel query letter we received that started out fairly promising, but lost us in the second paragraph. It's followed by a successful travel query letter:

Dear Ms. Geographic:

I love Paris! **[So what? So do millions of other people.]** In fact, I love it so much that the last time I was there I wrote down my experiences in my favorite bistros, boutiques, and beauty salons. **[This shows promise ... let's read more.]**

My book, *Paris in Any Season*, describes my favorite places and even rates them on a scale of 1 (bad) to 5 (good). **[She's lost us. If these are her *favorite* places, why would they be rated? Why would a favorite place be rated "1"?]** It gives you a real inside look at the "real" Paris. **[Says who? What are your credentials? What makes your view of Paris more interesting than any published book about the city?]**

Au revoir! Looking forward to hearing from you. **[It would help if the author told the agent or editor how to contact her by providing an e-mail address and phone number.]**

Megan Morris

Dear Ms. Geographic:

What is it about Paris that tourists love? Why is it the number-one travel destination for couples? What gives it that romantic atmosphere? **[This provocative paragraph sets up a reason for this book.]**

After almost 100 visits to Paris, my "second home," as an editor of the fashion magazine, *Chic Style* **[The author establishes her familiarity with the city, as well as her credentials.]**, I decided to discover the answer to this mystery. I set out to review the spots that make Paris romantic, chic, and beautiful: its bistros, boutiques, and beauty salons. **[The author clearly and concisely describes her book.]**

The result was an article I wrote for *Chic Style* that generated the most reader response in the magazine's history. You can view the article on the magazine's website, www.chicstyle.com. I expanded on the article in my book *Paris in Any Season*, perfect for anyone searching for a romantic spot to spend an afternoon, a little-known boutique to find that perfect scarf, or a salon where a haircut is transformed into a work of art. **[This piqued our interest!]**

If you would like to review the proposal, you can contact me at meganmorris@chicstyle.com or 615-555-1234. Thank you, and au revoir! **[A good closing, and she's included her contact information.]**

Megan Morris

The "How-To" or "Self-Help" Book Query

We receive more "how-to" or "self-help" query letters than any other nonfiction category. "How-to" encompasses any book idea that can make a reader's life better. We've found that the most common topics in the category are the following.

- **Financial and business.** These books include everything from investing advice to becoming debt-free to building a nest egg for retirement. This category also includes business narratives of corporations, profiles of business leaders, management books, and career advice. Books may focus on the psychological and emotional relationship readers have with money as well as steps to "financial freedom." Experience in money management and financial planning is essential, as is a business degree.

- **Diet and health.** Lose weight, lose weight, and lose more weight by (fill in the blank). Diet books have also expanded to include healthy diets, vegan diets, lactose-intolerant diets, and other specialized diet programs. Health books are condition-specific; they offer advice and treatment options. Topics such as seeking a balance in life, reducing stress, living with a chronic condition, and finding spirituality are also considered part of this category. Having credentials, a sizable client base, client results, and a solid platform are essential.

- **Sports and fitness.** This category includes everything from exercise secrets from celebrity trainers to exercise after 40, from body toning to dance, from playing tennis to win to understanding the rules of curling. Again, having credentials, a sizable client base, client results, and a solid platform are essential.

- **Lifestyle, gardening, decorating, and crafts.** This category deals with home life and personal interests. Having credentials and a platform are important. These books frequently have visual components, so make sure your work looks fabulous, and consider including a visual element in your query!

HOT OFF THE PRESS

The "how-to" or "self-help" book that helped start it all was a small volume called *How to Be Your Own Best Friend* by Mildred Newman and Bernard Berkowitz. Originally published by Random House, Inc., in 1971, the book found its way into late-night monologues, *The New Yorker* cartoons, and bookshelves worldwide. It's still available in a paperback edition.

Because "self-help" or "how-to" books are subject-specific, there is no one query letter that fits all. We have chosen fitness as our topic in the following query letters—first the bad version, followed by the good. Whatever your topic, make sure the elements of the good query letter are in place. (See Chapter 4 for an annotated example of a good "how-to" e-mail query about solving your money problems.)

Dear Mr. Friend,

No one likes to exercise, but I think I have found the solution. **[Really? Skeptical but curious, the reader goes on to the next paragraph.]**

I'm an exercise physiologist at Princeton University and I have found that working out only five minutes a few times a day can make a difference. I've wanted to share my findings with the world. Hence this book, *Fitness One Day at a Time.* **[The author mentions his experience, which is great. But he doesn't add much excitement to his program. In fact, it sounds boring.]**

You will be just as excited about this program as my case study subjects! **[People aren't "case subjects" or "case studies"! This already sounds boring—and more than a little off-putting.]** I will be happy to discuss my program and the business details at your earliest convenience. **[Nix the "business details." It's not appropriate at this stage. And please, if you're expecting an agent or editor to get in touch with you, don't forget to provide your e-mail address and phone number.]**

Thank you.

Martin Hopper, Ph.D.

Dear Mr. Friend,

If a scientist could figure out why we don't like to exercise, he or she would be eligible for a Nobel Prize. Even though we feel great after a workout, and despite it being so important to curtail certain diseases, we just don't do it. [**The provocative message is right up front.**]

I am an exercise physiologist at Princeton University. [**The author has a solid experience in fitness.**] I decided to tackle the problem by working with the student population at my university. [**He's providing research for further credibility.**] I've developed a five-minute exercise program that anyone can follow. The results at Princeton are amazing. This year's graduating class, for example, has lost 10 percent of their body weight since starting the program. [**The author has set up an unusual fitness program that separates it from the dozens of other exercise books currently in print.**]

My book, *Fitness 5 Minutes at a Time*, is all about getting the reader off the couch and out the door, but not by extolling the benefits of exercise, which are easy to tune out. Instead, I've focused on five-minute intervals that anyone can do, any day and at any time, and still make a difference in his or her overall health and looks. [**Easy to follow *and* written by an expert in the field? Slam dunk!**]

Please let me know if you'd like more information on my program. You can reach me at fitness@university.edu or 609-555-1234. I look forward to hearing from you.

Thank you for your attention. [**The author didn't forget the contact information or the polite closing.**]

Martin Hopper, Ph.D.

AGENTS' ADVICE

Practical health books belong in the health and medical section. Publishers expect them to be authored by a health-care professional who knows the topic well. Because physicians and medical experts aren't necessarily writers, often these books are actually ghostwritten by a health writer or journalist.

The Coffee Table Book Query

These oversized books are lavishly illustrated and designed and usually expensive. They can be art and architecture books, museum collection books, or books about collectibles, pop culture, or sports. They are intended for a sophisticated and devoted audience. Some publishing houses, known as *art publishers*, specialize in these books.

DEFINITION

An **art publisher** is a publisher that specializes in books that are often oversized with exceptional attention to production values. They are also often produced in limited quantities.

The query letter for a heavily illustrated, oversized art book must still begin with a compelling fact, and end with a gracious thank-you. The main distinction is that it has a clear and dedicated audience. The art book is more of a collector's item that people will treasure. The query letter can have a more formal tone and focus on the visual components.

Here are two annotated examples of art book query letters—first the bad version, followed by the good.

Dear Mr. Tisse,

Believe it or not, I have photographs that Georgia O'Keefe took that no one has ever seen! [**The fact that there are Georgia O'Keeffe photographs is very exciting, but "the believe it or not" makes it sound like the letter was written by a 10-year-old. And if you're going to misspell the famous artist's name, you might as well hang up your aspirations before you compose your query letter.**] They show that she was a great photographer as well a great painter.

The photographs are all original (Alfred Stieglitz didn't take them!) [**Name-dropping perhaps? And how does the author know Georgia O'Keeffe really took the photos—especially as her partner was one of the greatest photographers who ever lived?**] and are in all good condition. [**Poor grammar.**] I've written a couple of paragraphs on each one to help guide the reader. [**What makes you qualified to do this?**]

I'll be happy to show you some of the photographs. Just let me know where and when. [**A little too aggressive and informal for the subject matter.**] You can reach me at Casso@art.com.

Thanks! [**Ditch the exclamation mark. See the "written by a 10-year-old" remark above.**]

All best,

Nancy Casso, M.F.A.

Dear Mr. Tisse,

I have recently had the privilege of staging an exhibit of a little-known collection of photographs by Georgia O'Keeffe. I discovered this collection as curator of the Santa Fe Art League. **[The author shows deference to his subject— showing he takes this book very seriously. He also grabs the attention of the editor or agent: Georgia O'Keeffe was a photographer, too!]** The work is in perfect condition and can be easily reproduced. I have been appointed by the O'Keeffe estate to find a publisher for the work. **[An important fact in illustrated books.]**

The exhibit took three years to mount. **[This book has not been "thrown together."]** Many of the photographs have never been seen by the public before this exhibit—which caused great excitement in the art community and was covered extensively in *ARTNEWS* magazine and other art journals. **[This is a great plank in the author's platform. This fact alone would be reason enough to see the book!]** As an art scholar and great fan of Ms. O'Keeffe's work, I have prepared descriptive narratives for each of the photographs. **[The author shows that he knows the art world.]**

Please let me know if you would like to see my proposal and some samples. I can be reached at 999-555-1234 or casso@art.com.

Thank you in advance for your time and consideration. **[A bit more formal closing such as this one is appropriate.]**

Sincerely yours,

Nancy Casso, M.F.A.

The Current Event or True Crime Query

Truman Capote created a true crime genre with his acclaimed book, *In Cold Blood*. Today, the category literally fills rows of shelves in bookstores and newsstands everywhere, from the case of JonBenet Ramsey to the ongoing O. J. Simpson investigation. A good true crime story is as compelling to read as a novel, which means that the query letter must be equally compelling. True crime stories are by their very nature sensational. You don't need a lot of adjectives; let the facts speak for themselves when you write your query letter.

Here are two annotated examples of a true crime query—one that's weak, followed by a much better version:

Dear Ms. Spellane,

Remember the Church Men Incident? The crime that rocked the world? For the first time, I have the real story of what happened that fateful night. **[This starts out like a cheesy crime novel: "it was a dark and stormy night ..." Real facts would help cement reader interest, since not everyone may have heard of this crime. What was it, and when and where did it happen? Help your agent or editor place the crime and its importance.]**

I used hundreds of interviews to write about this gruesome crime. By the time you finish reading it, you'll be scared, sad, and angry that justice wasn't done. **[The author left out who he'd interviewed! And how can he really know how the editor or agent will feel?]**

I am so confident that you will want to read this, I'm sending along my book proposal under separate cover. **[There is nothing like flouting the rules and sending the proposal unsolicited to ensure you won't get a second chance. At this point, the editor or agent has most likely decided to write "Return to Sender" on the envelope when it comes. And if you want someone to get back to you, provide an e-mail address and phone number. Also note that this author never mentions the title of his book anywhere in this letter.]**

Thanks and talk to you soon! **[Ditch exclamation mark.]**

John Smith

Dear Ms. Spellane,

Twenty years ago, there was an incident in a Minnesota church that rocked the whole world. Everyone knows it as The Church Men Incident, but it was, in reality, much more than that. [**A provocative first paragraph.**]

My book, *Praying Out Loud: The Church Men Incident*, goes beyond the facts of the murders themselves to tell a story of deceit and corruption in a small town. From the mayor to the call girl to the family who didn't go to church that fateful day, all are implicated in this deadly incident in which five parishioners were killed by their neighbors. [**Relays the fact that this is a story with several layers.**] In hundreds of interviews with the victims, their families, the townspeople, the prosecutors and defending lawyers, and even the prisoners who knew the killers [**The author has done his homework.**], I've been able to reconstruct a story that started years before the incident—one that, if known, might have prevented this terrible crime. [**Ends with an attention-grabbing cliff-hanger.**]

May I send you my proposal? I can be reached at john@minnesnews.com or 612-555-1234. I look forward to hearing from you. [Contact information? Check. Thank-you? Check.]

Thank you for your consideration.

Sincerely,

John Smith

The Least You Need to Know

- Follow the basic rules when crafting query letters, but use your proposal to pull out the three to five major strengths for your query letter.

- Do your research and become knowledgeable about your category. Make sure you can answer the question: "Why does the world need my book?"

- Understand which books are selling in your category and why. How is your book different or better?

The Fiction Query Letter

In This Chapter

- The basic elements of fiction
- Basic guidelines for writing fiction query letters
- What to leave in and what to leave out of a fiction query letter
- Specific tips for writing queries for different genres
- Sample query letters

With nonfiction, as we discussed in Chapter 6, the idea is all-important. You need to convey the need and excitement of the idea and the reason why you are the perfect one to write it. Fiction is different. Your writing style and storytelling ability are as important as your idea, if not more important. Your query letter has to showcase your writing talent.

Fiction is also more complicated. On one hand, the theme may be universal, but the plot, the characters, the setting, the dialogue, and the other elements of your work must be unusual. Traditionally, fiction—including short stories and general novels—falls into a general genre or category such as mystery, romance, science fiction, thrillers, children's, and young adult. Fiction is classified this way in order for an agent or editor to properly market and sell it.

Elements of Fiction

Plots in fiction tend to reflect the human condition. Whether it's the Jane Austen heroine who wins the upscale hero against all the conventions of her day or the dateless high school nerd who turns into Bill Gates, fiction reflects our hopes, dreams, and fears.

Even the most unusual or commercial plot fits into one or a combination of five very basic *themes:*

- Romeo and Juliet: Forbidden love that ends badly

- Cinderella: A rags-to-riches fairy tale (or love that ends well)

- King Kong: Good versus evil (with a little Romeo and Juliet thrown in)

- Odysseus: A journey of self-awareness

- The Fountain of Youth: A treasure hunt (may be metaphorical)

A *plot* is the storyline. It may show a glimpse of another world (think *The Bell Jar* or *The Nanny Diaries*). You can use the man-versus-monster metaphor as a treatise on current events (think *To Kill a Mockingbird* or *Precious*) or a sci-fi thriller (think *District 9* or *Alien*). Your journey of self-awareness can be contemporary and glamorous (think *The Devil Wears Prada*) or classic (think *Catcher in the Rye*).

Your plot may be further categorized into *genres:* from sci-fi to literary, from historical to young adult, from mystery to romance. Each of these breaks down even further. A mystery may be a called a British cozy, police procedural, or thriller; a romance might be an historical romance, contemporary romance, regency romance, or paranormal romance.

DEFINITION

A **theme** is abstract; it answers the question of what your novel is about. The universality of your theme gives it the ability to touch others. A **plot** is the story you tell, the dramatic conflict central to your novel and the way you make a universal theme uniquely yours. There may be many subplots running through your work. A **genre** is the category your novel falls into so that agents, editors, and book sellers know who the reader is, how to package the book for that audience, and how to sell and market for these readers.

Characters are the people who populate your work. They may be heroic or villainous. The characters that come alive contain elements of both; they are shades of gray, not black or white—just as people are in real life. When creating characters, ask yourself these questions:

- Do they create the conflict and the tension in the novel?

- Are they memorable?

- Do their actions and dialogue advance the story?

Setting is where you place the work. It can be in a familiar locale, such as the small town in Sherwood Anderson's *Winesburg, Ohio,* or in a more exotic locale, such as the Far East captured in *Noble House* by James Clavell. Your novel could also be set in an imaginative world, such as those created by J. K. Rowling in the *Harry Potter* novels.

A sense of place is critical throughout your novel: Dennis Lehane captures Boston, Carl Hiassen does the same for Florida, and J. R. R. Tolkien perfectly captured a world he called Middle Earth, complete with regions, towns, and separate cultures.

Query Letter Basics

Despite its emphasis on storytelling and talent, many of the elements that make up a good fiction query letter are the same as for nonfiction. We summarize them here, but review Chapters 3, 4, and 5 for the basics on writing any type of query letter.

Keep It Short

A fiction query letter should be limited to one page if you are sending it snail mail, or four or five paragraphs if e-mailing it.

Do Your Research

Really immerse yourself in the category you are writing in. Read lots of works that are similar, study the section in bookstores and libraries, talk to readers who are passionate about your category, and attend related seminars or writers' conferences. Become an expert in your category. This is a business, and you need to be aware of trends and the qualities of successful books in each genre.

Get the Name Right

Unless your goal is to turn off an agent or editor, make sure you spell his or her name right and make sure they handle your category of fiction. Make sure you have the right e-mail address and the right company. People in publishing move around a lot, so even if you're sure a particular editor is still at the same house, do a quick double-check. Do an online search for the name. Check *Literary Marketplace* at your local library or, for more up-to-date information, go to publishing industry websites, such as PublishersLunch.com, publishersmarketplace.com, or Publishersweekly.com. (*Publishers Weekly* should also be available at your library.)

Establish a Connection

You will help your pitch if you can personalize the connection with the agent. If she handles Janet Evanovich and you write in a similar vein, that fact might make a strong opening line in your query. You should research and find out the agents who work in your genre. Your letter can be a template, ready to go to another agent or editor if you're rejected, but it shouldn't sound or look like it. Always write to one person only, not to a department or an agency.

AGENTS' ADVICE

Focus, focus, focus. Concentrate on your main project. We recently received a query letter that pitched two different ideas: a novel and a cookbook. Pick one and go for it.

Follow the Submission Guidelines

Agents and editors have submission guidelines for a very simple reason: they want you to follow them. If an agent specifically asks for a writing sample that is no more than 15 pages, don't send 25 pages. If, on her website, an agent writes that she isn't looking for new submissions, then don't send yours along, thinking you will be the exception. If an agent writes that he isn't interested in fiction, don't submit your mystery to that agency. Trust us. If the guidelines are on the website or in print, the agent or editor is serious.

Know Thy Recipient

If an editor is known for historical romances, she is not going to be the right or knowledgeable person for your sci-fi story. Similarly, if an editor is known for his sci-fi titles, he's not going to want to read a romance. Agents develop areas of expertise; they know the category and they have developed relationships with the editors and publishing houses specializing in them.

Find the right editor or agent for the right genre by doing the following:

- **Read publishing industry websites.** Although many are password-sensitive, you should be able to glean some information on editors who have recently acquired titles in, say, historical fiction.

- **Visit publishers' websites.** If you are writing a fantasy novel, you should know what is happening at TOR/Forge, Del Rey, and other science fiction houses.

- **Check out Internet booksellers.** You can learn a great deal of information from Amazon.com, barnesandnoble.com, and other Internet booksellers. You can sort your search by categories, bestselling titles, and other classifications.

- **Check out Facebook.** Although you cannot become a friend until he confirms it, you can get a global view of an editor's or agent's page if you are a member of Facebook. An editor may post his list of projects, likes, and dislikes. If he has a fan page or group, anyone can join that page.

- **Become a LinkedIn member.** Like Facebook, this is an invitation-only site, but it's more professionally driven than

Facebook. In fact, by becoming a member (which is free) and joining a group with similar interests, you can find out where an agent or editor is currently employed and the types of books she is interested in.

AGENTS' ADVICE

If you are a writer, it's always good to be up to date on publishing news. After all, your goal is to be part of that world. Although annual subscriptions to some publishing sites may cost you $100+, it can be well worth it. The industry news sources can keep you current on trends and topics of interest, such an eBook rights, downloads, and staff changes. We like to work with people who take the time to become educated about the business.

Proofread Your Work

It may be hard to believe, but a lot of people don't proofread their work. As easy as it is to double-check spelling and grammar with Word's spell-check function, there are writers who can't be bothered to spend the extra nanosecond it takes to make sure they have spelled things right. One quick glance at their work and they assume everything is spelled correctly. Wrong. Even if you use spell-check, it's easy to miss a typo or the incorrect use of a word. We cannot say it enough: proofread your work! Even better, ask one or two other people to read your letter before you send it out. Typos are a turn-off. Particularly in fiction, it's all about the writing, and poor spelling and grammar can nix the deal.

Start Your Letter with a "Hook"

Just like a nonfiction query letter, you need to grab the agent's attention right from the start in order for them to keep reading. The first few sentences have to be provocative, but unlike nonfiction, you don't need statistics or a one-line fact in order to sell your book.

Platform Still Matters

Your marketability is important when it comes to fiction. It's difficult to market fiction, so if you have anything to use to your advantage, it's important to let the agent or editor know; let the platform be the "hook." If you've been published before, won awards, or attended advanced writing programs, state it up front. Are you blogging and do people follow your work? Do you contribute stories to magazines? Have your previous books sold well? Any of these could demonstrate an ongoing audience for your work. If you have a huge Facebook fan base, say so right away. If you receive Tweets from famous authors, let the agent or editor know. All of these can help create a platform for your fiction.

End Graciously

Manners don't apply just to nonfiction. Being polite in closing your query letter is a golden rule. We appreciate thoughtfulness in both our fiction and nonfiction authors.

And don't forget to include your contact information! If the agent or editor can't reach you, you might as well have been rejected. He needs your e-mail address, phone number(s), and address (if your contact is via snail mail).

PUBLISHING PITFALLS

From the tone of an e-mail to the paper you use in snail mail, first impressions mean a lot for both fiction and nonfiction queries. Be professional. Forget smiley faces, cute e-mail addresses, or stationery featuring puppies or kittens.

Ground Rules Unique to Fiction

Fiction is much more arbitrary than nonfiction. Personal taste has a lot more to do with acceptance than with nonfiction. Its commerciality can be subtler: word of mouth can be an extraordinary selling tool. If you have attended a writers' workshop and received early advance praise from a published author, that's a powerful thing to add to your query letter.

It can be harder to sell fiction than nonfiction, especially if you are a first-time author. Part of a fiction writer's platform is longevity—their list of published works—although editors do also love to announce a debut novel by an unknown and help forge their literary career. Thus, the query letter must get to the point quickly, but must also be compelling reading in its own right.

The "Hook" Can Be a Short Excerpt from Your Book

Maybe you have a compelling first paragraph or an excerpt in your book that's so dramatic it can reel in the agent or editor's attention. Use it to your advantage! But one word of caution: make sure the excerpt is as good as you think it is. If not, you've lost your chance to impress. Get a second—even a third—opinion of your selection before submitting it as part of the query letter.

Your Role as "Expert"

As a novelist, your role as an "expert" is that of a master of writing and storytelling. Fiction writers need to be experts at identifying gaps in the market for currently popular topics or genres, then filling those voids compellingly.

With nonfiction, marketability is always associated with a void in the market, an audience to fill a need, and your expertise as the author. Not so with fiction. The platform is less about need and more about excitement: the desire to read a story about Hollywood, the enthusiasm for Victorian England, the passion for words that soar.

Think back. Have you done any book readings? Have you published other novels with favorable reviews? Have you received any scholarships? Been accepted to any writers' conferences? Make sure you put any experience or expertise upfront: a marketing platform cannot be created without individual planks. (Corny, but true.)

Dedicate a Paragraph to a Short Synopsis

The query letter is not the time to start with "Once upon a time" or to go into the names of every character, the nuanced subplots, or a chapter outline, one by one. Instead, think of the "elevator ride" test from Chapter 1. Try to make a concise statement about your book that you'd be able to read in the time it takes an elevator to go from your floor to the lobby.

PUBLISHING PITFALLS

Your fiction query letter should effectively answer the question, "What is your book about?" A very brief synopsis doesn't mean exaggeration, however. You have to position your book realistically so the agent immediately grasps who will read and like the work. Don't go "all Hollywood" in an attempt to describe your book. That means avoiding anything that reeks of "It's like *Avatar* meets *The Hangover,* but everyone is dead!" Or "It's like *Marley & Me* but about a cat." You get the picture.

Include a Sample from the Book

Here is where fiction query letters deviate the most from nonfiction. With a nonfiction book, agents and editors discourage your sending any attachments. If they're interested in your book, they will let you know and ask you to send a more detailed book proposal.

Fiction is different. Even if an agent or editor likes your concept, she needs to know that you can write. A small sample of your work shows her you can deliver.

Some editors and agents prefer writing samples to be embedded into an e-mail to avoid a possible virus when opening up and downloading files. Others will tell you in their guidelines that they don't want to see a sample. If they're interested in your book from reading your query letter, they will ask to see more and instruct you on how to send the material they wish to review, either by e-mail or snail mail.

Genre-Specific Approaches

Every genre has special themes, formats, plot options, or features, and if you want to write in that genre, you need to know what they are. If you're writing an Amish romance, for example, it's okay to have the Amish heroine fall in love with an "Englischer," but it's not okay to have her marry outside the faith. Either the love interest must decide to embrace the Amish ways, or the heroine must realize she loves someone inside the Old Order and her passion for the Englischer was just an infatuation. There are similar rules for every genre. (See Chapter 17 for more about genre fiction.)

Children's Books

You'll need to add the reading grade level if you're writing about a children's book. You should also specify if it's a picture book, or an early reader that has only a few words on each page. A publisher usually likes to match up a writer with an illustrator if you're not an artist yourself. If you are both writer and illustrator, it's important to include samples of both with your query letter.

Children's books are much harder than they look, and you must spend time researching the category, evaluating key comparative volumes, and fulfilling age-appropriate reading levels.

Young Adult (YA) Books

Let the editor or agent know what type of young adult book you are writing. Is it a coming-of-age book? A fantasy story? A novel about a teen grappling with real-life issues, such as addiction or ridicule? If this is your first YA, it will be important to demonstrate your "voice"; you need to show that you can write in a way that can relate to teenagers—and adults. In today's world, young adult books also appeal very much to adults: the *Twilight* series is a case in point.

Romance Novels

Publishing houses that publish romances may have strict guidelines for the category and subcategories. In your query letter, make sure to let the agent or editor know that you've followed those guidelines.

Science Fiction/Fantasy/Horror Novels

These types of books require imagination, and a query letter that starts off with an exciting two- or three-line excerpt can be a plus. With this genre, you can "drop names"; they tend to have a very loyal fan base and readers welcome the next Robert Heinlein or Orson Scott Card. Let the agent or editor know which authors you admire so he can get a better picture of your book's style.

> **HOT OFF THE PRESS**
>
> Winston Churchill once said, "Never, never give in." He was talking about war, but the saying holds true in anything you want in life—including getting a book published. One agent or editor may say "no" to your query, but the third or fourth one you write to may be so excited about your idea that he calls you on the phone and asks you how fast you can send your work!

Historical Novels

Being an expert in a certain historical period is a plus for this type of fiction. But that authority needs to be combined with the ability to tell a story that not only brings that specific time alive, but also tells a universal story of love, redemption, or good versus evil.

Humor Books and Humorous Fiction

Books that make people laugh are not necessarily fiction, but they aren't necessarily nonfiction either. They stretch the truth to be funny and it takes a great sense of humor to pull them off. In order to ensure your query goes to the right publisher, look at the humor section at your local bookstore or at its *point-of-purchase* racks to see who the humor publishers are.

Authors you would find in the humor section are not only those who write and illustrate cartoons about pets or other subjects. They also include writers such as Kurt Vonnegut and Christopher Buckley.

Writing humorous fiction calls for a delicate balance of satire, irony, parody, and good writing. It will take work to find an agent who gets your style.

Mysteries and Thrillers

As with science fiction and horror, a very brief excerpt from your book can be an effective way to open a query letter. Make sure your description of the book is enticing in the body of the letter as well. (See the next section for an example mystery/thriller query letter.)

The Bad, the Not-So-Bad, and the Good

Using a murder mystery as a framework, here are annotated examples of a bad fiction query letter, followed by a query letter that shows promise but still needs work, and finally, a good version. (We've only shown the body of the letters. You can find formatting basics for either e-mail or snail mail in Chapters 4 and 5.)

Dear Ms. Austen,

I am writing to inform you that I have two novels, one a young adult book titled *Screen Door Shutting* and the other, a science-fiction story called *Aliens I Have Loved*. [**Never pitch two projects in the same query!**]

I need find a publisher for them, and I am asking you to do this as my agent, to represent me and make us both some money! [**Talking about money in a query letter, even in an off-handed way like this, is always inappropriate.**] I know that you will be a great agent for my book and you will even sell it to the movies! [**Maybe, maybe not. But this author will never find out.**]

Please contract me as soon as possible so we can discuss my books **[Why? You have not said anything about yourself except that you have written two novels. Your letter-writing ability, along with the typos, does not convince us that you can write a novel.]**, which I am sendiking you under separate cover. **[Do not send any material unless you are invited to do so.]** You can reach me at 10 Downey Street, Ridgeworm, New Jesrsy, 02222 or call me on my phone. **[Include your phone number and e-mail address.]**

Thank you for your interest!

Sincerely, **[Even the closing has a typo.]**

Ellen **[First-name basis already?]**

Dear Ms. Austen,

And so it begins. As the screen door shuts, squeaking on its hinges, I can only sit there, staring at the tablecloth so closely it seems to move, red shimmering into plastic white. I am so tired, so very tired of it all. **[This book excerpt is not powerful enough to use as a "hook."]**

Thus begins my novel, *Screen Door Shutting*, a book about life and death and everything in between. **[This is just about as good as "A story of some people and what happens to them." It doesn't say a whole lot!]**

George McGrath is an old man when the book opens and the last screen door shuts. As he sits staring at the tablecloth, his life unfoldsfrom his years in Illinois as a scrappy lad to his years as a factory worker until he lost his hand, from his years on disability to the death of his great love, Mary, as he holds her. **[Nothing here shouts out, "Great writing!" And the typo in the text, "unfoldsfrom" instead of "unfolds from," suggests an unacceptable degree of sloppiness.]**

As requested, I've attached 15 pages of my novel so you can see my writing style. [**Good. The author has followed the agent guidelines.**]

I've never been published before and I'm not sure if this is good or not. [**Where's the platform? The visibility? Every writer has to start somewhere, but telling us you don't know if your work is good or not shows a decided lack of critical ability. If you can't evaluate your writing, preview it at a writers' group or conference submitting it to a publishing professional.**] But I did show it to some friends and they really liked it. I hope you will, too. [**Your friends love you. Of course they like your work—or at least tell you they do.**]

You can reach me at ridgeworm@novelist.net or call 222-555-1234; my address is 10 Downey Street, Ridgeworm, NJ 02222. [**Contact information: good.**]

Thank you in advance for your kindness and consideration. [**Good manners.**]

Sincerely,

Ellen Writer

P.S. Miriam Mistletoe says hello! [**Using a P.S. is too casual, and the fact that you have a mutual acquaintance who could recommend your work should go right up front. It's a major selling point in a query letter!**]

Dear Ms. Austen,

A mutual friend of ours, Miriam Mistletoe, suggested I contact you about my novel, *Screen Door Shutting*, a book about a murder that takes place in rural America in 1900. [**With a recommendation right up front, it guarantees that we will at least read this query. And because of this solid recommendation, adding an expert from the book is unnecessary.**]

Screen Door Shutting tells the story of Jane Rain, a 16-year-old girl whose body was found in the backyard. No one heard anything the night it happened, not her two brothers, not her parents, not the neighbors who lived so close you could hear them whisper as they moved from room to room. As the mystery of the murder is revealed, the family unravels, as does the town where the crime occurred. **[This brief description of the book has just enough to pique interest in an editor or agent interested in mysteries. It also shows some writing talent.]**

Although this is my first novel, I've had several short stories published in well-respected literary magazines, including *Granta* and *Glimmer Train*. **[Good platform. Despite the fact that this is a first novel, the author shows promise by being published in well-respected magazines.]** I've been teaching high school English for 12 years and belong to the local chapter of Mystery Writers of America. **[It doesn't hurt that the author has a passion for mysteries—and knows good English. It also shows the agent or editor a bit of personality without going overboard.]**

As requested, I have attached 15 pages of my novel so you can see my writing style. An entire manuscript is available for your review. **[Agent guidelines followed. And extra credit for letting us know the manuscript is complete.]**

You can reach me at ridgeworm@novelist.net or call 222-555-1234; my address is 10 Downey Street, Ridgeworm, NJ 02222 **[Contact information complete.]**

Thank you in advance for your consideration.

Sincerely,

Ellen Writer

The Least You Need to Know

- Be prepared to attach a brief, effective sample of your writing along with the query. Showcase your writing talent.
- It can be hard for first-time novelists to break into fiction, so if you can demonstrate your marketability, that may give you an advantage.
- Know your category inside and out by reading the top contributors to it.
- Understand what is happening in publishing—relevant trends and industry developments. Treat your writing like a business.
- Make sure you send your query letter to agents who specialize in the genre of your book.

Before and After You Click "Send"

In This Chapter

- A query letter checklist
- Playing the waiting game
- When and how to follow up
- What to do with feedback

You've done your homework: you have carefully and thoughtfully crafted your pitch. You've sought an objective critique. You've completed a final polish. You've double-checked your grammar and spelling. Done and done. You have taken that last deep breath and you're ready to click "Send" or mail your query letter.

But wait! You just remembered that you hadn't changed the "Mr." to a "Ms." Or you forgot to add that writers' conference you attended three years ago. Or, whoops, you realize you didn't sign your letter. That's why it's important to have a checklist and go through it diligently before you send each letter. Once you have sent off your letter, it's gone. There may be no second chances with that particular agent or editor. You get one chance. So make the most of it and do everything right.

Checklist: Is It a Winning Query?

Even if you have forgotten to dot all your proverbial i's and cross all your t's, it doesn't mean that your query will be rejected. But why increase the odds against you? Look over the following checklist to make sure you've done everything possible to make your query a winning one.

AGENTS' ADVICE

Thanks to your research, you should have a solid submission list. But take a second and look at the list. Identify a select few agents or editors to test your idea on. Don't blanket the entire publishing community with your first submission. You might get valuable feedback from an early round of submissions that will help you improve your presentation in the second round.

Did you …

- ❏ Follow the query "do's" and "don'ts" in the previous chapters?
- ❏ Follow the agent or publisher guidelines?
- ❏ Make sure the agent or editor's name is spelled correctly?
- ❏ Make sure the name of the literary agency or publishing house is spelled correctly?
- ❏ Make sure the agent or editor address or e-mail address is correct?
- ❏ Write only to one agent or editor in each letter—not a mass mailing?
- ❏ Add your contact information, including phone number(s), address, e-mail address, website, and social media links (if appropriate and applicable)?
- ❏ Use a professional-sounding e-mail address?
- ❏ Use an informative or intriguing subject line (e-mail query)?
- ❏ Start the query with a strong "hook" (such as compelling data, a need for the work, or a provocative question)?
- ❏ Open your letter with a recommendation to make a connection (if applicable)?
- ❏ Add experience and/or expertise in your topic, and avoid adding unrelated experience (nonfiction)?

❑ Add any pertinent "platform" information, including any media, publications, corporate sponsorship, blogs, or conference participation?

❑ List any awards or citations, prior publication history, or endorsements from other published novelists (if applicable)?

❑ Provide key biographical information?

❑ Add one or two lines about the competition (if relevant)?

❑ Avoid exaggerations or meaningless assertions?

❑ Double-check statistics or claims (if applicable)?

❑ Make sure any embedded links work (e-mail query)?

❑ Make sure your expertise and passion for your work is evident?

❑ Aim for a short query letter (limited to one page, if possible, or 150 words for an e-mail)?

❑ Double-check your query against your proposal to make sure you covered the three to five key points of your project?

❑ Clearly identify what you have available for review if there is interest (a proposal and sample chapters or a complete manuscript)?

❑ Only submit one topic or genre per submission letter?

❑ Close with a "thank you"?

❑ Use spell-check and grammar-check?

❑ Format the letter correctly?

❑ Sign the letter?

❑ Have qualified people proofread the letter?

❑ Use white or light-cream paper, professional-looking stationery, type as a Word document, and enclose a self-addressed stamped envelope for a reply?

❑ Make sure the agent or editor is the right one for your genre (fiction)?

❑ Keep your plot description short (fiction)?

❑ Attach a compelling excerpt or sample if requested in the agency guidelines?

❑ Include a sample visual if it is pertinent to your project?

If you checked everything off the list, you are ready to submit. Now you can take that deep breath and send your query letter!

> **PUBLISHING PITFALLS**
>
> Make sure everything is set up before you send your query letter—your outgoing phone messages for your home and cell and your website, if applicable. Make sure your voicemail is professional and clearly identifies you. You might have a professional e-mail address, but your cell phone or house phone message might be more adorable or funny than polished, such as your kids' voices, a clever "You know what to do" line, or the latest Usher song. Either change the message or use a different phone for professional use.

The Waiting Game

Be prepared to wait to hear back about your query. It's not easy to be patient, but agents and editors are busy people and they're swamped with submissions. Many agency sites clearly state how long you must be prepared to wait for a response. Don't contact the agent or editor just a few days after you've sent off your letter, thinking you have a good ploy. We've heard them all, including: "Did you receive my query letter?" "I was afraid you might not have received my query." "I forgot to mention that I [know your colleague/received an award/ read an article about my subject]."

Let's face it, if the agent or editor hadn't received your letter, you would have had it "returned to sender" or returned to your inbox. And adding a fact after your submission is, unfortunately, too late. Add it to your letter for the next round of submissions if your initial query is rejected.

Valid Reasons for Early Contact

That said, there are some real reasons to reach out to the editor or agent you have recently written:

- **A recent addition to your experience.** If you've just received an invitation to speak about your subject at a major conference or got word that your short story has been accepted for publication at a prestigious literary journal, or been approached to appear on national TV about your topic, let the editor or agent know. These are not excuses, but significant and important enhancements to your platform.

- **An introduction to a colleague, friend, or close family member.** If you have, say, just been to a cocktail party where you met the agent's client, business partner, or best friend, let her know. (Even better: ask the client, business partner, or BFF to let the agent or editor know you have just met.)

- **If another editor or agent has expressed interest in your book.** If you are sending out multiple query letters, you should say so in your letter. This way, if several agents request more material for review (lucky you!), all the parties are aware of the multiple submission.

- **A change of address.** If your contact information has changed, it's important to let the editor or agent know right away.

AGENTS' ADVICE

Referrals from other clients are a leading way that editors and agents get clients, so use your connections.

Keep Track of Your Submissions

It's essential to keep track of the agents or editors to whom you sent out your query letter. Make sure you list the date you submitted your query letter and, if applicable, the version you sent. Keep a log of rejections and any feedback you receive. The goal is to keep improving your query letter and submission strategy. This way you'll know when it's appropriate to follow up, as well as avoid any embarrassment caused by sending the query letter to the same person twice.

Stay Positive

Every writer we have ever known has been rejected at one time or another. It's almost an initiation into the world of writing. Publishing can be a tough game and can require a thick skin. It takes patience, persistence, and professionalism.

The best way to keep negative feelings at bay is through action. Keep working on your novel, your proposal, and your platform. Keep reading industry journals and other books in your category. Sign up for a writing workshop. And, above all, stay positive! If you want to be a writer, you need to work at it. If you're rejected, simply review and revise your query and try again.

When to Follow Up

Although your query letter is one of the most important things in your life right now, remember that your query letter is in a huge queue waiting for review.

AGENTS' ADVICE

We receive hundreds of query letters every month. Even though we like to respond as quickly as we can, it's just not possible. We not only have the need to find new authors, but we also have the responsibility of ensuring that our current authors get the best representation. But no matter how busy our day, a smart query letter jumps to the head of the line every time. Your job is to create that smart query.

The best way to determine when to follow up with an editor or agent is to review submission guidelines. If it states eight weeks for submission review, it means you may have to wait at least eight weeks before following up with the editor or agent.

If there are no specific timelines listed in the guidelines, a good rule of thumb is to wait six weeks before contacting the agent or editor by e-mail. Remember to log in any follow-ups. After two attempts without receiving a response, move on.

What to Say in Your Follow-Up

When it's time to follow up, be straightforward when you write the agent or editor. Don't pretend that you haven't been biting your nails and fantasizing about your bestseller. (Editors and agents know that.) That doesn't mean you should be dramatic in your follow-up, but rather to the point. In other words, don't begin your letter with something like, "Have you read my book??? I've been waiting frantically." Or: "Not that I care (NOT), but have you finally read my letter?" Or: "Please, please let me know if you've read my letter!!"

Keep it short, professional, and to the point, as in the following follow-up letter:

Subject line (if e-mail): Query Letter, Title, Dated January 10 Follow-Up [**This is clear and to the point. The current date of the follow-up letter should be around March 10 to show that you've been waiting for approximately two months, if specified in the guidelines. Also, by referring to title and the original date of the submission, the agent or editor will be able to check his e-mail inbox more easily to see the status of your original letter.**]

Body of letter (e-mail or snail mail):

On January 10, 2010, I sent you a query regarding *Baby Talk*, a book I am writing about teaching your baby sign language. [**Again, clear and to the point.**] I thought I'd write again to ensure you've received it. [**Okay, we know that this is a "ploy," but it's also a polite way of asking, "Why haven't I heard from you?"**]

As a working psychologist who spends a lot of her time on the lecture circuit [**You don't have to repeat your query letter, but working in a little about your platform doesn't hurt.**], I certainly appreciate how busy you must be. I just want to reach out and inquire whether you would like to receive more material. I would be honored to join your extensive list of

---

authors who have written about parenting. **[Clear and to the point and a call to action.]**

Thank you again for your consideration. **[A polite closing!]**

Sincerely,

Julia Delaney

When They Offer Feedback

Repeat after us: feedback is good. Unfortunately, not every writer believes it. Some writers reject feedback as criticism. But agents and editors work on a lot of books and they can offer valid direction. Salespeople look at rejection as one step closer to a sale. This might be a healthy way for you to look at it, too. Think of it this way: if an editor or agent took the time to send you feedback on your book idea rather than a rejection form letter, he believes enough in your book to suggest how to make it better. Just because your query is rejected doesn't mean it is a bad idea; it may be market conditions that prompted the decision. Or perhaps an agent can't take on another sugar addiction book at this time.

Is the editor or agent correct in his assessment? One way to know is if there's a consensus of opinion. If more than one agent writes back with the same suggestions, chances are that you should make them. But if your instincts say "I'm not sure," or "I don't know if I agree," then wait to see if other editors or agents feel the same way. Send out the query letter to the next agent or editor on your list. Of course, if you decide to ignore the feedback, but you keep getting rejected, then perhaps you should listen and try a different slant.

Does it mean you have to toss your idea away and start fresh? No. It just means you may have to adjust your book's focus, your query letter organization, or your platform.

The Least You Need to Know

- Before sending out your query letter, make sure it's perfect and includes everything you want it to.

- Unless you have a valid reason to contact the agent or editor early, be prepared to wait for a reply.

- Continue to develop your work, your connections, and your marketing platform so that your next round of queries is stronger.

- Follow up with an editor or agent according to her guidelines—keep it short, straightforward, and professional.

- Feedback is meant to help you. If an agent or editor takes the time to send you suggestions, consider them carefully.

The Book Proposal

Your query letter was a success—and you're that much closer to your goal of getting published. Now, more than ever, you need to make sure that the next step—sending in your book proposal—is perfect. In this part, we start with the basics you'll need to write a successful proposal, then take you step-by-step through an example, from the attention-grabbing first page in the overview through your writing sample—and everything in between. We'll show you how to seamlessly detail the market need for your book, its audience, and the reasons why your book is better than the competition. When we are done, you'll know everything we know to make a book proposal sing and sell.

Book Proposal Basics

In This Chapter

- Why you need a book proposal
- What to consider when you are developing your proposal
- Collaborating with others
- Details of the collaboration agreement
- The components of a book proposal

A powerful book proposal is the critical foundation to your success in publishing, and preparing and writing it is a complex endeavor. Before you put pen to paper in an attempt to write the perfect book proposal, you need to know the basics of a winning proposal. You need to know what a book proposal is, its components, and how it is structured before you can build it. You need a blueprint for success.

Why Have a Book Proposal?

A book proposal is not just a longer query letter. It must contain information on the book's content, its relevancy, its competition, and details on your platform and marketing strategies. A book proposal is also your essential presentation of your book idea: you must put your best foot forward in writing style and capability. It must show that your idea can sustain a book-length work and that you have the ability to pull it off. The proposal has to be convincing and persuasive.

A proposal is often harder to craft than the actual book. You have to conceive of the entire scope of the book—its structure, content, and flow—and state the selling material to support your presentation. Unlike a query letter, which is one page, in a book proposal you will use as many pages as needed to best showcase your project. But remember, this is a book proposal, not a book, and you need to choose every word carefully. Have you answered the following questions?

- What is the concept of the book?
- Why are you qualified to write it?
- Who will buy it?

Picture an editor and agent reading your proposal. The project must come alive on the page; be persuasive. You cannot meet with the editor or agent face to face to explain your proposal or hope to get on the phone to embellish its content. The proposal itself must do the selling.

We've been in the book-publishing industry for decades, but no matter how many proposals we have seen, we always look at a new one with fresh eyes. We always turn the page wanting our enthusiasm to build and our excitement to stay constant. Contrary to popular opinion, editors and agents are not cynical snobs who delight in saying no. Rather, the majority of us are eager to read something that feels like a winner and takes us to another place. We all love to read, which is why we are in this field to begin with. And we all want to help authors with talent and great ideas find their place in the world.

Developing Your Proposal

There are several elements that are instrumental in a successful book proposal. A book proposal should not only showcase your writing, it should also make your credentials come alive. It will explain the unique qualities of your work, give a look at the competition, help an agent or editor visualize the look and feel of your book, and show your marketing ideas. Ask yourself the following questions:

- Will this proposal idea maintain interest throughout? Will it reflect what was presented in the query letter?

- Will this proposal have a unique slant on new material on the subject, one that separates it from other books in the market?

- Can I demonstrate that this book will have a wide enough audience to warrant its being published? Are books in this category selling?

- Do I as the author have the talent to pull the book off? And does the writing sample reflect my talent?

- Is there enough content or does this read more like a magazine article than a book?

- Do I have a powerful marketing plan that will help convince a publisher that the book will appeal to the public?

- Do I as the author have a strong enough platform so that I can appeal to a wide audience, which will translate to sales for the publisher?

If you are struggling with any of these questions, one solution might be to look for a partner to help you better develop your project. If, for example, as a writer you don't have a compelling style but your idea would likely be a commercial success, we may suggest hiring an editor, ghostwriter, or collaborator to help you to actually write the book. On the other hand, if you have a great writing style and content expertise but don't have the credentialed authority to give the project the necessary credibility needed to be persuasive in a competitive marketplace, we might suggest you find an expert in the field to collaborate on some level—as a co-author. If your writing style and credentials are both in place but you are concerned about the strength of your presentation, it's often helpful to have a freelance editor review and polish your proposal.

Partners in Writing

A collaboration arrangement can be a fast and effective way to make your book project stronger. Assess your weaknesses honestly and seek out a writing partner who is strong in the areas where you're weak. If your writing needs help, perhaps you can bring in a free-lance editor or ghostwriter to help you with the writing. If you lack the professional credentials necessary to be successful, especially in the fields of health, science, and business, you should explore part-nering with an appropriate expert. Financial arrangements between writing partners are varied but are generally the responsibility of the originating partner. Fees come out of your pocket, but arrange-ments between the parties may be made so that such expenses can be recouped when a publishing contract is secured.

Co-Writer

Some authors resent the idea of having to share their book with someone else. After all, it's *their* idea and they have done all the hard work on the topic. This is absolutely true, but if no one is going to buy the book, it doesn't matter how much of an expert the author is or how much work he has put into his project.

In a collaboration, the author of a book is considered the expert or authority in a topic. The co-writer is the one who does the actual writing. A good collaboration is a symbiotic one: the co-writer needs the author's authority to get published, and the author needs the co-writer's talent to get people to read it. One cannot sell without the other.

We have many writers on our roster who have specialties in different fields, from medical writing to popular culture. When we suggest a co-writer to an author, we not only look at the writer's experience in the area, but whether or not the co-writer and author are compatible. A good relationship is important not only for writing the best book possible, but for the mental and physical health of both parties— and ours, too! You may want to research and find your own expert by searching the Internet, checking professional organizations, and reviewing journals in your topic area to find out who is doing research in your field of interest.

Ghostwriter

The reason a ghostwriter is called a ghostwriter is quite simply because he or she is "invisible," writing the book proposal, and often the book itself, anonymously. The only people who know who the actual writer is may be the author, the agents, the editor, and the publisher.

A ghostwriter we know once agreed to speak at a middle school about the process of ghostwriting a book. She had the largest audience of any speaker. Why? With a title like "ghostwriter," the students were expecting someone who wrote tales of horror and gore. They were disappointed (but ultimately liked what the ghostwriter had to say).

Freelance Writer or Editor

Writers-for-hire or freelance editors also write anonymously, but are paid a flat rate for their work. They don't receive any money on book sales and are paid for services rendered. The main difference between an editor and a writer-for-hire is the amount of writing done. A writer will usually do more of a rewrite whereas an editor will more likely edit and polish the proposal or the book.

The Collaboration Agreement

If an author is working with a co-writer, we always suggest a collaboration agreement, which establishes each person's role, the financial arrangement, acceptability of the work, and timelines and due dates. Collaboration agreements are as varied as the parties and situations involved. But in addition to the usual contract legalese, all of them spell out specific expectations of the parties to the agreement. Most literary agents will help their clients draft a formal collaboration agreement, or some writers choose to retain an attorney to help them.

Advances and Royalty Splits

If a co-writer is asked to rewrite a proposal, or writes an initial proposal before it comes to us, an equitable arrangement is usually one where the co-writer gets a fee upfront that may be recoupable by the author when the book is sold, if that co-writer will also write the entire book. Once that fee is repaid, usually through the publisher's *advance*, the *royalty* share of a book, if that is part of the arrangement, can range from 10 percent or even a 50/50 split. All terms are negotiable and should be clearly spelled out and agreed to before the actual work gets underway. If the writer is "for hire," there will be no advance or royalty. She is paid a flat rate that is detailed in the collaboration agreement. Be sure the document clearly spells out who has ultimate ownership of the material, the copyright holder when the material is published, and protections against plagiarism.

DEFINITION

An **advance** is the amount of money a publisher pays an author upfront when the book is placed under contract for publication. It's called an advance because it's an advance to the author of future royalty earnings. **Royalties** are monies paid by a publisher for each copy sold. Royalties are paid once the advance has been recouped in sales after the book is published. Royalty rates are negotiated by the agent and depend on format and means of publication, such as hardcover, trade paperback, mass market, e-books, audio books, foreign licensees, and so on. Publishers typically report and pay sales and royalty earnings twice a year.

Literary Agent Commission

Literary agents work on a commission basis. Typically their commission is 15 percent of all receipts from the sale of the book, which includes the advance and all royalties earned from book sales and *subsidiary rights*. Agents don't receive commission if they don't sell your work. Any expenses the agent incurs in the process of selling the work are recouped as detailed in the author's agreement with the literary agency.

DEFINITION

Subsidiary rights (or **sub rights**) are the sales made that license the rights to the book or part of the book in other formats to print periodicals, magazines and/or eBook companies, phone apps, digital downloads, movie and/or TV companies, audio publishers, and foreign publishers; and merchandise such as calendars, gift cards, and games developed from the work. All of these rights are separate negotiations. In some cases authors retain certain rights, and in others they are shared with the publisher.

Writers' Credit

Who gets cover or copyright credit for the book? If there is more than one author, and depending on the role of each contributor, whose name appears first on the cover? These arrangements should be worked out in advance and clearly spelled out in the collaboration agreement. There are many options for this relationship. If a co-writer has been working with an author right from the beginning, the cover and title page may grant a full share of credit and the names appear together linked by the word "and," usually with the authority's name appearing first because that name adds marketing weight. If the co-writer was brought in later or contributes a smaller amount, then the key author's name appears first and may appear in larger typeface, and the word "with" may separate the names. If the co-writer is ghostwriting the book or is a freelance editor or writer-for-hire, credit may be given in the acknowledgments section in the interior of the book. The name will not appear on the cover, title page, or copyright page of the work.

The Parts of a Proposal

Proposals are as different as the people who write them. Sometimes a person's platform is so strong that an in-depth marketing section belongs up front. Sometimes the content is so provocative the book's Table of Contents should be one of the first things an agent or editor sees. In short, an author has to be flexible and determine what her most saleable items in a proposal are, and arrange the organization of the proposal accordingly.

But no matter how unique a person and his idea, there are 10 elements that must always be in a proposal, usually in this order:

- **Cover letter** (one page). This is not a repeat of your query. Rather, it's a reminder that the agent or editor wanted to see your proposal. (See the "Cover Letter" section later in this chapter.)

- **Title page** (one page). This is one clean, concise page that contains your book title (and subtitle if applicable), your name, and your contact information. Think of it as the first page of a presentation—which it is. (See the "Title Page" section later in this chapter.)

- **Proposal Table of Contents** (one page). This is a listing of all of the parts and page listings in your proposal. It shows that you have put time into the structure and organization of your proposal. It will also help an agent quickly find key elements like your About the Author or Competitive Review sections. (See the "Proposal Table of Contents" section later in this chapter.)

- **Overview** (two to five pages). This section is the most critical: it's the first impression you will give an editor or agent. It's an "executive summary" of the content and the subsequent sections in your proposal and your book. (See Chapter 11.)

- **Expanded Table of Contents** (four to six pages). This section provides an agent or editor with detailed content material of each chapter in the book. It helps her understand how you envision the organization and development of material and, more importantly, that you have enough material to make a book. (See Chapter 15.)

- **About the Market** (one to three pages). How well do you know your audience? How well can you convince an agent or editor that you know your book's market? Discuss those points here. (See Chapters 10 and 13.)

- **Competitive Review** (one or two pages). This element is a part of your About the Market section, but so critical that it should be clearly defined within it. This section includes exactly what it sounds like: information on any competing books—and how your book is different. (See Chapters 10 and 13.)

- **About the Author** (one or two pages). This is your chance to "blow your horn"—but selectively. Focus on pertinent facts about your life experience and career that can enhance your expertise in your subject. (See Chapter 14.)

- **Platform marketing section** (one or two pages). The all-important platform should not get short shrift. It has a strong influence on an agent or editor's decision to accept or reject the proposal. This section is a continuation of the "About the Author" with an emphasis on how your experience today and in the future can help promote your book. This section highlights your position in the pertinent marketplace and how you can promote yourself and your book in that specific market. It contains all your marketing ideas and connections. (See Chapter 14.)

- **The writing sample** (one to three chapters). You not only need to show why your book is vital and how it is set up, but you also need to show an agent or editor how well you can write it. That's where this section comes in. It can be a selection, or one or two full chapters from your book, whichever you feel best represents your writing skill. (See Chapter 16.)

Getting Started

Writing your query letter was just a warm-up for the *real* work: your book proposal. This is so important that we've devoted Part 4 to helping you perfect each of the last seven elements we mentioned in the previous list. The first three elements—the cover letter, title page, and Proposal Table of Contents—are relatively quick and easy to do, so we'll take a look at each of them here. Try your hand at them to get your proposal off to a good start.

Cover Letter

Agents and editors may receive hundreds of book proposals a month on top of hundreds of queries and, as excited as they might have been when they received your query letter, they might not recollect who you are when you send in the requested proposal. A simple one-page cover letter with your name, the title of your book, and a brief description of the book theme and your platform will refresh their memory and remind them that they were interested in seeing your work. (Don't forget to attach the proposal!) Because your contact information is on the title page of your proposal, you don't have to repeat it on your cover letter. You can also use memo-length stationery if you're sending your letter via snail mail.

The following example shows a short and to-the-point cover letter:

Dear Ms. Johnson,

Thank you so much for your interest in *Meltdown: How the Financial Crisis Changed the Middle Class*. My book offers a 10-step program to rebuild your retirement portfolio. As requested, attached is my proposal, including details on the book as well as a more in-depth description of my research about the decline of the middle class. Early adopters of my program are showing a recovery of their savings at record rates. I have continued to expand on my seminar business and speaking engagements. I will deliver my 10-step program in 20 locations this summer. You can view the testimonials on my website: www.rebuildtoday.com. The manuscript is complete and available for your review.

I look forward to hearing from you. And thank you again for your consideration.

Sincerely,

Lisa Berry

Lisa Berry

Title Page

The title page should spell out the book's title, subtitle, and possibly a key selling line of the book, as shown in the following sample. Typically, the title is centered on the page and in a larger type size than the proposal text type size, such as 14 or 16 point. The subtitle and key selling line appear centered below that in a slightly smaller type size. Follow that with the line "A Book Proposal By" also centered on the page. That is followed by your name, your co-author's name if applicable, along with key credentials (educational or significant business title), also centered. Double-space this information, as shown on the next page. Your contact information should be single-spaced and set off flush left in a column; include your name, address, phone number, cell phone, fax if applicable, e-mail address, and website if applicable.

Here is an example of a title page:

Meltdown

How the Financial Crisis Changed the Middle Class

A 10-step program to rebuild your retirement portfolio

A Book Proposal By

Lisa Berry, Ph.D., MBA, CFP

Lisa Berry
100 Oak Terrace
Greentown, Ohio 54545
575-555-5555 (home)
575-555-6666 (cell)
575-555-7777 (fax)
lisaberry@xyzmanagment.com
www.rebuildtoday.com

Proposal Table of Contents

Unless you're writing a novel, your book will have a Table of Contents. Does your book proposal need a separate Table of Contents of its own? It may seem like overkill to type up a Proposal Table of Contents, but, in reality, it can make your work look more professional and makes your proposal more functional. A Proposal Table of Contents with page references lets the agent or editor know that you have compiled all the necessary elements. In today's world of sound bytes, RSS feeds, and customer reviews, a short "here is what's inside" makes your book proposal more accessible. The Proposal Table of Contents should be short, as shown in the following example. Keep in mind the unique features of your book. If your bio is especially impressive, move up to your About the Author section; the About the Market section would appear early in the presentation if you have a national media opportunity. There is some flexibility in the ordering of the proposal pieces.

Meltdown

How the Financial Crisis Changed the Middle Class

A 10-step program to rebuild your retirement portfolio

Proposal Table of Contents

I.	Overview	Page 1
II.	About the Author	Page 5
III.	Platform and Promotion Opportunities	Page 7
IV.	About the Market and Audience	Page 9
V.	Competitive Review	Page 11
VI	Book Table of Contents	Page 14
VII.	Expanded Table of Contents	Page 15
VIII.	Sample Chapters	Page 19

Don't Forget the Guidelines

If an agent asks to see your book proposal as a PDF (short for Portable Document Format), do not send a Word doc. If an editor asks to see your book proposal electronically, do not send it via snail mail. If the guidelines don't contain this information, you can e-mail the agent or editor and ask. You won't be a bother. Remember, he or she is interested in your project.

If the agent prefers snail mail, make sure you include a self-addressed stamped envelope (SASE) in your package if you want your materials returned. Otherwise, you run the risk of never getting your material back. An SASE should be the correct size and have the appropriate postage.

The Least You Need to Know

- A book proposal is a crucial component of your project presentation. Whereas a query letter piques an agent or editor's interest, the book proposal must sell the idea and help seal the deal.

- The unique material and your strength as the expert author should persuade the agent that your project is winner.

- If your writing is lacking or you require a partner for expertise, bring in an appropriate co-writer, ghostwriter, freelance writer, or editor.

- If you do bring in outside help, think through the terms of the collaboration arrangement: the financial agreement, the timing, and the workflow.

- A book proposal can be tailored to the subject and the person writing it, but it should always include the essential components.

Pre-Proposal Marketing

In This Chapter

- Doing online research
- Checking out the bookstores
- Mastering your category
- Understanding the competition

A proposal is a sales tool designed to generate interest and present your book to a third party. But before you sit down to write your proposal, there is critical research you must do to gain expertise about your project—what we call pre-proposal marketing. This will result in a proposal that's a professional document showing the agent that you are knowledgeable about your category and your specific book.

Marketing is as much a part of your book proposal as the sentences. Marketing for your proposal includes understanding the competition in the category and how your book can be positioned in comparison to those other titles; building your platform so your mastery of the subject makes you a desirable author for the work; researching the potential audience for the book; and reviewing your contacts list for people who might have appropriate celebrity or credentials to write an introduction, foreword, or endorsing blurb for the work. Once you've done your homework, you will have everything you need to begin to write your proposal.

Researching the Competition

A competitive review is not only important for positioning your book, but it's also a key piece of the actual proposal document. Ask yourself the following questions as you research the competition:

- What are the important books on my topic?

- Which titles are the category leaders and which ones are selling?

- What sets my book apart? Does it fill a need that the other books don't have?

- Where will my book be shelved in the bookstore? Most stores shelve a book in only one category. For example, will a book titled *Raising a Vegan Child* be found in the cooking, health, or parenting section?

AGENTS' ADVICE

When we consider a book proposal, we look at the level of writing and how solid the marketing component is. Pure and simple, we are determining whether or not your book can sell. We ask ourselves: "Who will read it? Will it sell? Where will it go in the bookstore? Which publishers are acquiring in this area?"

Online Opportunities

A good place to start your research is online bookseller websites where you can find books on any category. The lists can be sorted in various ways, such as bestselling in the category, by author, or by subcategories.

If you want to find out about your competition fast, simply go to Amazon.com, barnesandnoble.com, Borders.com, and the smaller regional chains like Powells.com and tower.com, and type in your topic under "Search." A number of books should pop up. Click on the one you want to investigate first and you'll be redirected to that book. Here's some information you can find on Amazon about the competing book:

- Name and title of book.

- Amazon's ranking of the book. Keep in mind that this number only pertains to Amazon sales, not local bookstores, boutiques, discount chains, or other online stores. Also, these numbers change all the time, and numbers can change radically from a small volume of sales. The ranking in your category is what matters.

- Publisher and publication date.

- Book category.

- Book description (called flap copy on hardcover books).

- Other books written by the author.

- "People who liked this book also liked" list of books.

- "Buy this book and a related one together" section (which can help facilitate your search by clicking on the other book image).

- Book statistics, including size, cost, and *ISBN*.

DEFINITION

An **ISBN** (International Standard Book Number) is a code that's used for cataloguing and inventorying a specific book. The first number details if the book was produced in the United States, the next three to five numbers pinpoint the publishing house, and the last set of numbers signifies that book only. Each book is assigned a unique number. For each edition of a book—hardcover or paperback—a new ISBN is assigned.

- Key phrases found in the book.

- Customer reviews. This sometimes provides an observation of what is missing from a book, so it may provide an opportunity for you to see what customers think is good and bad about a particular book and give you the chance to fill a perceived need.

- Published reviews.

- A "search inside this book" application.

The "search inside this book" option is a great tool to use to evaluate the competition. Usually you'll be able to see the front cover, Table of Contents, foreword and/or introduction, a chapter excerpt, and an index. Read what you can: it can help you dig deeper into the competition, give you ideas for other search words to use to discover the competition, and help you discover what the book has to offer. Features not covered in competitive works could become your key sales hooks.

Online Extras

An online bookstore will also give you a list of its current bestsellers overall and in specific categories. You want to learn about the publishing business in general. What are people buying, and what are the current trends?

Don't forget to check any "listmanias." These customer-driven lists can also be a source to find competing titles.

Other Venues

Researching competing titles on Amazon.com, barnesandnoble.com, Borders.com, and other sites is a good first step, but is no substitute for spending time in an actual bookstore. Taking a book off a shelf, flipping through it, and seeing the range of titles in the category makes it more real. It can help stimulate new direction in your own topic. Bring your book's Table of Contents with you for comparison. Does your project cover new research? Does it take a unique view of a subject? Do you have new things to say? Does your bookstore research show you that you need to further refine your own work? Check where other books on your topic are being shelved. How are the published books packaged—with a gigantic, glossy photograph of a celebrity author or targeted bullet points of financial information for a business book? When your book is published, it will most likely find a space where you identify your competition. How does your project stack up against the already-published competition?

Your Local Bookstore

A local bookstore is a great place to network while you research the competition. The owner or manager can give you a good sense of the books that are selling in your category and what readers are looking for. These booksellers are often a good source of fiction trends, too: Are paranormal or historical romances currently more popular? What are the local book clubs reading? Visiting the store now and then and getting to know the owner may also give you entry once you are published for an author signing or reading event.

The Big Book Retailers

A large chain bookstore, such as Barnes and Noble or Borders, may offer greater scope. You can pull off the shelf as many books as you can carry and set them down next to a comfortable chair. For the next few hours, you can easily take notes as you browse through the books. Buy books in your category to study at length. Remember, you are supporting your industry; you'll want readers to purchase your title someday soon!

The Book Review Section of the Newspaper

Some of the competing books you find online or at the book-store will also be found in the book review of the newspaper. But the paper gives you one thing the others don't: reviews by professionals. Reading what another author or book reviewer says about a competing book can help you formulate ideas for your own, as well as give you an in-depth description of the book. Special sections of newspapers often provide review coverage of titles in those specific categories, such as business, finance, gardening, cooking, and lifestyle. If your book fits one of these categories, keep an eye out for what's new in the marketplace.

If you are writing fiction, there are a lot of category-specific publications and online review sites you can research. Become familiar with them and regularly check them out.

And don't forget the ads! Book ads can also give you valuable information about the competition.

HOT OFF THE PRESS

What helps distinguish your fiction and educate an agent is if you can make an apt and accurate comparison of a bestselling title or popular author to your own work. You want to be able to introduce your novel with a comparison like, "For the readers of *The Devil Wears Prada*, my novel, *Never Shop on Monday*, gives another insider look at the fashion world as they follow the hilarious misadventures of Adrienne Burton, personal shopper to the stars."

Professional Magazines

Publishers Weekly, Library Journal, or *Kirkus Reviews* are examples of other great professional publications that will help your research. You may not be able to access them online, but your local library should have these publishing industry journals in the periodical section. These journals have reviews of upcoming books and archived reviews of older titles. *Publishers Weekly* also offers articles about publishing trends in the industry.

Books in Print

Published by R.R. Bowker, *Books in Print* (BIP) lists all printed publications. The print edition rapidly becomes out-of-date as new titles are published all the time. But today's *Books in Print* can be found online at www.booksinprint.com with more current information.

Libraries and bookstores can access *Books in Print* for title searches. You might not be able to find out how many copies of a competing title have sold, but you can find out how many competing books there are as well as their titles. This research might give you a clue about new books coming out in your category—that is, books not yet published or found in the bookstore.

Is the Medium the Message?

Sometimes events or programs in other media outlets provide support for your book concept. Let's say you are a master beekeeper and you want to write a book about beekeeping. You can look for competitive books beyond the bookstore in order to promote your project. Has the Discovery Channel just produced a documentary on raising bees? Use this information to your advantage.

Turn it around. Be sure to include information about the television program, the YouTube video, or the online blog about the topic to show consumer interest. Think of these productions as further reasons to publish your book. After all, if the topic is popular enough to warrant a television show, it means that people are interested in the topic. And a book can detail facts that cannot be covered on television; it can dive deeper into a topic.

Competition Is Welcome

Keeping to our beekeeping example, there are approximately 650 items on bees available on Amazon. Not all of these books are competition for your book. There are picture books for children about dancing bumblebees, kids' books about Transformer bumblebees, books that use bumblebees as a metaphor for a completely different topic, and even bumblebees that aren't books at all (Burt's Bees cosmetics and "Flight of the Bumblebee" sheet music).

Let us say that we can narrow the field to six direct competitive titles to your beekeeping book. They, too, deal with etiology, history, and science—just like yours. These competitive books can be used to advantage. They should be mentioned in your proposal only if they sell well and show interest in the topic.

Become the Resident Expert

Now that you've identified the books that are direct competitors, jotted down their title and author, and compiled a working knowledge of their popularity, you are ready to analyze the data.

The challenge here is to show why your book is different—and better. Spend as much time as needed to become fully acquainted with the books. The agent and editor will expect you to be the resident expert on what is happening in your area. There is an expression, "Keep your friends close, but keep your enemies closer." In other words, the more you know what the competition looks and sounds like, the better able you will be to differentiate yours from the pack.

Now for the interesting part! What makes your book different than the others? What makes it stand out? Consider the following:

- **Scope.** This is the stage where you evaluate what your book will cover and, in doing so, how it distinguishes itself from the competition—its unique features, new research, and fresh approach. The key competitive titles on beekeeping, for example, may concentrate on the dynamics of collecting pollen or, perhaps, the hierarchy of the hive. Will your book talk about organic beekeeping? Will it be the only one that shows you how to go from pollen in the hive to produce honey for the table or recipes for creating beauty products using honey? Will your book have new research on colony collapse disorder?

- **Crafting your sentences.** Strive to say things like, "The only book that …," "The first book to …," "The most current book on the subject to …." Your book offers a view of the subject that captures a wider audience than the competition.

- **Authorship.** Who wrote the other books? An amateur back-yard beekeeper? Are your credentials better? Are you an entomologist? Nature writer? Are you a leading authority on organic beekeeping? Do you offer a more current or contro-versial view on the topic? Set up your credentials.

- **Style.** Your view of the material and manner of presenta-tion might offer a more popular or accessible coverage of the topic. For example, competitive titles read like textbooks, stuffy and academic. But your book uses the friendly, hands-on tone that has drawn hundreds to your presentations on backyard beekeeping and makes your website and blog the most visited beekeeping site on the web.

- **Illustrations.** The competition might have full-color photographs, but your vision for your book is to include very detailed line drawings that are more insightful and easier to see on an iPad or Kindle screen and create an attractive, reasonably priced gift book. What do you have that they don't? This electronic edge can translate into more sales.

Keep your analysis nearby. When it comes time to write the competition section of your book proposal, you will be better prepared (see Chapter 13).

PUBLISHING PITFALLS

It may be your instinct to criticize the competing books while you build your book up, but avoid this tactic. Showing why your book is better without bad-mouthing the competition positions you in a much more positive light and spotlights your professionalism.

Before You Write the First Word

Now that you have done your research, think about how you are going to organize your proposal and your book. Here are a few additional items to think about before you actually begin writing your proposal:

- **Focus!** Have a clear organization in mind. Keep your book proposal on the right path. Don't meander.

- **Remember the reader over your shoulder.** The great poet Robert Gray said that writers should always remember their readers reading along as they write. Make sure your language is accessible for the audience you're trying to reach.

- **Let your passion show.** Does your knowledge and love for this topic come through?

- **Banish any exaggeration.** Don't misrepresent yourself or the facts. Dramatic presentation is one thing, but exaggerations or outright misleading statements or lies are quite another. You can keep an agent or editor turning the pages with your clarity, your focus, your good idea, and your marketability, but not with falsehoods. If, for example, 3 million people worldwide have the medical condition you are writing about, then don't say 30 million in the hopes that an editor or agent will be impressed. Like plagiarizing on a test in college, exaggerations and lies will get you nowhere. Agents and editors can check these stats as easily as you, and you can bet they'll do so before even turning the page. Once you've blown your credibility, your proposal doesn't stand a chance, no matter how good it is—and you'll never be able to submit a proposal to those agents or editors again.

The Least You Need to Know

- Researching your competition is not only important to positioning your book, but also a key piece of the actual proposal document.
- Use online bookstores, local bookstores, and large chains, libraries, and the Internet to find titles that may be likely competitors.
- Ask yourself, "Why is my book different?" when you find a competing book. Use competition to your advantage to identify a niche that works for you.
- Become the resident expert about your topic to show why your book is different—and better—than the competition.
- Think carefully about how you are going to organize your proposal and your book before you do any writing.

The Nonfiction Proposal

In this part, we take you step-by-step through an actual proposal, from the first page in the overview, through a detailed Table of Contents and powerful writing sample, and all the essential elements in between. You will learn how to expertly introduce your bio and credentials, detail the market need for your book, organize your marketing platform and present the reasons why your book is better than the competition, and effectively select the writing sample that puts your ideas and writing in the very best light.

The Book Proposal Overview

In This Chapter

- Understanding why an overview is so important
- Learning the elements that make up a winning overview
- Writing an overview that shows your enthusiasm!
- Overview do's and don'ts

Before you go any further, take a moment to pick up a book and read the first few pages. Do the words grab you right from the start? Do you find yourself becoming absorbed in the story? Do you want to read more? Whether it is a romance novel or an auto repair manual, those first few pages have to draw you in.

It's not that much different for a book proposal. Those first few pages have to grab the agent's attention and make her want to turn the page. It has to be provocative, compelling, and readable. If it were a newspaper, it would be the front page headline.

This is no small feat, but it's doable. We see proposals that grab us right from the start at least once a week. With the right tools, you, too, can make the agent or editor want more.

Introducing the Overview

A critical section in the book proposal is called the overview; it introduces the book to the agent or editor, and pinpoints its relevancy and immediacy right from the start. The overview is the summary of the entire book.

An overview also includes a review of the most pertinent and compelling selling points of the project, including your platform, competitive titles, if any, and specific markets that would be interested in you and your book.

AGENTS' ADVICE

"Why this book?" When writing the overview, you should always ask yourself this question. Is there an audience for your book? Is it relevant? Does it fulfill a need? This is the information we are looking for when we read a proposal.

Each book is different and each book proposal has its own individual stamp. However, each one needs to start with an overview of the book. Try to keep it to no more than three to five pages. Let's take a closer look at the elements that the overview should include.

The Quick Hook

Grab the agent or editor's attention right from the start with a quick hook, using a compelling first sentence, statistics, marketing information, or questions that show why the world *needs* this book now. The hook itself should be in the first sentence, although you can add a second (and rarely, a third) sentence to support it if necessary. We're talking about a hook here, as in a hook that gets a fish to take the bait, but you should also think of that first sentence as a hook in boxing: if you can get a knockout punch with the hook, go for it! But if you need a second sentence to get that one-two punch, add it. What you *don't* want to do is clutter the first sentence with so much detail it obscures the hook itself. Here are some examples of hooks that just don't cut it, and how to improve on them:

- **A bad quick hook:** This book proposal has everything you ever wanted to know about olive oil.

  Boring! We know this is a book proposal already, and the subject? Yawn.

- **Making it good:** From the olive groves in Italy to Spain to California, my book will be the first to rate the different varieties of olives and detail the process of growing and harvesting the fruits. I will tell the story of processing the harvest to create the world's most popular olive oils and provide authentic recipes for each variety.

  Are olive oils interesting? Yes, because this overview is a comprehensive study of the subject, it takes a global view, and it offers useable deliverables—recipes for the home cook.

- **A bad quick hook:** There are women who win races in the sixties and are not even out of breath. How come? Why not you?

  It is poorly written. Are you talking about a person in their sixties or the decade?

- **Making it good:** Joanne Smith, a 65-year-old, is the national champion racer in her age category. Picture her running through the ribbon of a finish line, her arms up in victory, her face beaming. In *Run for Your Life*, Ms. Smith shares her anti-aging secrets and training routines so you, too, can accomplish more than you ever dreamed at any age.

  This hook goes right into the author platform. You immediately learn that this woman is 65 and has beauty and fitness secrets she wants to share.

- **A bad quick hook:** The Merriam-Webster Dictionary defines tinnitus as a sensation of noise that is caused by a bodily condition and typically is of the subjective form that can only be heard by the one affected.

  Starting any book proposal with a definition is usually a deal-breaker. It is static and shows a lack of imagination. It also may be undecipherable. What is the book?

- **Making it good:** We hear with our brain, not with our ears. Nothing proves this more than tinnitus, a condition in which sounds, usually ringing or buzzing, literally come from inside the head.

It starts with a provocative fact that immediately jumps to the topic of the proposal: tinnitus. It pulls you into reading the next sentence.

The Longer Hook

The opening will grab attention. The subsequent paragraphs have to keep it. These next few paragraphs should expand on the initial quick hook. Now start adding statistics and a peek at what will solidify the author's claims and bring in a large audience. Here is an example of a longer hook for a diet and exercise book that not only holds the reader's attention, but makes him want to turn the page:

> You used to dance all night. Your metabolism never seemed to quit. But now you not only yearn to take a nap in the middle of the afternoon, you *need* one to stay awake for an evening out. What happened?
>
> Finally, here is a program to help you feel 20 again and get you back on the dance floor. Dr. Janice Neweight of Princeton University created a regime that both promises and delivers renewed energy and the added benefit of weight loss. Backed by the scientific and medical communities and complete with solid data from hundreds of studies, *The LifeBliss Program* by Dr. Neweight has proven results regardless of age, body, blood type, or sex. The benefits are seen in a matter of weeks.

Your Credentials and Platform

Detail the reasons why you are the right person to write this book. Add pertinent platform information here, such as other published works, interviews, and group affiliations that not only give you credibility, but also show how the book can be *positioned* to sell. This should be no more than a paragraph or two of compelling data;

you'll have a chance to expand on it in the About the Author section (discussed in Chapter 12).

> **DEFINITION**
>
> **Positioning** is exactly like it sounds: "positioning" your book in a market so the audience will find it. This is done by first differentiating your book from the competitors and demonstrating the unique need it fills. Make valid comparisons and contrasts to established books. Positioning helps the agent understand comparisons for your book.

For example, using the earlier tinnitus proposal, let's look to see how the author brings in the fact that he's an authority on the subject who is well known both from conferences all over the world and through his blog, and that he's someone who completely understands the condition because he suffers from it himself:

> I know how important this subject is. As a neurologist for 30 years at Mt. Hebron Hospital in Manhattan, I have seen thousands of patients with the condition. I have also lectured on tinnitus at neurological conferences all over the world, and, at the last calculation, 346,000 people read my blog, "It's Not All in Your Head," every week.
>
> But it's not just my experience in the field that makes me a good candidate for writing this book. I am also someone who has suffered from tinnitus his whole life and was desperate for relief.

Potential Markets

Potential markets for the book include specifics on the audience you are trying to reach. Again, try to hit hard here and be concise; you'll have plenty of room to say more in the About the Market section of the proposal (see Chapter 13). A couple of strong paragraphs, or a compelling paragraph followed by hard-hitting bullet points, is all you need here. Using statistics can help reinforce the need for your book in the marketplace. See how data is used effectively in the following example to demonstrate the need for a book on tinnitus:

Why a book on tinnitus? Because there is no other book currently on the market that is written by someone who knows the subject from both sides. A large audience exists. Consider these facts:

- Approximately one in five Americans suffer from some form of tinnitus.

- Over 12 million find tinnitus so problematic that they need to see their doctors to get relief.

- There are too many misconceptions about tinnitus: from "it's all in your head" to "get used to it."

- Many physicians don't know how to treat tinnitus; they aren't aware of the many different treatments out there.

My book, *It's Not All in Your Head*, offers holistic, proven relief from this syndrome, providing empathy only possible from someone who truly knows what it is like to suffer from it.

A Discussion of the Competition

Don't ignore the competition. Instead, show why your book is different from it. You will review the competition more comprehensively later in your proposal (see Chapter 13), but for now, you are demonstrating your knowledge of the category and the positioning for your book. The following example about an imaginary mental disorder (OPD) gives you an idea of how to discuss the competition in a realistic fashion that still puts you on top:

People seem to be waking up to this common but misdiagnosed disorder. There are two other published books on OPD, but neither detail *both* OPD's psychological and physiological ramifications as well as treating it holistically—until now.

The Book's Structure

Remember, this is the overview. You might make a reference to the book's structure only if it is a critical component of the book. For example, it's important, if applicable, to note that, say, my book will include original art, fit into a golf bag, or include 100 recipes, or that it is a sequel to my previous publication.

Let's get back to our example of midlife metabolism management, *The LifeBliss Program*, for a look at how a book's structure and content may be presented:

The LifeBliss Program is simple.

Dr. Neweight provides a questionnaire to establish current health levels and future goals. She provides targeted four-week food plans. The plan includes five small meals each day with fruits and vegetables at the center of the plan. Along with your meal specifications, Dr. Neweight provides exercise plans, including five short minutes of yoga-centered meditations, called Bliss Moments, which reduce stress and curb your appetite.

PUBLISHING PITFALLS

As you evaluate the organization of a book, the scope of content should become clear to you. It's most important to be sure you have enough to say. Is your idea sustainable for a full-length book? A good idea may make for a fascinating magazine piece, but may not be transferable to a book-length work.

Delivery Dates

At the end of the overview you may want to add a realistic statement of the length of time it will take you to complete the manuscript. Six months? One year? Don't exaggerate; be realistic.

Other Information

Include any other information that may be relevant to your book, such as access to primary "never seen before" references, the name of the authority who will be writing a foreword, if applicable, and/or any interviews you may be conducting.

Enthusiasm!

It's common sense: if you aren't excited about your topic, how can you expect anyone else to be? Make sure your enthusiasm translates to the written page. All our examples reflect the author's passion for her topic. Following is another example that puts this proposal at the top of the list, with another excerpt from the diet book:

Every 10 years or so, a new idea for weight loss emerges that takes the public by storm. The fact that these programs are not always substantiated by solid scientific and medical research is not important to most people. Reality is irrelevant. It's the *promise* of weight loss in 10 days, or 30 days, that counts.

Dr. Janice Neweight of Princeton University has created a program that both promises and delivers weight loss and renewed energy. *The LifeBliss Program* is backed by the scientific and medical communities and solid data from hundreds of studies. And it has proven results regardless of age, body or blood type, or gender.

The benefits are seen in a matter of weeks.

The LifeBliss Program is a regimen built on adding more plant-based food to your diet. Dr. Neweight's 20 years of cutting-edge research and her work as a nutritionist in private practice has led to the creation of a program that has the support of the AMA, the ADA, and the major health insurance companies. It's a program that not only promises results, but delivers them.

Over 1,000 clients have followed this program and lost at least 10 percent of their body weight in one month. All have shown improved bio-markers. Their results and stories will be interspersed within the pages of this book.

The LifeBliss Program offers more than weight loss. It improves vitality and restores energy ... for life.

Do's and Don'ts of a Successful Overview

To summarize, keep in mind these do's and don'ts when writing your overview:

- Do keep this section brief, to the point, and focused on top-level information. You can add supporting data later.

- Do remember the importance of the hook. You must reel in the agent or editor with irresistible bait or deliver a knockout punch.

- Do make sure your overview conveys why your book is different from the competition, why there's an audience for it, and why you're qualified to write it.

- Don't overwhelm the agent or editor with verbiage at this point. Remember that you're dealing with a busy professional; respect his time accordingly.

- Don't drift from the point, become familiar or chatty, or let yourself get sloppy. In the overview, every word counts.

- Don't leave out a critical component, such as your built-in audience of 50,000 e-mail names or membership in a relevant industry group or your awards. In the overview, you need to bring out the big guns.

A Winning Overview

At the end of a good overview, the agent or editor should have a description of your book, an understanding of its scope, the features that make it different from other books, and the reasons why you are the best person to write it. Congratulations! You've hooked your reader. In the next five chapters, we'll show you how to reel him in.

The Least You Need to Know

- Think of your overview as a three- to five-page summary of the book told in a provocative way.
- The elements of a good overview include a brief description of your book, your credentials and platform, your audience, and your competition.
- Tell your story with enthusiasm.
- A successful overview is focused and to the point, and reels in the agent or editor with a compelling hook.

About the Author

In This Chapter

- Establishing why you are the right person to write this book
- Highlighting your qualifications
- Do you have expertise in a specific topic?
- About the Author examples

Think of the About the Author section as your biography, in 250 words or less. The agent needs to be introduced to you by scanning your one- to two-paragraph bio about who you are and why you have expertise in the area you are writing about. They need to know if you have related publishing and/or media experience, even if it's on other topics. And they need to see additional support for your credentials in the form of an attached resumé/CV if it boosts your bio.

In this chapter, we'll explore the elements that make up the About the Author section and offer suggestions to make it get noticed.

Let Me Introduce Myself ...

Think of the *About the Author* section as a formal, factual introduction to you. When we say "formal," what we really mean is that it should sound as though it has been written by a third party, such as a book reviewer or movie critic.

One of the mistakes first-time authors often make is to write their About the Author section in the first person. This section is almost always written in the third person: "He has" or "She has," not "I have." Why not write in first person? It sounds amateurish. Keeping your bio in the third person creates more of a tone of expertise and authority. And because experienced writers present their About the Author section in third person, writing yours in first person sends up a red flag to agents and editors that you're a newbie.

Sound intimidating? It's not. Think about it this way: by writing in the third person, you gain distance from your own story. It's actually a lot easier to write about "his" or "her" life in a concise, compelling way than it is to write about *your* life. That's because it lets you look at the person you are writing about as an author and expert, not just as you. It works! Try it and see.

Start with a Resumé

The easiest and most efficient way to put together your About the Author section is to start with a resumé. You may already have a business resumé, or, if you're an academic, a curriculum vitae (CV). Your resumé should be professional and well crafted. If you have a weak resumé, you will have to work to enhance it. Suppose you're a stay-at-home mom who's developed a fantastic program for other stay-at-home moms to get their act together, like the FlyLady, who built an Internet presence into a successful book line. Or you're Julie Powell, a secretary, who decides to start a blog and ends up writing a successful book, which is turned into the movie *Julie & Julia*. In either case, your resumé may have originally been unimpressive, but your ultimate achievement is amazing.

Why start with a resumé? A well-written resumé is tightly focused, and a good About the Author section should be, too. A resumé also gives you an at-a-glance format where you can review your work experience, education, awards and honors, publications, memberships in professional organizations, and related experience. And, as we'll see, these can all contribute to a strong author bio.

> **AGENTS' ADVICE**
>
> A resumé that relates to your book topic can strengthen your book proposal. For example, if you're an entrepreneur who launched your first company while in college, went on to start five more companies before you turned 40 (one of which is a Fortune 500 company), and you're now writing a book on the secrets of successful start-ups, a section in your resumé will summarize those achievements.

Putting Together Your Bio

To write a good About the Author section, you need to set aside everything you thought you knew about writing a biography: the year you were born, where you went to school, who you married, how many kids you have, where you work, what you have been doing the past few years. When it comes to the About the Author section of your proposal, you want to include only what is pertinent to why a publisher would take you on as the author of this particular book. Yes, that can include major and significant events in your career, as well as degrees, credentials, publishing history, awards, speaking engagements, and memberships in professional organizations. But you need to weight the presentation of your experience to the particular project you're proposing.

What Belongs in Your Bio?

Still wondering what to include in your About the Author section? The following checklist will help. If you check "yes" to any of these items, it belongs in your bio. If you check "no," leave it for your fans on Facebook.

- Do I have a career in the field I am writing about?
  ___ Yes ___ No

- Do I own a business, have a practice, or have a client base in the field I am writing about? ___ Yes ___ No

- Do my degrees add credibility to my subject? ___ Yes ___ No

- Am I a recognized expert in my field? ___ Yes ___ No

- If I've published any books or articles, are they relevant to my topic? ___ Yes ___ No

- Does the number of my published works add to my credibility? ___ Yes ___ No

- Does mentioning my job add to my perceived authority? ___ Yes ___ No

- Have I done research in the topic on which I'm writing? ___ Yes ___ No

- If so, has that research been published? ___ Yes ___ No

- Has it been published in a prestigious publication? ___ Yes ___ No

- Have I been interviewed on TV or the radio or featured in newspapers or magazines on the topic of my book? ___ Yes ___ No

- Am I the spokesperson or a spokesperson for an organization related to my book's topic? ___ Yes ___ No

- Do I hold or have I held a significant office in that organization or another organization connected to my topic? ___ Yes ___ No

- Have I spoken to large audiences, spoken often, and/or spoken to organizations related to my book's topic? ___ Yes ___ No

- Do I have a blog and/or website related to my book topic? ___ Yes ___ No

- Has my blog or website received a significant number of hits? ___ Yes ___ No

- Have I received any awards or honors connected to my book's topic? ___ Yes ___ No

- If not, have I received any major awards or honors that would add to my perceived authority? ___ Yes ___ No

- Have I taught classes on the subject of my book?
  ___ Yes ___ No

- Are my city/town, birthplace, or former places I've lived relevant to my book? ___ Yes ___ No

- Are my travels relevant to my book? ___ Yes ___ No

- Do I have a hobby or a vocation that is connected to my book? ___ Yes ___ No

- If so, am I considered an authority among fellow hobbyists? ___ Yes ___ No

- Do I have any personal experience that enhances my subject? ___ Yes ___ No

Look over your "yes" answers again. They all point to the same thing: relevancy. Like your platform (see Chapter 14), your About the Author section is meant to sell you to an editor or agent. It should show why you are the right person at the right time to write this book; you have established that you are an expert or authority in your field.

Calling Attention to Yourself

Your qualifications are highlighted by any job, research, hobby, degree, award, personal experience, and more that is relevant to your subject. Let's go over what works and what doesn't in these categories.

Career

If the work you do is relevant to your book, include it in your About the Author section. For example, if you're the creative director of an advertising agency and you're writing a book about successful marketing, it should definitely go in your bio. If you're a financial consultant writing a book about debt reduction, put it in your bio. But if you're a landscaper writing about Labrador Retrievers, leave it out. However, if your career makes you more marketable, it's smart to put it in even if it's not technically relevant to your book. If you're an Air Force captain, it shows that you have qualities of leadership, initiative, and responsibility from life experience. The same is true if you head a successful company, chair a department at a prominent medical school and developed a breakthrough medical technique, founded your own consulting company, or are an entrepreneur who's developed a popular search engine, social networking site, or successful web-based business.

> **PUBLISHING PITFALLS**
>
> Many would-be authors fall into the "too much information" trap when they write their About the Author section. Agents and editors want to know how your expertise and experience can help them market your book. They do *not* need to know the year you were born (unless you're writing a book on people born in that year), the ages of your children (unless you are writing a book on family-related issues), the number of cats you've adopted from animal shelters (unless you're writing a book on living with shelter cats), or if you are married (unless you're writing a book on marriage).

Education

If you're writing in a technical or medical field, it's especially important to have a strong educational background in your subject area. An agent will have a difficult time selling you and your book if you don't have the degree(s) to back up what you are writing about, even if you've done extensive research. And the better the school's reputation in that field, the better for you and your book. A book on Constitutional law from a graduate of Harvard Law School will be easier to sell than a book on the same topic from someone whose law degree came from night school. A book on perennials will be easier to pitch if you have Master's degrees in horticulture and landscape architecture. If you have an MBA from a preeminent business school, it will help you sell your book on making your small business work in today's economy. If your education is relevant, by all means note the awards, honors, scholarships or fellowships, and other relevant data, such as that you graduated at the top of your class. Advanced degrees usually indicate a level of professionalism and ability, so provide this information if relevant.

Relevant Hobby

Perhaps your expertise for your book doesn't come from your job or your education, but from what you do when you aren't working. If it's relevant, it belongs in your About the Author section. Perhaps you want to write a book on appliqué quilts. Your day job is in nursing, but you happen to be a prize-winning quilter who goes all over the country teaching classes on your particular technique. Or you're an engineer who wants to pitch a book on motorbike touring. You've been to all 50 states on your Harley Davidson and have the photos, a popular blog, and interviews with famous bikers to prove it. Both of these examples show that, while your topic isn't your career field, you know your subject and can write about it with authority. But remember to keep it relevant: the fact that you love to knit does not belong in your proposal for a book on pottery.

Publications

If you have been published in the past, it shows an agent that you have writing experience, you have been able to get your work into print, and you have the follow-through to finish what you start. Include any previously published works, providing titles, publishers, and dates of publication. A publication history is an important plank in your platform (see Chapter 14). If you have self-published books, provide titles, publication dates, and sales data. Your agent particularly needs to know about any books you have previously published, as your previous book sales will affect an acquiring editor's and publisher's perception of your future marketability. If you've contributed chapters or sections to books, list those as well under "contributed to."

Don't limit your list just to books. If you've been published in magazines, have a newspaper column, publish your own newsletter, or write for a relevant or prestigious professional publication, this is all content for your About the Author section. But again, remember that little word "relevant." If you have been previously published in a less well-known venue, such as your local paper or a local magazine, you don't have to list the name of the paper. You can simply say, "She has also been published in numerous newspapers and magazines." (But only if "numerous" is true.) If you do have an extensive list of published articles or publications, use the Internet to organize and catalogue your work. This allows you to create a link for easy access by an agent to peruse your publication history.

Personal Appearances

You don't have to read this book to know that adding your latest appearance on national media programs will help sell your book. On the other hand, you may not realize that even speaking once or twice at a local chapter of Mothers Against Drunk Driving (MADD) can add credibility if you're writing a book about teenage alcohol abuse. If you're regularly invited to speak to groups of stylists or cosmetologists as a recognized expert or, say, a celebrity stylist, this can add real strength to your bio if your book is about creating personal style. This indicates that you are regarded as an authority or spokesperson in your field.

Prizes and Awards

If you have received any accolades for the work you have done on your subject, they definitely belong in your About the Author section (as well as your overview and platform!). But again, list these only if they're pertinent. Winning a trophy for golf has no bearing on your book about type 2 diabetes, but winning an award for your work on blood sugar control definitely does. An exception is if you've won a truly prestigious or national award.

AGENTS' ADVICE

If you have a website, blog, or Facebook page dedicated to your subject, you should definitely add it to your bio. If you can document its popularity, all the better. And, of course, list any related websites you contribute to and related blogs where you guest-blog. But please, skip your personal Facebook page, as it's likely not relevant.

Research

If your subject requires in-depth study, show that you have what it takes to do it well. For example, if you're writing a book about Amelia Earhart, saying that you have access to her family's private letters gives you a definite edge. If you're writing a book about Renaissance art, adding that you researched and curated a museum show of Renaissance landscapes or have had access to private collections of Renaissance art in Florence and Rome can make the difference between rejection and acceptance. If you're writing about the secret life of Anne Boleyn and can say that in the course of your research you have access to private historical documents, your bio gains instant authority. On the other hand, writing that you have done extensive research on Japanese irises does not belong in the bio for your Japanese vegetarian cookbook.

Personal Experience

Because most About the Author sections are written in the third person, writing about personal experience is usually not an issue. But if you're a dietician writing about lifestyle and you have lost and gained weight your whole life, it can add an empathetic dimension to you and your platform. Or if you're a psychiatrist who has suffered from depression himself, you should add this to your bio for a book on men and depression.

Geography

If your travels or current location are related to your subject, add them to your bio. For example, if you are writing a travelogue about London, it helps that you live there now, lived there for many years, or have vacationed there every year for the past two decades. If you're writing a book on the history of country music and live or have lived in Nashville, you should say so.

Playing to Your Strengths

Let's look at some examples of strong ways to position yourself in a specific topic area. You can see how they would help an agent, editor, or publisher visualize you as the author of a successful book on the subject.

Business

Being able to show a strong work history and background is crucial to getting your book published. For example, you hold a senior position in a Fortune 500 company, head your own consulting company, have an MBA from a preeminent university, are a celebrated scholar in economics with an endowed chair, or have won a prestigious award in your field. Linking this to publications increases the strength of the proposal, so be sure to include details if you've published articles for your distinct market, or self-published a book used in your business and used as a textbook by a local college.

Health and Nutrition

Authors can come from different areas of expertise in this topic area. You could, of course, be directly involved in the field: a doctor, specialist, nurse, physical therapist, acupuncturist, psychiatrist, dietician, pharmacist, or dentist. You could be a journalist who specializes in health issues, a fitness trainer, a medical researcher, a professor at a medical school, even a lawyer who specializes in medical ethics or malpractice. Or you could be a patient who's made a miraculous recovery or lost 100 pounds thanks to medical intervention or special mind-body techniques.

For example, suppose you're a journalist who specializes in health writing. To position yourself strongly, demonstrate expertise in your subject area through your current job (senior editor at *Healthy Living*); your publishing history (health-related articles and columns published); your degrees and advanced degrees (in journalism and/or health writing); a new media aspect (blogging on the topic on WebMD.com or about.com, for example); your collaborations on previous books or other publications with doctors, hospitals, etc.;

corporate writing for hospitals; or newsletters for nonprofit health organizations or professional organizations.

HOT OFF THE PRESS

You can also team up to write a book with people whose strengths complement yours: a bariatric surgeon with a dietician or health writer, for example. Other possible partnerships would be a specialist in Chinese medicine with a chef who specializes in healthy Chinese cooking, or a spa owner with her top facialist.

Pop Culture

Show your pop-culture savvy through your participation: Do you cover social media for a website, blog, TV show, newspaper, or magazine? Do you have your own active blog? Do you have professional experience on the topic, such as having performed on the rock-and-roll circuit or managed a band? Do you have a radio show or appear regularly on talk radio? Are you a content manager for a publication, website, or show that focuses on pop culture? Are you the founder of a famous fan club? Do you teach a course on pop culture, interview pop figures for radio shows, or know or have access to celebrities?

Parenting

Once again, you need to show your credentials in this category. Are you the creator of a parenting website? Have you made appearances on TV and/or radio as a parenting expert? Other examples of relevant credentials include contributing to iVillage or *American Baby* or *Parents* magazine, an alliance with a famous medical expert, academic credentials, personal experience, or membership in related professional organizations.

Cooking, Lifestyle, and Crafts

What qualifications do you need for this book category? Here are some good ones: you are an editor or contributor to shelter (home and lifestyle) magazines, websites, etc.; you own a restaurant or cookware shop; you're a chef or caterer; you have relevant professional degrees and work experience (for example, in fabric design or interior decorating, or you've graduated from a renowned culinary institute and worked in famous restaurants); you display and sell your creations on your own website or through other websites like Amazon, eBay and Etsy, catalogs, and/or stores; you've been featured in magazines, interviewed on radio or in newspapers, and/or been a guest on TV shows; you've won competitions (such as quilting competitions or cook-offs); you attend and display your work at craft shows; you belong to relevant professional organizations.

History and Science

In these areas, you need the credentials to give your book authority: previous works of serious nonfiction, reference, or narrative; appropriate degrees, preferably from prestigious schools; a body of academic research, papers, and publications; or access to the relevant material. Do you lecture or teach in the field? Have you won awards for your work? Have you made discoveries, written a textbook, or invented something? Are you a recognized authority on the topic? Are you interviewed on TV, do you have a radio show, or are you regularly called on as the expert on a show? Are you quoted (again, as an expert) in articles and reports? Have you contributed to documentaries? Are you the science writer for a news website? Do you have your own website? Professional organizations add weight here, too.

Fiction

Any qualifications you can bring to bear here will help you: degrees in creative writing, prizes, professional organizations, attendance at conferences, attending or teaching writing programs, publications, and endorsements from successful authors in your genre, for example. Have you authored or ghostwritten previous books? Do you have a blog where you show off your writing skills? Do you have any genre-specific credentials, such as writing for or editing a romance magazine or founding a mystery-writing club?

Children's Books

Here are some appropriate things to list in this category. Do you have any relevant academic credentials, such as a degree in child psychology, children's literature, or creative writing? Do you have experience writing for the age level you're aiming for, in books, magazines, or online? Have you won any awards for your writing? Do you have experience editing children's books or teaching creative writing with an emphasis on children's books? Do you have related writing experience, in fiction or nonfiction? Do you have contacts with, or have you previously worked with, any children's book illustrators? Do you belong to any relevant professional organizations?

You can see how to apply these examples to any field of writing. Take another look at your About the Author draft and make sure you've put down the right information.

An About the Author Example

Now that you have the elements you need to create a successful About the Author section, let's put them together so you can see the whole picture. Sally Walker, our hypothetical author, is a professor of exercise physiology who wants to write a book on fitness at any age. She may have what it takes to write the book outlined in her proposal, but it's hard to tell from her About the Author write-up:

Sally Walker [**No credentials?**] is professor of exercise physiology at Boston College. She is also Phi Beta Kappa. [**From what institution?**] Dr. Walker has authored many articles. [**Where were they published, and what were they on?**] She has also received awards. [**From whom, for what?**] She is also the author of a book about dancing your way to health. [**What is the title, who published it, when? Did it sell well? Did it result in any publicity and appearances?**]

Dr. Walker has also been interviewed in the *Boston Globe*. [**This is a good addition: getting interviewed is a nice plank. But what was she interviewed about?**] Sally [**Too informal, and** it's also inconsistent since "Dr. Walker" is used elsewhere] has also received recognition for her charitable work [**Nice, but not necessarily relevant. Is her charitable work on teaching fitness? If not, it doesn't belong here.**] She has two children and a husband who is very fit. [**Cute, but not relevant. Does she help her husband stay fit?**] She received an award from the Quilting Club of America for her beautiful handiwork. [**Again, not relevant.**]

You can find out more about Dr. Walker on her website. [**She's forgotten to include the address. And overall, the content is choppy and awkwardly written.**]

Let's give Dr. Walker another chance to sell herself and her book idea with a stronger About the Author write-up:

Sally Walker, Ph.D. [**Putting the author's name in bold is not necessary, but it does emphasize the author's name and credential.**], is professor of exercise physiology at Boston College. A Phi Beta Kappa graduate from Columbia University and a member of the American College of Sports Medicine [**Excellent professional credentials; the author is obviously well versed in her subject.**], Dr. Walker has authored many articles in scientific journals and presented papers at numerous national and international scientific conferences. [**She is no stranger to public speaking—a real plus for her platform.**] She received a Public Service Award from the National Institutes of Health in 2004. [**Excellent! This can mean she has contacts in high places—which can further help her platform.**] Dr. Walker's work on fitness at any age was highlighted in a special 2005 [**an important addition: the date of the publication**] issue of *The New England Journal of Medicine*. She is also the author of *Fitness Flair* (Roundtree Books, 2007), a book about dancing your way to health, which has sold 45,000 copies to date and is still in print. Publication of *Fitness Flair* resulted in an excerpt in *Prevention* magazine and 35 invitations to speak at conferences nationwide. [**The author's credentials are strong and support an agent's or editor's faith in her delivery of a solid second book.**]

Dr. Walker has appeared on numerous local television shows and has been profiled in the *Boston Globe*. [**She doesn't forget local appearances, but also doesn't make a big deal about them.**] You can find out more about Dr. Walker on her website, www.drsallywalker.com. [**She remembered the address this time.**]

The Least You Need to Know

- Use your About the Author section to position yourself as the right person to write your book.
- Start with a resumé to help you determine what parts of your life and work history are relevant to the topic of your proposal.
- Keep your About the Author section brief and to the point.
- Include awards, public and media appearances, degrees, previous publications, and other supporting information to demonstrate your authority in your field of publication.
- Avoid personal information that has no bearing on your proposal's subject.

About the Market

In This Chapter

- Why establish the market for your book?
- What goes into market research
- How well do you know your market?
- How to write the Competitive Review section
- Market section examples

Why should we take on this project? This question is in the fore-front of our minds every time we read a proposal. We ask ourselves: "Who will buy this book?" "How big is the potential audience?" "Which publishers have an interest in this category of book?" "Can we picture this book in the bookstore?" If the proposal overview piques our interest, we review the rest of the proposal to answer those questions.

These questions all relate to a book's potential market, the potential customers for your book. After all, the reason publishers buy books is because they think the books will sell in the market and make them a profit. The reason we sign an author is because we think he or she will sell, both to publishing houses and in the market.

If this focus on marketability strikes you as irrelevant, then you might want to consider self-publishing (see Chapter 18). Some writers can't or won't do the marketing required by today's publishing envi-ronment. But before you do, ask yourself: wouldn't you like for all your hard work to make you some money? If so, doing your market research and writing a book with the best chance of selling well and being widely distributed and promoted by an established publisher is in your own best interest as well as your agent's and publisher's. Everybody wins, including your readers.

The Importance of the Market

The About the Market section is one of the most important sections of your book proposal. Your writing might be wonderful and your concept solid, but without demonstrating a working knowledge of your audience—their likes, dislikes, and needs—as well as the competition for your book and places where it can be sold beyond the standard brick-and-mortar and online bookstores, you just won't make the cut. Do your homework and make sure you know your audience and why they will want your book. Demonstrate a solid knowledge of the other books on your topic and how yours is different and better. And think about nontraditional sales venues for your book.

Why Research Your Market?

As agents, of course we're knowledgeable about our markets. Keeping up with the latest market research, book-buying trends, and insider publishing moves is part of our work. So why do we want you to research the market before you send us a proposal? Here's an example. Suppose you're a passionate self-taught backyard gardener who's fallen in love with the idea of making compost and all the great things compost can do for your garden. So you send us a book proposal on backyard composting, announcing that you're the first person ever to think of writing a book on this exciting subject! (We know this sounds wildly exaggerated, but we and every other agent and editor we know have received scores of proposals exactly like this.)

What do we think when we get a proposal like this? That the author can't be bothered to even go to a bookstore or online to Amazon and check out the competition. Even the most superficial research would show that at the time of this writing there are 24 books on making compost in print, that none have come out since 2008, and that only one is in the Amazon Top 1000 books list.

All of this data could prove extremely useful in shaping a proposal and marketing pitch, especially coupled with some stats, easily found through Internet searches, about the percentage of gardeners in the United States who use compost. And once you'd done the research, you'd conclude (as would any acquiring editor) that your best bet for a compost bestseller would be a book that presented an easy new system of composting, emphasis on *new*.

The bottom line is that agents and editors need to see a reason for the book and a clearly defined market for the book. The emphasis is on identifying a trend and capitalizing on it.

Show You Know Your Subject

As experienced professionals, we can see if a writer has talent, but we might not always know how marketable a book idea from this author really is. Because many of our authors write books on practical nonfiction, we know that market very well. But we might also be intrigued by a proposal on, say, vampires or the Knights Templar or the real King Tut.

Of course we know how popular those subjects are. And we know which publishers are likely to be interested. What we *don't* know is how your proposal stands out from the crowd, and why the audience that wants books on vampires or the Knights Templar or King Tut would pick up your book instead of somebody else's.

You are the expert here. And "expert" implies being aware of the competition, reading it, analyzing its strengths, and pinpointing its weaknesses. Agents want to work with professional, smart people, so come prepared.

If the agent doesn't know the specifics about a given book-buying market, she counts on the author to fill her in on the market, the audience, and the competition. Even if the agent is familiar with a particular market, it doesn't mean she knows every detail. The agent expects authors to do their homework. It shows that they are serious and committed professionals. Helping the agent out here makes it easier for her to help *you* out further down the line.

> **AGENTS' ADVICE**
>
> Professional authors *always* do their market research before submitting a proposal. It's another way of proving to agents, editors, and publishers that you really are on top of your subject and committed to your book. So many projects we see do not clearly articulate the need for the book. Make a case for your project by showing how it will stand out and be differentiated in the marketplace.

We're Here to Help

If you're putting together your first book proposal and have never done market research before, you may feel overwhelmed. But don't panic. We don't expect you to do *all* the market research on your own. In fact, we know you often can't. Yes, you can go to bookstores and research the competition, go to Amazon and barnesandnoble. com and check book popularity on those sites, and review industry publications and dig up stats to support your proposal. But there's one thing most authors can't do, and that's access Nielsen BookScan.

Nielsen BookScan is a subscription service that allows subscribers to see exactly how many copies of a given title have sold over time, as well as week-by-week sales and by region. BookScan has changed the face of proposals in terms of making sales claims. You submit a proposal and say, "My previous book on morphing adobe widgets sold 200,000 copies!" An agent accesses the BookScan account and sees that the true figure is closer to 2,500 copies. The acquiring editor and marketing committee at every publishing house will do the same and discover what the actual sales are. Game over.

But BookScan can also be your friend. You're convinced from your research that there's an eager market for your book on the healthy diet for Asperger's Syndrome. In your proposal, you pass along the top-ranked Asperger's titles based on your research on Amazon and barnesandnoble.com; an agent may run them through BookScan and find that you're right, the sales figures are substantial. This provides solid bedrock for your proposal from a marketing perspective.

> **PUBLISHING PITFALLS**
>
> You can subscribe to Nielsen BookScan yourself, but be warned that there is a hefty subscription for a service you may need only once every couple of years.

Assemble Your Market Research

The goal of market research is to prove to an agent, acquiring editor, and (ultimately) publisher that there is an audience for your book, that your book will stand out from the competition, and that there are secondary markets for your book. Let's look at each aspect in more detail.

Know Your Primary Market

A book market is made up of readers, your potential audience. Although you briefly discuss your market in your proposal overview (see Chapter 11), you need to reserve three to five pages of your proposal to discuss and explain your market and evaluate the competition.

Define Your Audience

This sounds easy enough, because we hope you have been thinking about the audience for your book since the beginning. For example, people who write books about weight loss are thinking of the millions of people who want to lose weight. But in reality, defining your audience takes some research. It's not enough to say, "My book is for the millions of Americans who want to lose weight."

Why? This describes your book, and the literally thousands of others competing with it, books written by weight-loss clinics, doctors, nutritionists, fitness experts, celebrities, bariatric surgeons, or winners of *The Biggest Loser*. What do you have to offer that Jillian Michaels, Curves, Dr. Phil, and The South Beach Diet don't? If you are lucky, the answer is a weight-loss book targeted to an audience that the competition is not reaching, or is not satisfying.

Where did you go wrong here? Your statement "My book is for the millions of Americans who want to lose weight" is so general and superficial that it's meaningless. Further, it completely ignores the distinct markets within the weight-loss market. (Think about it: if there was one weight-loss solution that worked for everybody, there would only be one weight-loss book.) Generalizations don't help your case for proving that there's a viable audience for your book. In this case, it appears as though you haven't done the basic online research to see *how* many millions of people are overweight! This is definitely not good, for you or your book's prospects.

So let's break this market down. There are people who have health problems where weight loss is essential to their treatment (for example, cardiac patients were the inspiration for *The South Beach Diet*—both the diet itself and the book by the same name). There are people who follow very specific programs, such as Weight Watchers, Curves, or Jenny Craig. There are people who have been overweight since childhood, and others who have found themselves putting on pounds for the first time in their lives after a few years at a desk job. There are new moms who want to lose the pregnancy weight. There are women who suddenly find they gain pounds after menopause. And what about those guys who were high-school athletes, but have traded their six-pack abs for six-packs and have the beer bellies to prove it?

Your book can't be a panacea for everyone. Instead, the more tightly focused it is on a likely audience, the more it will appeal to a publisher, especially in an already-crowded market like weight loss. Ask yourself again: Who are you writing for? What do you as an author have to give these people that they can't get elsewhere? Once you have refocused on your book's core mission, take a new look at the stats.

Forget about grandiose statements; they are not convincing or compelling. Exaggerated claims simply indicate your lack of expertise or ability to connect with your defined market. How do you solve that? Read on.

Find Statistics

When it comes to finding statistics to back up your claims, search engines like Google are a nonfiction author's best friend. Simply type in the topic and hundreds—perhaps thousands—of possible websites will pop up as potential sources for statistics.

Don't be afraid to be specific when you type your query. Refine your search and use keywords to drill down to the specific information you need to support your proposal. "Number of men in America under age 40 who are morbidly obese" may take you to the stats you need, as more keywords help you sift through the sea of websites. Don't get discouraged, and be prepared to spend a lot of time at this stage of your research. You may have to play with the wording of your search phrase a number of times to find the data you actually need. Keep refining your search for documentation, and keep track of websites you think have lots of good information as possible resources for marketing your book.

Must-Have Stats

You can define, and refine, your audience base through a savvy use of statistics. You'll need demographics to provide a general overview of the audience, then qualitative data to provide audience specifics. Here are examples of weak, better, and strong uses of demographics and qualitative data to define an audience:

- **Demographics.** These broad-stroke statistics include everything from gender, age, and nationality to economic status, level of education, religion, geographic location, and political leanings. The best numbers are found in the niches and more focused audiences, so refine your audience research to match the audience you hope your book will reach.

  Weak use of demographics: Overweight men and women everywhere from all parts of the nation will need my book. [**Too broad and general. No statistics offered, no real demographics. You aren't making your case.**]

  Better use of demographics: Sixty million Americans are overweight, and the number of men and women are almost equal: 35.5 percent of women versus 32.2 percent of men. Even though more than a third of American men are overweight, most weight-loss books are aimed at women. [**Interesting numbers. Not everyone knows that the percentages of overweight men and women are almost the same. But the second sentence is tacked on with a generalization ("most weight-loss books") rather than a supporting statistic.**]

  Strong use of demographics: Sixty million Americans are overweight, and the number of men and women are almost equal: 35.5 percent of women versus 32.2 percent of men. Even though more than a third of American men are overweight, 90 percent of weight-loss books and programs are aimed at women, leaving almost 30 million overweight men unsure of where to turn for help. [**Now you're working the numbers to support your proposal, a weight-loss book tailored specifically to men.**]

- **The qualitative component.** The demographics show quantity, but they don't show qualitative data, the statistics that help indicate the reasons *why* the potential audience has a need for this book.

Weak use of qualitative data: Today, morbidly obese people are increasingly turning to bariatric surgery after less invasive attempts to reach a normal weight have failed. **[Again, too general. No supporting statistics. This sounds more like an ad than a statistical observation.]**

Better use of qualitative data: So far, most morbidly obese people who have chosen to have bariatric surgery performed have been women. But the number of men who opt for this procedure is on the rise, and is expected to reach almost half a million in 2011. Yet there's no information on bariatric surgery aimed specifically at men. **[This goes further, and includes a startling statistic as well as showing that there's an opening in the market. But it still doesn't go far enough.]**

Strong use of qualitative data: According to www.bariatricsurgery.info, interest in bariatric surgery has increased by 40 percent since 2002. Women in their late 30s who weigh 300 pounds or more are the most likely candidates for bariatric surgery. But recent trends indicate that morbidly obese men—276,000 in 2009 alone—are also choosing this surgical procedure. The numbers are expected to rise to more than 450,000 in 2010, and continue to skyrocket for the foreseeable future. My book, *Bypass for Men*, will be the first book directed toward men's specific postoperative needs. **[Excellent presentation of the market for a potential book: shows a viable need that the author's book will fill.]**

Secondary Markets

Bookstores—both online and brick-and-mortar—are not the only markets where your book may be sold. Customers for your book may search other outlets. A book on improving your golf swing might be picked up by pro golf shops. Specialty stores like Restoration Hardware may carry a decorating book, and an organic vegan cookbook may be available in natural food stores. (Whole Foods, for example, has an aisle devoted to cookbooks and cooking products.)

Today, publishers expect authors to identify and even deliver secondary market opportunities for their work. It can be a huge advantage to have concrete opportunities stated in your proposal. ("I can sell at least 1,000 books each year in my clothing boutique.")

Other secondary markets include these:

- **Conferences, seminars, or lectures.** Many people want to write a book as a supportive tool and additional source of income for their regular business. For example, a financial planner who has an established national seminar business might want his own book to sell at these events. A doctor specializing in hormones may want a book on his program to share with his patients. The owner of a fitness franchise may develop a workout book to sell to her club members.

- **Institutions.** Schools, associations, and the like can be a very lucrative source of book sales. The financial planner who has an association with a national investment firm may arrange a large sale to the firm on publication. The doctor may also have a university position, which offers the opportunity for classroom adoption of the book as well as a chance to sell the book at national health conferences. The health club owner's book may find another market on shopping networks or infomercials, or it might be used in training physical therapists.

If you can identify any other markets where your book may be sold, you should add them to this section of your proposal. Concrete examples are convincing. "I have sold 10,000 copies of my self-published book, *Lovable Leftovers*, at Tupperware parties in the Atlanta area in 2009" will convey a strong potential market for your book. But avoid generic promises like "every bookstore and airport will want my book." Publishers know how to reach those outlets; your goal is to identify appropriate and unique opportunities for your project, and to deliver on them. Wishing is not marketing.

The Competitive Review Section

Another essential element of the marketing section of your proposal is the *Competitive Review*. This is where you examine published books that fall into the same category as your work, and you evaluate how your book compares and contrasts with those works. You will want to identify the top sellers in the category and make the case that your book is needed because it offers something your competition doesn't. This section is your opportunity to share an overview of the existing books in your category.

DEFINITION

The **Competitive Review** presents a comparison between your proposed project and the books on the topic that are already published. The big point is that you want your agent, editors, and marketing committees to get an understanding of what's available in your category, what's selling, how crowded the market is, and where the opportunities are.

Adding a Competitive Review section to your About the Market section demonstrates that there is an audience for your type of book. But it can also imply that the bestseller has covered all the bases, so why should your book be published?

Know that no one book can cover everything. New developments, products, discoveries, and audiences make sure of that. Your job is to familiarize yourself with the content, style, and depth of information in each bestseller. Summarize its strengths and weaknesses. Then go after those weaknesses in your Competitive Review. What does your book have that the competition doesn't?

Seeking Out the Competition

This part is easy. First, go online to Amazon.com, barnesandnoble. com, and Borders.com and, under "Browse," type in your subject and sort by subcategories and bestseller rankings.

Once you've identified the competition and printed out the pages with descriptions, reviews, and rankings, you need to see the actual books. Take a trip to your local bookstore, browse through your topic's section, and study the competitive titles. Pull out your printouts or a list of top-selling titles and make sure you pay close attention to all of them.

If you're serious about writing your book, you'll probably want to buy some of the competitive titles to have as ready references (or check them out of your local library). Make notes about the content and style and your impressions of each book, including its strong and weak points. Another resource is *Books in Print*, which you can find online, at your public library, and on your bookstore's database.

The Competitive Review is a great checkpoint for any aspiring author. Let's say you have a brilliant idea for a backyard bird-feeding book. You know about a number of books on the topic, but yours is different because it's organized in a handy and appealing month-by-month format. You head to the bookstore and see that two month-by-month bird-feeding books have come out in the past year. Now you have two choices: come up with a new way to make your book different, or find another topic. This might be disheartening, but it's a critical juncture for figuring out the unique qualities for the book you want to write. Take the time to do some research and think about your approach.

But let's say your research is more rewarding. You see that there are at least a few bestsellers in your category, but your book offers something none of them have. Good for you! Now your job is to show what that is, and why it will sell, to your agent and acquiring editors and publishers. It's time to write the Competitive Review.

HOT OFF THE PRESS

Nothing breeds success like success. If there are other books in the market that are or were bestsellers, they should be noted in the Competitive Review section. The success of *The South Beach Diet* and *The Beverly Hills Diet* may help make a case that your glamour-diet book, *The Aspen Diet,* will succeed.

Writing Your Competitive Review

The general rule is to select 5 to 10 significant titles to present in your Competitive Review section. Don't leave out any bestsellers, but don't add obscure books for the sake of filling out the list, either. The goal is to give a top-line overview of the category.

If your work is a niche title, you may choose to identify the leading books in the general category (such as baseball or languages) and then select a few narrower examples (such as all-star pitchers or Spanish verbs). Just make sure the niche titles you select relate to the book you're proposing.

When you write up your competitive review, title the page as such and then proceed to list each title with the same data you'd see in a bibliography: title, author, and publisher, date of publication, format, and price. Next, provide a brief overview of the book, including its strengths and weaknesses, and say how your book is different. Mention any sales statistics you can find ("#1 *New York Times* bestseller, #21 on Amazon, #3 on Personal Finance Amazon book list," "chosen for Oprah's Book Club"). You should list the competition in order of success and relevance.

Let's break it down:

- **Title and author.** Each entry begins with the title, subtitle, and author of the work.

- **Publisher and publication date.** This information indicates what publishing houses have an interest in the subject, or may already have that book-buying market covered and won't want another book on the topic for a year or two. The pub date is important, because it shows if books that are old are still holding on to bestseller status, indicating long-term selling patterns.

A category that's led by an older title may indicate that there's a market for a current book. If there are many books that have similar (recent) publication dates, it may show that the market is saturated or in need of a new approach. For example, job-searching guides were different in the Internet age of the '90s than they were in the '80s, and have changed again now, in light of the recession. If your work is topical, this may offer an opportunity for you to exploit.

Another opportunity presents itself if there hasn't been a book on your topic in a while, but you can show that interest is rebounding. If the last book on making terrariums came out in 1976, but you can show statistics to prove that terrarium setups are the hottest sale items at Michael's and terrarium plants are the number one sale items at specialty greenhouses nationwide, you have a viable market. Ditto with homegrown mushrooms or sprouts, or the 200 best recipes for Amish Friendship Bread. If sales numbers are available in the public record, add them here.

Let's look at what it takes to create a compelling competitive review:

- **Format and price.** Format refers to hardcover, oversized paperback, mass market or children's book, spiral-bound, e-book, audio, etc. The price indicates the retail cost of the book. This information aids in identifying suitable or typical packaging of the category.

- **Summary of the book.** The best way to construct a short description of the competitive book is by looking at it in a bookstore or library. Reading someone else's review seldom gives you the talking points you need to contrast it with your own book.

- **One to three sentences on why your book is different.** This is the crux of this section, the rationale for why your book should be published. Here are some tips:

  - *Don't exaggerate or lie.* Trust us, agents and editors will check, and your book idea will end up in the scrap heap of history.

- *Don't omit a book.* If a book is almost the same as yours, don't leave it out, especially if it's a bestseller. Instead, highlight how your book will play on the bestseller's popularity while still offering something new and different. There is room for more than one book on a bestselling subject.

- *Be concise.* This isn't the place to ramble. Agents, editors, and marketers are very busy people. It's up to you to do the summarizing so they can take in the salient points at a glance.

- *Showcase the differences.* Say what makes your book stand apart. For example, "Although widely read, *Fat!* focuses on obesity in general. My book is specifically written for men by a male doctor who has beaten his own weight issues."

- *Stay positive.* It's tempting to say that a competing book is poorly written or doesn't live up to its promise, but unless the book has been widely panned, you're not taking the best approach with this analysis. Instead, stick to the strengths and weaknesses of the book and how your project differs. However, it's acceptable to point out if a published work is legitimately out-of-date.

- **Sales information, if available.** Sales figures are difficult to obtain and often confusing. But you should always include the Amazon sales ranking and any public information on a title's sales history.

HOT OFF THE PRESS

Amazon.com offers a sales ranking for every book it sells. When you go to a specific book's Amazon page, scroll down to "Product Details" where you'll see the Amazon sales ranking clearly marked. A book's sales ranking is sometimes further delineated by specific genres or subcategories. Although Amazon.com sales rankings are only indicative of its own online sales, it's a good indicator of how well a book is doing in the online market at that time. Barnesandnoble.com also lists sales ranking in its product details. You can note both sales rankings in your analysis, but list Amazon's first, as it's the more popular site.

Competitive Review: Two Versions

Following are two examples of Competitive Review sections for a proposed book on honey called *Honey from the Hive*. Let's start with the Competitive Review you never want to write, in the following annotated example:

Recently Released Books about Honey and Honeybees: **[There are more recent books on the market, but why aren't they mentioned here? And why are there only 2 books listed when there are at least 10 that are compelling? There is no need for a head like this in a Competitive Review. Just list the relevant books.]**

Stealing from the Hives by Elizabeth Henry. Simon and Smith, 2001 (trade paperback, $18.95), Amazon ranking 24,023. A biography of honey, the sweet liquid gold that seduced the world. **[Commentary sounds like a gushing ad for the book, not an incisive comparison to the author's book.]**

Bees in North America: How the Honeybee Pollinated America, by Robert Jones, The University Press of North America, 1998 (hardcover, $24.95). A cultural look at beekeeping in America published by an academic press and not designed for the trade audience. **[Then who is it published for? And what relevance does it have to a book on artisanal honeys? Also note the inconsistencies in punctuation, and the fact that the first book has an Amazon ranking, but the second book does not.]**

These books further the public's appetite for information on honeybees and honey, but in no way are competition for *Honey from the Hive*, a book on the deliciousness and diversity of artisanal honeys across America. **["In no way" is a red flag to agents and editors. Every book that sells in your subject area is some form of competition. And using a word like "deliciousness" in a Competitive Review is far too informal. The whole About the Market section should be all business.]**

Rare and Collectible Books on Honey: [**Rare books, collectible books, and out-of-print books shouldn't be in a Competitive Review unless they duplicate the content of your book closely or exactly. If so, simply add the title to the list of competitive books and note that fact in your commentary on the book, as well as the fact that it's out of print and its information is outdated. Don't make a separate category for it.**]

The Complete Book of Honey, by Dr. Anna Snow, Charles Thompson: New York, 1965 (hardcover, $12.95).

Honey: A Collection from Around the World, by Dr. Anna Snow, Rainbow House, 1968 (hardcover, $13.95).

Both these books need to be updated; they are out-of-date and have few photos. My book will be current and fully illustrated.

The previous version is an unprofessional Competitive Review that doesn't do the author any favors. Important books have been overlooked, irrelevant books have been added, the discussion of the titles is uneven, and even the way each book is listed is inconsistent. It gives the impression that the author doesn't know the competition and has thrown in a few books willy-nilly.

Now let's give *Honey from the Hive* a second chance with the following Competitive Review. (The author will list additional books in the actual Competitive Review, but we include only her first three here.) Note that the author provides an overview to position her book before she begins delving into the competition. This reminds readers of the proposal of her book's distinctive features and positioning, and they can take this sound bite into their reading of each competitive book's analysis.

Competition for *Honey from the Hive*

Because *Honey from the Hive* is not about beekeeping itself but rather is an overview of the breadth of artisanal honeys available in America, I haven't included any beekeeping guides in this Competitive Review. The beautifully photographed in-depth interviews with artisanal honey crafters and the presentations of their favorite recipes make *Honey from the Hive* more similar to books on artisanal cheeses, breads, beers, and wines than any book on bees, beekeeping, or honey currently on the market. But since those books aren't competition, I've listed the closest contenders below:

Honey: A Connoisseur's Guide with Recipes by Gene Opton (Ten Speed Press, 2000, revised ed., 144 pages, paperback, $14.95, Amazon ranking 830,256). This book discusses the wide range of available honeys and provides 82 recipes that include honey, as well as sources for hard-to-find honeys. It has no illustrations and is out of date. *Honey from the Hive* will be lavishly illustrated with 200 color photos and will be thoroughly up to date. Its focus on the producers of artisanal honey, with their stories and favorite recipes, gives it a more intimate and inviting format than the "here are the kinds of honey and here are honey recipes" approach of this book.

Honey: From Flower to Table by Stephanie Rosenbaum and Caroline Kopp (Chronicle Books, 2002, 120 pages, hardcover, $18.95, Amazon ranking 557,247). This beautifully photographed book is an introduction to honey: how it's made, harvested, and used in cooking and crafts. It also provides the history and lore of honey. But it lacks the focus on artisanal honeys and their producers that is the heart of *Honey from the Hive*.

The Backyard Beekeeper's Honey Handbook: A Guide to Creating, Harvesting, and Cooking with Natural Honeys by Kim Flottum (Quarry Books, 2009, 168 pages, paperback, $24.99, Amazon ranking 64,554, it is the #4 book about bees in the Amazon subcategory). Kim Flottum is a recognized authority in the world of beekeeping. His book *The ABC and XYZ of Bee Culture* is an industry standard, and his magazine, *Bee Culture*, is the most popular periodical for backyard beekeepers. This book extends his focus from beekeeping to cooking, and is aimed at backyard beekeepers. *Honey from the Hive* is aimed at everyone who loves honey, even if they will never keep bees themselves. And its focus on the range of artisanal honeys and unique setup, with chapters devoted to individual artisans and their own distinctive honeys and recipes, is quite distinct from the "produce it–harvest it–cook with it" approach of this book.

The preceding Competitive Review is thorough and professional, with the information consistently presented. Most important, it clearly lays out how the author's book, *Honey from the Hive*, compares to competitive titles.

Think Positive!

As you offer your statistics, data, and conclusions in your Competitive Review, the passion that makes you want to write and publish your book can get lost in a forest of numbers. Don't let this happen. Make sure your tone remains positive and enthusiastic in every section. Your book has something great and distinct to offer that will draw readers like, shall we say, flies to honey. Think about why your book is different and better. Then take a deep breath, smile, and add that competitive review to your proposal.

The Least You Need to Know

- Research your audience so you know the market intimately.
- Provide compelling demographics and qualitative data to prove there's a viable audience for your book.

- Don't tear down your competition to make your book look great. Instead, highlight the strengths and weaknesses of the competition, and show how your work will contribute to the topic instead of duplicating what is already out there.

- Never omit a title in your category because you think it is too much like your book. Agents and editors will know that you either did it on purpose or that your research was sloppy.

- Make sure you know the competition for your title thoroughly and you can convincingly show an agent, acquiring editor, and publishing committee why, even with these other books in print, there's a market for your book.

The Platform Marketing Section

In This Chapter

- Why your platform marketing section is so important
- The six essential "planks" of a platform
- What to consider when building your platform
- Why and how to market yourself
- A sample platform marketing section

You've done your research and written your overview. You've crafted an effective About the Author section. You've analyzed the competition and you've accurately determined your market. Now it's time to write another critical part of your proposal: your platform marketing section.

Where your About the Author section shows why you are qualified to write the book you're proposing, your platform shows why people, preferably lots of people, will buy it if *you* write it. Together, they give an agent or acquiring editor the tools he needs to sell your book to a publisher.

Platform Makes Perfect

Why is a good *platform marketing section* so important? Because book publishing is a business, it's an expensive business, and from the publisher's perspective, every book is a risk. (Unless your name is, say, Malcolm Gladwell or Mitch Albom.) If a publisher commits to publish your book, they will invest a lot of money producing and promoting your book. And of course, they will want a return on their investment.

A platform proves that you can bring a ready-made audience to the table, and that you have effective ways to reach that audience once the book is published. A great platform is like a promise of profitability. And it's a book publicist's dream, because it gives her a strong start in promoting the book through your personal and professional contacts.

> **DEFINITION**
>
> A **platform marketing section**—or simply, platform—is the author's ready-made market. It gives an overview of media experience and contacts; the size of your current audience; your e-mail list; the success of your previous efforts; and any related opportunities for promotion, such as a product that could be author-branded or endorsed and used to promote your book.

If you've read the earlier chapters, by now you should be able to define the audience (the market) for your book. Next you have to show how you can successfully reach that market.

A Platform's Six "Planks"

A platform isn't as straightforward as "I have a doctorate in this" or "I've taught my Pilates program to 6,000 women." You need to include different facets of your outreach campaign to show that you're a go-getter who'll be a full partner with a publisher in marketing your book. There are six elements that can create your platform and will make an impression on an agent or editor.

Media Experience

If you have been on television or radio, or have been interviewed in a magazine or newspaper, put it in your platform section. Even if you think your appearance on a local cable show is not that noteworthy, include it in your platform. Even a column in your small-town community paper about the knitwear you make and sell at a neighborhood boutique can emphasize your expertise and your ability to reach readers. You have been interviewed about the topic, and you should emphasize that. Any media exposure is important, because it shows an agent or acquiring editor that you're comfortable with media appearances (or interviews) and that you have what it takes to get them on your own. Of course, media experience in your book's subject area adds extra points to your platform.

We have found that the platform is the most misunderstood section of a proposal. Potential authors forget to write down their promotional experience, and it's only through talking with them that we find out important things that were overlooked. For example, a fitness instructor writing about exercise was sponsored by a national insurance company to create an employee fitness program, or a cook writing about homemade preserves has her own commercial line of jams that are sold in Williams-Sonoma. These experiences not only helped us sell the authors' books to publishers, but they opened the door to book sales at businesses and Williams-Sonoma stores across the country.

Social Media Marketing

Social media marketing is a hot trend in book marketing. It could be the easiest, fastest, and cheapest way to construct your platform. Do you have an online presence, a devoted readership, a fan base? If you have a website, blog, Facebook page, Twitter following, e-newsletter, or extensive e-mail list that relates to your topic, then you have an instantaneous way to reach your audience and promote your book. If you have a dedicated YouTube site that links back to your website and streams videos, or if you use podcasts and videos on your site, say so. If your audience is impressively large, say so. How many fans are following you on Twitter? How many comments do your blog posts get? If the number is impressive, use it. If you sell your product through your website and/or other locations like Amazon, eBay, and Etsy, how well has it sold? The larger the audience for you and your products, the better it is for your book's sales. If you don't have your own established outlet, you may want to investigate using other successful social media sites. Perhaps you can post a piece from your book on breastfeeding on popular mommy blogs, for example.

Previous Publications

Although you will have listed any other significant books or articles you've published in your About the Author section (see Chapter 12), you should reiterate the list here, especially if the books or articles pertain to the subject of your proposal, and/or if the books have sold well.

Speaking Engagements

If you address large, national, or prestigious groups, include the size, scope, or prestige in your platform. If you're represented by a speaker's bureau, you should be sure to mention that. Also, if you have a regularly scheduled list of events, provide this information as well with the number of attendees. Publishers value this level of professional outreach, and providing a detailed summary enhances your platform. For example, the fitness instructor we mentioned earlier had spoken at her local YMCA's annual 5K event. That may not be an engagement of monumental proportions, but it does show that she is in demand in her community and, most important, it proves that she is able to speak in public. If you're asked to be a guest lecturer at a university, to address a business group or organization, or to give a presentation or workshop, make sure you note it in your platform.

Product Tie-Ins

If you have your own product line or endorse products, this is another venue that your book's publicist could use to promote your book. Your publisher might even want to create a tie-in to a product if it's a good fit. For example, make-up guru Bobbi Brown's books are cross-promoted with her own line of branded cosmetics. Celebrity fitness stars often have their own lines of branded exercise equipment, workout clothes, shoes, DVDs of workouts, and CDs of exercise music. Golfing, tennis, and basketball stars have their own lines, too, and many athletes endorse unrelated products such as beverages and cereal. And then there are celebrity chefs with their branded lines of cooking equipment and special seasonings, sauces, and dressings. All of these items offer additional opportunities for the publisher to promote a book product.

Continuous Exposure

Sure, it's thrilling to have an article accepted in the *New Yorker* or have your landscape featured by the gardening columnist in *The New York Times* or make a guest appearance on *Martha Stewart Living* or *Iron Chef America*. This is great publicity, and you should highlight it in your platform. Your presence nightly or weekly on a TV or radio show or your ability to generate headlines and interest enables you to build a loyal following, an audience for your book. You need to be pitching yourself constantly. To begin, you may have to start with local opportunities such as the local paper, a small radio station. The mantra in marketing is to start local to go national. All these can build a loyal reader/fan following. Play these up, especially if the numbers support your claims. The ultimate goal may be to get yourself posted on media listings so you are called as an expert for relevant commentary on appropriate topics.

> **AGENTS' ADVICE**
>
> If you've been published on a website, in a magazine or journal, on an op-ed page, quoted in a blog, or interviewed for an article, you will want to send the link to your agent or editor. Mention the coverage in your platform section, and show the proof by attaching a link to the articles, or the actual articles themselves if they are requested.

Assembling Your Platform

To make sure you list all the relevant components, review the following checklist. You'll see some familiar questions from the About the Author checklist in Chapter 12. But we have included them here as well, because this time the purpose is different. Before, you were trying to establish credibility. This time, it's all about marketing.

- Have I been interviewed on TV or the radio or featured in newspapers or magazines on the topic of my book?
  ___ Yes ___ No

- Will the show commit to have me as a guest or interview me about my new book project? ___ Yes ___ No

- Do I have useful connections with celebrities, other experts in my field, or other public figures who would be willing to invite me to guest on their shows, speak at their conferences, or provide cover quotes for my book? ___ Yes ___ No

- Do I have my own radio or TV show? ___ Yes ___ No

- Will I be allowed to promote my book project on the show?
  ___ Yes ___ No

  If so, how large is its audience? _____

- Do I have a regular column in a newspaper or magazine or on a website? ___ Yes ___ No

- Will I be able to include the book title in my byline?
  ___ Yes ___ No

  If so, how large is its readership? _____

- Do I have a blog and/or website? ___ Yes ___ No

  If so, is it/are they related to the topic of my book? Can I feature part of my book on an ongoing basis?

  _____

- Has my blog or website received a significant number of hits? ___ Yes ___ No

- Do I promote my topic on Twitter? ___ Yes ___ No

  If so, do I have a significant number of followers?
  ___ Yes ___ No

- Do I have a dedicated YouTube site that promotes my topic and links to my website? ___ Yes ___ No

- Am I a spokesperson for an organization related to my book's topic? ___ Yes ___ No

- Will they support the book and buy copies and promote the book to their members on their website? ___ Yes ___ No

- Have I received any awards or honors connected to my book's topic? ___ Yes ___ No

- If not, have I received any major awards of honors that would add to my perceived authority? ___ Yes ___ No

- Have I taught classes, seminars, or workshops on the subject of my book? ___ Yes ___ No

  If so, where, how often, and how well attended have they been? _____

- Can I line up speaking engagements around the time of publication? ___ Yes ___ No

- Do I sell, promote, or endorse the sale of any products related to my book? ___ Yes ___ No

- Can information about my book be added to the products for cross-promotion? ___ Yes ___ No

- Do I have any products that are branded with my name? ___ Yes ___ No

- Do I have contacts that could arrange manufacturing opportunities for branded products? ___ Yes ___ No

- Do I have contacts for product endorsement? ___ Yes ___ No

- Do I have any other contacts that could help me promote this book? ___ Yes ___ No

- Do my degrees add to my book's marketability? ___ Yes ___ No

- Is there a chance that my book might be used at my university or at universities or high schools around the country? ___ Yes ___ No

- Can I effectively contact prominent alumni about market options for my book? ___ Yes ___ No

- Do I have a career in the field I am writing about?
  ___ Yes ___ No

  If so, am I a recognized expert in my field? ___ Yes ___ No

- If I've previously published any books, will their sales and/or reviews, awards, and the like promote sales of a subsequent book? ___ Yes ___ No

- Can the number of my published works (books, articles, etc.) be used to boost sales of this book? ___ Yes ___ No

- Have I been published in a prestigious publication?
  ___ Yes ___ No

- Do I hold or have I held a significant office in that organization, another organization connected to my topic, or any organization with a large membership? ___ Yes ___ No

- Will they buy and promote the book? ___ Yes ___ No

- Have I spoken to large audiences, spoken often, and/or spoken to organizations related to my book's topic?
  ___ Yes ___ No

- Is there a relevant news event that I can respond to in a major publication that will bring attention to my book's topic? __ Yes __ No

Look over your "yes" answers. Maybe you will have more than you think. You might have never thought of yourself from a marketing perspective before, but now that you look at the answers, you may realize that your thriving eBay business, cooking-from-the-garden workshops, or pet-troubleshooting workshops are surprisingly successful and fit into your platform. Or that your cottage industry of smoking and marketing your own chipotle peppers or your jewelry-making business has found an enthusiastic niche market that is eager for recipes or directions. Your book is on its way!

AGENTS' ADVICE

Keep a piece of paper on your nightstand for a week, and jot down all associations and affiliations you might use to bring value to your platform: your job, alumni association(s), hobbies, clubs, memberships, organizations, volunteer activities, church, and the like. Don't overlook previous jobs and affiliations when you make your list.

Putting It in Perspective

Let's turn to some real-life examples of super-successful platforms. These aren't meant to intimidate you, but to inspire you to put on your marketing hat and think creatively.

When Gary Heavin, the founder of Curves, a fitness franchise, writes a diet or fitness book, he can make some pretty eye-popping claims. In his platform, he can say that his book can be marketed through his 10,000 Curves franchises to their more than 4 million members. He could also promote the new book on the Curves website, in the quarterly Curves magazine, *Diane*, that is available free to all members, and through the popular Curves diet workshops.

But Curves' impressive numbers pale in comparison to songwriter Jimmy Buffett's empire. Many of Buffett's contemporaries in mellow rock 'n' roll are now broke, dead, or selling real estate. But Jimmy Buffett appears to have been blessed with the marketing acumen of the (unrelated) Warren Buffett when it comes to brand extension.

First, Jimmy Buffett developed his own distinctive "Gulf and western" sound, creating a laid-back, tropical paradise in his songs that drew a legion of loyal fans, called Parrotheads, who attend all his concerts and buy all his paraphernalia.

This proved to be a goldmine for Buffett, whose 30-plus recordings and CDs have earned him 8 gold and 9 platinum or multi-platinum albums. But the music was just the beginning. Not only was Buffett shrewd enough to create a genre of music that offered an easygoing fantasy to the hard-driven Yuppies whose lives were more Manhattan than Margaritaville, but he was able to parlay the popularity of his distinctive style into branded products that played off his music, including T-shirts, license plates, footwear, and other paraphernalia, Land Shark Lager, and Margaritaville Tequila, margarita mixes, and shrimp. Not to mention his two restaurant enterprises, a chain of Margaritaville restaurants that he owns, and a chain of Cheeseburger in Paradise restaurants, operated by an affiliate of the Outback Steakhouse franchise. (Both are named after popular Buffett songs.)

All told, Jimmy Buffett's various enterprises make him a reputed $100 *million* a year. Is it any wonder his first three books became instant bestsellers? Of course not: he had a huge platform to market them.

You say you don't have a platform? Perhaps you have the expertise to write about your topic, but not the exposure to promote it. But it doesn't mean you won't *ever* be published. It just means you need to get to work *now* to create a compelling platform.

> **AGENTS' ADVICE**
>
> Work on creating your platform even while you're writing your proposal and book. In today's publishing environment, without a strong platform it's an uphill battle. It takes a lot of phone calls, e-mails, and asking. Work through the checklist and suggestions in this chapter and see what sort of platform you come up with. Look closely for gaps that you can strengthen before you submit your proposal.

It's All About Marketing Yourself

Writing a platform may sound like a lot of work, but what about *building* a platform? You may have thought that getting a book published was about writing, not marketing. Do you really have to market yourself? The short answer is yes, unless you're already famous (or infamous), in which case your fame *is* your platform. (But in that case, publishers will probably be coming to *you* and begging you to write a book, not the other way around.)

Look at it from the publisher's perspective. Bookstores, with their packed shelves, may look like they stock every book there ever was. But the truth is far different: bookstores have only so much shelf and display space, and they want every inch of that space to be profitable. As a result, bookstore buyers turn down any books they think the store can't sell, and if a book isn't even going to make it into the stores, it won't make it into print from a major publisher. Publishers need to be able to show the bookstore buyers proof that there's an audience waiting to buy your particular book on low-fat cooking as opposed to every other low-fat cookbook on the market, and the platform makes that argument for them.

But that's not the whole story. Imagine your book sitting on the store shelf. What are the chances that someone will wander into the bookstore or be browsing the Internet and pick up your book out of the thousands of others available? And the reason they will do that is because they know you through your platform, and they want to see what you're saying. Publishers love it when you can up the odds in their favor (and yours, too, don't forget) by delivering that ready-made audience along with your manuscript. In a busy world with so many things fighting for our attention, you want your readers to go out and look for your book.

Maybe you think marketing and promotion are drudgery as opposed to the creativity involved in developing a book idea and then writing the book. But marketing is an art, and we're here to tell you that it's every bit as exciting as writing. Marketing can also be a lot of fun as you brainstorm ideas on how to gain exposure for yourself and your book. You'll surprise yourself by what you come up with when you let yourself go and the ideas start coming! And who knows, you might open up a whole new income stream from your efforts, such as becoming a regular columnist for your paper or contributing articles to magazines or selling your creations online.

Ideas to Get Your Platform Going

Here are some tools that will build up your platform quickly. And there's more good news: they'll impress a potential agent or acquiring editor.

Sell It Yourself

Many people publish a book to support, market, and expand their existing business. These people have a built-in platform through their client base. What is your corporate reach in this case? You may have national and even international outreach.

Create Your Own Website

Websites have become so *de rigueur* that they're almost like a college degree: you need one before you can get your writing job. The good news is that you don't necessarily have to pay someone to get your site up and running. There are do-it-yourself website programs that are easy to create and that look very professional. Many companies offer this software; ask at your local office-supply store, ask other people for their recommendations, or check online reviews. Some of these companies also host your site, updating it as necessary and keeping track of the "hits" you receive.

HOT OFF THE PRESS

There is no great mystery about getting a web address. You can actually own a domain name for less than $10 per year. You can register your website through Google or other search engines and no one else will be able to use it. (But don't forget to renew your domain name every year.) Be sure to register both .com and .net. We suggest that you copyright your website name before building the site to make sure it's exclusive to you. Branding your site to your book title is helpful. Ease of recognition is crucial so that your audience can find you.

Start Blogging

Blogs can be an excellent way to leverage your ideas into a book. Setting up a blog is very much like a website, but it provides interactive comments and reviews. Audiences can sign up for RSS "feeds" in which they receive e-mail alerts when you have written a new post. You can see how many people have come on your blog each day and what posts they have read, as well as track how many hits (views) each post has gotten over time.

If you add a statistics counter like SiteMeter to your site, you can even see the location of your visitors (quite a thrill when they come from all over the world and from across the United States). SiteMeter and other statistics counters like StatCounter are free, and they also send you monthly reports summarizing your blog's activity.

Blogs are easier to create and maintain than websites because the blog hosts (the two largest are Blogger and WordPress) make it easy to choose your blog's heading and style with a few clicks. And you can embed photos, videos, or widgets on a blog without having to create a menu or a new page.

Answer all comments that appear on your posts (unless, of course, they're spam). Readers appreciate that you've taken the time to read their comments and responded to them, and will come back to see what you've said, and return again. Keep it interactive. You are building a following one at a time.

Visit other blogs that post on your topic and leave comments on their posts. The blogger and people who visit the blog will see your name and your blog's associated with the comment, and they might head to your blog to check it out and find themselves coming back for more. You may even want to attend a blogging convention in your field to further your contacts.

PUBLISHING PITFALLS

Don't be disappointed if your blog doesn't attract stellar numbers. It takes time and effort to build up a blog following. Post often, preferably daily, but at least several times a week, to give visitors a reason to come back often and see what you've been saying (or doing, if it's a blog about parenting, cooking, crafting, woodworking, gardening, or the like).

Become a Contributor

Besides having your own blog and website, you can become a contributor on other people's sites. If you see a blog or website on your topic with multiple contributors, see if you can join them. Many of these sites are eager to have people they think are a good fit adding content, and it's a great way to increase your exposure.

Speak on Your Subject

One of the quickest ways to build a platform is to speak on a platform. Research the organizations and associations where your topic would be welcome. If you are writing about depression, check out a local Bipolar and Depression Support Alliance chapter. If you are writing about cardiovascular disease, check out your local American Heart Association chapter. If you grow herbs, see if there's a local chapter of the Herb Society of America. Become a member and offer to speak at one of their meetings. Try to put together a six-month schedule of speaking events.

If you attend conferences and speak at them, this can be a huge boost to your platform. How many do you attend each year? Are they local or national? How many attendees are there? How many attend your talks? Could you sell your book at these conferences? Try to brand your book to your presentation if appropriate. The same holds true if you attend and speak at trade shows and other professional meetings.

You can also speak on your topic to civic and business organizations, offer to give a talk or presentation at your local library, or see if area museums need speakers for a presentation. For example, if you grow culinary herbs and have built up a business selling herb blends and edible herb wreaths, you could give a wreath-making demonstration at a living-history museum, speak on how you built your business to a small-business organization, and give an evening presentation on herb blends at the library.

Look into joining a speaker's bureau, which will help you line up speaking engagements. Organizations like Toastmasters (www. toastmasters.org) can help you polish your speaking skills.

Teach

Does your community have an adult education program? Does a nearby college have continuing education classes? Can you offer seminars at conferences on your book topic?

Don't overlook other teaching opportunities. If you're a master gardener, offer to teach at a community garden or garden centers. See if any area elementary schools have or are thinking about planting gardens and offer to teach the students about gardening. If you're a Reiki Master, see if local hospitals or wellness centers would let you teach Reiki to patients undergoing treatments. Perhaps an organizing store would let you teach a class on clutter control.

One of the best ways to build up your expertise (and your platform) is by demonstrating your ability to teach your subject. Keep in touch with your students by e-mail updates and through your blog and website. Capture names and e-mail addresses at every event. They will be useful at the time of publication.

Use Social Networking Sites

Social online networks are not just social. YouTube, Facebook, LinkedIn, and Twitter all provide great vehicles for your platform:

- **YouTube.** One of our authors began developing her platform with a series of YouTube videos on honey. She filmed herself cooking with honey, making soaps and candles with honey, and making a mixture of honey for homespun medicinal use. If you're going on YouTube to promote yourself and your topic, be sure to act like a professional and make sure your videos are of professional quality.

- **Facebook.** Use your page to promote your platform and your book. This is an opportunity to mix your personal and professional worlds, but we caution you to keep the content professional at all times. You might consider setting up a Facebook page for your professional interests.

- **LinkedIn.** Because this is more of a professional site, a profile on LinkedIn is a great platform-builder for business, career, and finance books, and a source, for example, for a financial-management expert looking for customer testimonials and speaking engagements. If your book topic is also your business, LinkedIn can provide great exposure.

- **Twitter.** Twitter is an excellent way to reach a large audience, because your tweets are short and punchy, while a blog post might be longer and require more time commitment on the part of readers. As with blogs, the more often you tweet, the more followers you're likely to have. And, just like you do on your blog, make sure you respond to all comments.

AGENTS' ADVICE

It's important to remember to promote yourself through your platform. This is not the time to be shy. Agents need to know as much as possible about you and your network of contacts. Even more important, they need to see that you're comfortable appearing and speaking in public, because your publisher's publicist will almost certainly try to set up some appearances on radio, newspaper interviews, and maybe even TV appearances for you. Better get used to the limelight! But be self-aware, if you need media training in order to effectively promote your work, seek out professional advice.

Expand Your E-Mail Address Book

An extensive list of e-mail contacts is well worth noting in your platform. Several publishers have mentioned that 40,000 is considered a strong number. Start a company newsletter that will enable you to create an e-mail list and capture e-mail names. You can send e-mail "blasts" to the entire list, building anticipation for your book, announcing speaking engagements and upcoming classes and presentations, announcing the book's pub date, and of course promoting any bookstore appearances and book signings.

Get Quotes

You have seen the quotes on the back cover and front pages of books, praising the author and her book or books. These cover quotes are major sales tools for your publisher. If you're writing a book on hair styling and you're a "stylist to the stars," who can get Mariah Carey, Angelina Jolie, Miley Cyrus, and Jennifer Lopez to give quotes about how you make their hair look fantastic, you are likely to enhance book sales. Perhaps one of your celebrity clients or contacts might be approached to contribute an introduction to your book.

But what if you're not connected to anybody famous? What if you haven't even started writing your book yet? No worries, you can still get good testimonials.

You don't need to have already written your book in order to get a good quote. Provide satisfaction surveys when you teach a course or have a local speaking engagement, and get permission to use any comments. If you provide a service or sell a product, ask customers to fill out a customer satisfaction form, again asking permission to use any comments. ("After just one hypnotism treatment with Dolores, I was able to give up smoking. I'd been a heavy smoker for seven years and it's now been two years since I touched a cigarette. Dolores is a lifesaver!")

You can use these quotes on your Facebook page, in your blog, and on your website. Most important, you can use these quotes and testimonials in your platform marketing section. It shows you have a following.

Brand Yourself

If you're the spokesperson for a brand, it's instant proof of your marketability. You can also brand your book by seeking brand alliances. Would AARP brand, support, or offer to sell your book, *Growing Old, Staying Young?* Would Orvis lend its name to your book, *Fly Fishing for Families,* or be willing to pick it up for their catalog, website, and fly-fishing schools? This is very powerful marketing, and will add huge stature to your platform. It also shows your willingness to get out and find markets for your book, as you will be able to sell books through their vehicles.

PUBLISHING PITFALLS

If you get a chance to speak at a meeting, you will need to be prepared with a solid presentation. If you can display some of your quilts or jams, bring plants or blueprints for chicken coops, or bring some examples of the products you use to a presentation on restoring antiques, it will help make your talk a hit. There might be "no such thing as bad publicity," as the quote goes, but there is bland publicity. A poor speech will do nothing for you, your platform, or your audience. But a good speech can open the door to regular speaking engagements and increase your confidence, so that you are all set to speak *after* your book is published.

More Food for Thought

Before you write your platform marketing section, think again about possible contacts. We suggested earlier in the chapter that you keep a pen and paper by your bed for a week and write down any organizations, associations, and the like that might prove helpful in terms of selling or promoting your book (and you). Now it is time once again to put pen to paper and think about anyone or any place that can help sell your book:

- Do you have a famous connection or know someone who has a famous connection? If so, ask if you can use his name to help promote your book.

- Do you know anyone who has connections with key opinion leaders or organizations? For example, maybe a colleague at work knows the president of the Culinary Institute of America, and you are writing a cookbook. Or maybe you have a friend who is married to a writer on WebMD and you're writing a book on fitness.

- Is there a key date or anniversary you can include in your marketing efforts? For example, the hundredth anniversary of Mark Twain's death is a perfect opportunity to market your Mark Twain biography; a book based on the leadership skills of General Eisenhower may be best promoted and sold on the anniversary of D-Day.

- Are there any organizations or corporations who would be interested in selling your book? Perhaps you are writing a book on building a dream bathroom and you know a regional manager at Home Depot. Maybe this manager can get you a meeting with someone at corporate headquarters who would be interested in buying a certain number of copies of your book to sell in their stores, giving you a built-in audience and a great platform. Perhaps a query to the American Heart Association would result in an opportunity for you to sell copies of your book on fitness for heart health on their website, or result in their buying a bulk quantity to give out as gifts in their annual Heart Runs.

HOT OFF THE PRESS

Try to keep your platform marketing section to one or two pages. You want to detail your experience and potential book-selling opportunities, but not repeat the facts from the About the Author section of your proposal.

A Platform Marketing Section That Sells

In the following annotated example, it looks like Jane *could* have a strong platform, but her information is so vague that it could turn out to be mostly hot air. She's not helping an agent, acquiring editor, or publisher tell if she really has what it takes.

Sample Marketing Section

"Jane Smith is a great personal trainer." —A-list celebrity **[It's great to have such a famous endorsement, but she needs to say more.]**

"Jane Smith's programs are based on sound scientific ground rules." —A professor at Harvard **[Who? What does the professor teach? Needs more detail.]**

Jane Smith is a certified personal trainer who has extensive experience in working with clients from all walks of life. She trains a lot of celebrities, corporate executives, and television experts. **[It would help if she names some of these people. Right now, her claims are too broad—and they could be exaggerations.]**

She also has experience teaching fitness classes at Market City and Lose Weight Now corporate headquarters. **[Great! But is there any way to leverage these contacts into book sales?]**

Jane has been a frequent speaker at the YMCA. **[YMCA where? Needs to be more specific.]** She has appeared on *Good Morning Charlotte*. **[What is that? A TV show in North Carolina? Needs more description.]** She is in the process of creating an exercise video series. **[She and many others; what makes her series unique?]**

Jane has been quoted in national magazines. **[Which ones?]**

In the following version of her platform, Jane displays the savvy of a professional. We can see at a glance that her book will be easy to pitch to publishers. In your own platform, of course, use real names ("Professor Ellen Hays, M.D., Ph.D., Division of Exercise Physiology ...," "the Jonas Brothers"), not descriptors as we've done here.

Sample Marketing Section

Foreword from an A-list celebrity:

"Jane Smith is a great personal trainer. I have personally trained with her for the past four years and she is always motivating, enthusiastic, and creative so I don't get bored. I love her program! The chance for other people to share what I already know about Jane will make an amazing book." —A-list celebrity [**Not only is a famous celebrity promoting Jane, but the quote is really promotable. Perhaps the celebrity can be approached near publication time to provide a foreword.**]

Additional endorsement for book jacket:

"Obesity has reached epidemic levels in this country. Anything and everything must be done to help Americans stay fit. Jane Smith's expertise in this arena is brilliant. She is the gold standard and the real deal." —Exercise specialist, Division of Exercise Physiology and Science, Harvard University [**Another great testimonial—this time from a professor—showing that Jane not only attracts the famous who want to be fit, but her program is grounded in science.**]

Media appearances:

Jane Smith's work has been quoted in *The New York Times*, *Chicago Sun-Times*, *The Los Angeles Times*, *Women's Day*, *More Magazine*, and *O: The Oprah Winfrey Magazine* online. *Women's Day* plans to do a feature of her around the time of publication. The author plans to write an op-ed piece about the book for National Fitness Day, April 3. [**This paragraph shows that Jane is a professional who knows how to promote herself. At this point, we would be saying, "Let's call her today!"**]

Promotional opportunities:

Jane Smith is a certified personal trainer who has extensive experience in working with clients from all walks of life. She trains Hollywood A-listers and sports professionals who are frequent guests on the *Today* show and MSNBC. They have agreed to do workouts with the author around the time of publication on national shows. **[Great promotional facts. They also tie back to and reinforce the testimonials above. And the author has remembered to refer to herself in the third person, which looks professional, rather than saying "I'm a certified personal trainer," etc. Good job!]**

Brand extension products:

The author is in the process of creating an exercise video series that has attracted national sponsorship, including Reebok, Nutrisystem, and diet pill manufacturer Novalitis. **[More strong promotional material.]**

Corporate support:

The author teaches fitness classes at Market City and Lose Weight Now corporate headquarters, and both organizations have generously offered to purchase books in bulk (minimum order 2,000 copies) on publication. They further agree to promote the book on their websites and newsletters. **[This is a key platform plank. Jane has the promise of large corporations purchasing her book in bulk—which means guaranteed sales!]**

Speaking events:

Jane Smith has been a frequent speaker at YMCA annual conferences, as well as teaching for 10 years at her local North Carolina branch. She has 20 major speaking events in place for next year—see the attached appearance schedule. **[This shows that the author will be able to sell copies of her books at events for years to come.]**

The Least You Need to Know

- Your platform shows a publisher that you can be a full partner in generating sales once your book is published.
- Create your promotional platform before you even begin to write your proposal.
- Use your contacts to leverage your platform.
- Take advantage of the promotional possibilities available cheap on the web.
- Don't be shy about "blowing your own horn." Take advantage of all appropriate opportunities to better the chances of having your book published, as long as you can support your claims with names and numbers.

The Expanded
Table of Contents

Chapter
15

In This Chapter

- What is an Expanded Table of Contents?
- How to create an Expanded Table of Contents
- How to organize your book into parts
- The components of the chapter descriptions
- Using bullet points
- Expanded Table of Contents samples

Most writers start with a skeletal Table of Contents (TOC) and refine it as they write their book. They develop catchy and appropriate part heads and chapter heads, a tight list that is often included in the proposal. An essential element in the proposal is the Expanded Table of Contents that builds on the basic Table of Contents page.

We get a lot of proposals that start out with a bang. The writing style is catchy, the cover letter hooks us, and the overview keeps us turning the pages. Yes! This is a live one, a great idea backed by great writing style. The author has done her homework: the competitive review is compelling, and she has a strong platform. Looks like we have a winner—until we get to the Expanded Table of Contents, the detailed outline that summarizes the book. Then it becomes clear that there's no substance; it's just another person with a good idea but no clue how to turn that idea into publishable reality. And if a person can't write a compelling outline, there's little hope that writing an entire book, much less a *good* book, will result. Too bad: another one for the rejection pile.

This is what the Expanded Table of Contents, which gives a brief supporting description for each part and chapter title, is intended to do: put the flesh on the bones of the original TOC. If the expanded version doesn't excite an agent or acquiring editor, it's an indication that you don't really have a vision for your book. Don't let this happen to you and your book. You've already come up with a clear, focused concept that you think stands out from the competition. You've written an overview and thought through a concise Table of Contents with appropriate part and chapter titles. Now it's time to put more details and substance in it.

The Big Reveal

The *Expanded Table of Contents* is a summary overview of the content that is included in each chapter. Under each chapter heading, a paragraph or two codifies what will be covered in that chapter. By reading all these chapter descriptions an agent can see the arc of the book: the beginning, the middle, and the end. Further, she will be able to tell how the content is organized and how much material is covered in each chapter, and identify the fresh thinking and highlights of the content.

DEFINITION

The **Expanded Table of Contents** (or Expanded TOC for short) includes part and chapter summaries, each with a heading or title, providing a synopsis of each section's content. A part of the book proposal, the Expanded Table of Contents gives the agent and publisher the opportunity to evaluate the content and organization of the book.

The Expanded TOC is your chance to prove that you not only have the vision, but the logic and dedication to carry your book through to its conclusion. It's a concise way to show exactly how you plan to make the book work, part by part and chapter by chapter. And—if you've brought the agent or editor this far into the proposal with you—it's a certainty that he'll read the expanded outline, so this gives you a chance to hit him again with your writing style and publishing savvy. The Expanded TOC is the perfect marketing tool, *if* you know how to work it.

To an agent, an acquiring editor, and a publisher, the Expanded TOC demonstrates the substance of the work. To a first-time author, an Expanded TOC is especially important to show they understand what it takes to create an entire full-length book. Can you visualize the entire work from this piece? Is there solid research? Is there enough content for each chapter? Does the book seem organized? Does the narrative read smoothly? This is the piece of the puzzle that assures the folks who are putting time, effort, and money behind your success that you have what it takes to turn an idea into a marketable manuscript.

And it's not just a key piece for your eventual publisher: by working through the Expanded TOC, you can focus on the content and quality of your book. You can test the solidity and originality of your book idea as you flesh out the chapters and parts. It's an excellent checkpoint that lets you test the strength and logic of your concept and correct any weaknesses before you even begin sending out the proposal.

 PUBLISHING PITFALLS

If you're struggling with your Expanded TOC, take a deep breath and regroup. If it doesn't make sense to you, it certainly won't make sense to your agent and publisher. You *must* be your own objective critic before you add the Expanded TOC to your proposal. Take the time now to read and re-read your outline to make sure it's logical and compelling. Be ruthless in dealing with any weaknesses in the outline. Never forget that agents and editors are experts when it comes to finding weaknesses in a proposal. Make sure your Expanded TOC sticks to the point and doesn't wander off into meaningless or unnecessary asides.

Creating the Expanded Table of Contents

If you're not sure how to start, try identifying 5 to 10 key points in each chapter of your book, then create a bullet for each key point. Then turn each bullet into a narrative of one to two paragraphs that presents your material in an orderly and progressive way. The

Expanded TOC shows not just that you know what you're talking about, but that you know how to explain it to readers who are interested but probably *don't* know what you're talking about. Your Expanded TOC will give acquiring editors and their publishing houses a good idea of your skill in conceiving the book as a whole piece, breaking down into parts (the individual chapters), and handling the material appropriately for the audience. The challenge is to keep the writing lively even though there is a lot of content in a condensed version.

If your Expanded TOC fails to live up to the promises you've made in your overview, you may be asked to try again. But you don't want to risk a rejection based on your first try. You need to show through your Expanded TOC that *your* book is the best yet on the topic.

Your Expanded TOC is not set in stone. You may find that the organization changes as you write your book. Your agent, acquiring editor, marketing committee, and text editor may all have suggestions for better structure and content. (Remember, publishing is a process, not an event.) The purpose of the Expanded TOC is to show that you have a vision for your book, but you remain flexible about input from publishing professionals.

A successful Expanded TOC needs to be clear and concise without being boring. Sound like a challenge? Yes. But, based on our experience, we have compiled a list of tips that will help you combine clarity with content:

- **Keep it short.** Your chapter-by-chapter outline typically runs from two to six pages total for all of the chapters. You need to describe what is in each chapter, but please don't write the actual book. Keep it short, but not too short. The title alone is not enough. Let's hope it's great and catchy, but here's where you need to flesh it out with a description. Your chapter description should contain about 100 to 125 words. Ideally, each chapter description should be one paragraph with three or four bullet points of content information.

- **Give it a logical organization.** Your Expanded TOC is designed to show the flow of your book. Make sure your organization makes sense, and that it also makes *business* sense. (As in, it helps a publisher sell more copies of your book.) For example, if you're writing a book on cardiovascular disease, you might be tempted to start with the anatomy of the heart, then "funnel down" to a section on risks and symptoms, and end with treatment and sustaining a good, healthy quality of life. But this organization is predictable, and you may find in your research that many competitive titles take it. Your goal is to achieve a fresh approach. But if somebody buys your book because he has heart disease, he doesn't want an anatomy lesson; he wants solutions. So you might opt to start your book with a chapter titled "Five Ways to Prevent and Reverse Heart Disease," then move on to explanations and sustainable treatments.

- **Name your chapters well.** Giving your part and chapter titles targeted headings will help your book appeal to the reader and stand apart from the competition. Don't randomly call a chapter something you think is clever if the reader can't tell what the chapter is about. Titles should be informative. For example, in a weight-loss book, a chapter called "Jump Start" could mean anything: jump-starting your exercise program, jump-starting your metabolism, or crash-dieting for quick weight loss. "Jump-Start Your 10-Pound Weight Loss" is much more specific.

- **Be bold.** In addition to naming each chapter, keep the title and description separate by putting the title in bold or in a different typeface. This not only separates the chapters more effectively, but it also makes your Expanded TOC easier to read (see the sample later in the chapter).

- **Add variety.** There are no hard-and-fast rules about how you should write your chapter descriptions. What you don't want to do is begin each chapter description with this hackneyed line: "In this chapter, I will ...." Starting a chapter description with a question is fine. Just don't start *every* chapter description with a question. It can become tedious. Mix it up; keep it interesting. You want an agent to see that you know your subject inside and out and you want to keep your reader engaged while writing about it.

- **Show your confidence.** It's not enough to say you are an authority on a subject; you need to *show* it through concise, clear sentences, a mastery of the subject, and a confidence in each chapter's contents. Selectively quoting statistics, study results, and your experience that you will be using in your work will help reinforce your credibility and demonstrate that you have something valuable to add to your field.

- **Keep your writing sample separate.** If your writing sample for the proposal comes from, say, Chapter 4, don't repeat what the agent will be reading when she gets to that section of your proposal. Simply state next to the chapter listing that "Chapter 4 is the writing sample," or "See page 20 for writing sample." If you're submitting an excerpt of a chapter as your writing sample, describe the chapter in the usual fashion, but be concise; don't parrot the sample text. Add at the end of the chapter description that "excerpts from this chapter are included as a writing sample." (We discuss the writing sample in detail in Chapter 16.)

Organizing the Book into Parts

If you're writing nonfiction, you've probably organized your book into broad parts, and then grouped your chapters under each part. This organization helps the reader navigate through the book. Bear in mind that a book that's easy to navigate is a book that's more likely to be read (and bought). Your first task when creating the expanded outline is to define the parts, making each clearly distinct from the others while tying them together. Here's a good example from a hypothetical biography of King Henry VIII:

> **Part I: Defender of the Faith**
>
> **Part II: Bewitched by Anne**
>
> **Part III: Good Queen Jane**

> **Part IV: Bereft of God and Man**
>
> **Part V: England after Henry**

Now, create a sentence or two after each part title to clarify its scope. Here's an example of using parts:

> **Part I: Defender of the Faith:** The young Prince Henry was considered a perfect knight, the flower of chivalry, when he asked Princess Catherine of Aragon's hand in marriage. He was also such a staunch Catholic that the Pope named him Defender of the Faith. Little did any of them know what fate had in store.

Writing Your Chapter Descriptions

Each expanded chapter summary supplements the chapter title with a short descriptive paragraph of at least two or three key descriptive sentences each. This format enables the agent and editor to visualize each chapter and assess how the book is organized and how the content flows. It will give them an opportunity to see what's new and exciting about each chapter, as well as how the chapter fits into the part section and into the book as a whole.

Using Bullets to Expand on Narrative Content

If you're writing nonfiction, bullet points at the end of each descriptive paragraph give the agent, acquiring editor, and marketing committee something to latch on to in terms of potential marketing points. Of course, you should only use them if you have something noteworthy to add to each chapter. For example, if you're writing a book about nutrition during pregnancy, you might want to include a few recipes from each chapter as bullet points after the chapter description. If you're writing about celebrity child-rearing, you might want to include some names of the celebs you're interviewing as bold bullet points.

PUBLISHING PITFALLS

Don't fall into the trap of thinking you can just list bulleted talking points about the topics readers will find in a particular chapter. Bullet points are sometimes added to a chapter description, but only after several sentences of narrative description.

Expanded Table of Contents Examples

To help you visualize some of the key points in an Expanded TOC, we have created two annotated sample excerpts of the same hypothetical proposal for a book about teenage depression. The following excerpt from an Expanded TOC falls flat, while the second version shows a well-prepared Expanded TOC.

Expanded Table of Contents (Partial)

There Is No Normal:

The Truth About Teenage Depression

Introduction: The Face in the Mirror

The introduction will educate the reader to childhood depression. [**Overstatement: this is too broad and not descriptive enough. And it's not grammatically correct: "to" should be "about."**] You will also learn about my experience. [**Your experience doing what? This chapter needs a lot more information.**]

Part I: Through the Mirror [**This part title doesn't make any sense because it doesn't reveal the content or organization. The author also needs to add a couple of sentences here to describe what's covered in this part.**]

Chapter 1: Teenagers Today

This chapter is about teenagers today [**Don't state the obvious; avoid useless repetition. Each sentence must reveal something new.**], what they like and what they don't, what

---

they want and what they don't. [**Again, repetitious and too general. There is nothing here that says why this book is different, nor does it demonstrate good writing. But the bigger point is, what does this have to do with children who suffer from depression? If you're trying to set up what normal is, explain that here.**]

Chapter 2: What Is Depression?

Everything you wanted to know—and more—about depression that I have learned as a clinical psychologist and Associate Professor at Brown University. [**Although the author does refer to his authority, the phrase "Everything you wanted to know—and more ..." is a cliché that seems to trivialize the subject.**]

Chapter 3: Symptoms of Adolescent Depression [**This sounds like a textbook, and the title is bland.**]

The symptoms of adolescent depression are outlined here:

- Withdrawal from family and friends

- Erratic and irrational behavior

- Loss of appetite or overeating

- Insomnia or oversleeping

- Drop in school grades

- Anxiety

- Feelings of hopeless and helplessness

(This chapter is excerpted in my writing sample.) [**The bulleted list is good, but it's missing the first few sentences that introduce the content of the chapter and set up the list to follow.**]

Part II: When the Mirror Breaks

Chapter 4: Other Disorders [**What does this mean? What does the reader learn from this heading? Unfortunately, not enough.**]

Every two out of ten diagnoses of childhood depression are masked as a learning disability or ADHD. [**The use of statistics isn't helpful here because we're not sure exactly what they refer to. Statistics are good, but they have to be clearly sourced and easy to understand. Does the author mean that depression is misdiagnosed when the child really has a learning disability or ADHD, or the reverse? And because this book is specifically about teens, "childhood" is too broad a category. Another omission is that the disorders should have been spelled out in the heading.**] Lots of children have depression combined with one of these disorders. [**How many? The author should use a statistic here, too. And, again, keep the focus on teens. If girls and boys have different stats, it would be intriguing to point that out here.**] This chapter delves into learning disabilities, drug abuse, and ADHD …. [**This is a lot to cover in one chapter. Drug abuse doesn't fit with learning disabilities and ADHD.**]

Chapter 5: Drug and Alcohol Abuse [**How does this tie back to depression? The title needs more explanation while still remaining concise.**]

A lot of teenagers try to self-medicate when they feel depressed. They will take drugs or drink alcohol, often with terrible results. This chapter goes into the details of this. [**This description simply sets up the obvious. What about drugs or alcohol? How can a parent see the signs? Substantiate this statement with clearly sourced statistics. "A lot" just doesn't cut it. Not only that, but the book ends abruptly here without a wrap-up chapter or any sign of closure. This is a definite "No"!**]

Expanded Table of Contents (Partial)

There Is No Normal:

The Truth About Teenage Depression

Introduction: The Face in the Mirror

Is your teenager depressed? Or is he or she "just acting out"? This chapter provides a behavior checklist to help pinpoint teenage depression, and introduces a condition that is often misdiagnosed. **[Questions can be a good lead-in to the subject at hand. In this case, they are also used to describe why this book is different, and the checklist offers readers an action to help them move forward and relieve their frustration.]** I explain how my findings and techniques are based on my 30 years of research and clinical practice as a clinical psychologist and Professor of Psychology at Brown University. **[Even though this is repeated from the overview and platform sections of the proposal, it sets up the premise and authority of the book. It's good to reinforce the expertise of the author.]** This introduction also briefly explains how the book is organized. **[Clearly and concisely explains what this chapter is about and how the book is organized without repeating anything that will have been in the overview section.]**

Part I: Through the Looking Glass: **[An interesting metaphor, and a stronger title. It will be up to the successful author to sustain it effectively. Note how the author has also added some descriptive text.]** This section shows you how to determine if your teen is struggling from depression and needs professional help or is simply acting like a crazed, aggravating kid. Sometimes it's not easy to tell the difference!

Chapter 1: Teenagers in the Twenty-First Century [Bolding the chapter titles helps them stand out from the text.]

Teenagers today face enormous stresses and challenges. This chapter describes life as a typical teenager today and the cultural differences from their parents' childhoods. [**This would pique reader interest.**]

Chapter 2: Is Your Teenager Depressed?

Here readers will learn exactly what depression is, and is not, focusing on the brain, the chemical roots of depression, and the influence of the environment. [**The key here is to set up the foundation of the topic.**] The chapter includes a brief quiz for parents to help them determine if their children are depressed or just stressed, or a combination of both. [**Quizzes are always interesting; they engage the reader and help make the book more interactive and personal.**]

Chapter 3: A Cry for Help: Signs of Trouble [This title says it all; you know what the chapter will deliver.]

This chapter is a guide to the signs of trouble that all parents need to be alert to. The symptoms of adolescent depression are described, along with assessment tools to see if your child fits the description. They include the following:

- **Withdrawal from family and friends**
- **Erratic and irrational behavior**
- **Loss of appetite or overeating**
- **Insomnia or oversleeping**
- **Drop in school grades**
- **Anxiety**
- **Feelings of hopeless and helplessness**

(Writing sample included from this chapter, see page XX.) [**Short, sweet, and clear.**]

Part II: When the Mirror Breaks: **[This part title success-fully keeps the mirror metaphor going.]** Troubled teens often suffer from multiple disorders and/or drug and alcohol abuse. This part of the book helps parents identify what's really going on, then provides 16 proven ways to help your teen through these turbulent times.

Chapter 4: A Dual Diagnosis: Depression Plus Learning Disabilities and ADHD [This title presents parents with the possibility that their teen isn't struggling merely with one problem or another, but could conceivably have both. It also clearly explains what the reader will find in the chapter.]

Every two in five teens diagnosed with depression also suffer from other disorders, including learning disabilities and ADHD, according to the nonprofit Partnership for Solutions. **[Good use of statistics to make your point. Mentions where the statistics come from.]** This chapter helps parents find out which, if any, of these conditions influence or accentuate their teen's depression. **[This sentence neatly ties the subject matter of the title back to the subject of the book and successfully shows how the book's organization builds from the general to the more specific.]**

Chapter 5: Drug and Alcohol Abuse: Depression's Dysfunctional Partners [A provocative title. And the topic deserves its own chapter, because it's one that would be a huge concern for parents, the audience for the book.]

Like their adult counterparts, depressed teens will try to self-medicate when they're experiencing feelings of hopelessness and helplessness. **[A solid introduction to the chapter.]** They will turn to drugs and/or alcohol to escape. And that's just the first part: drug and alcohol abuse often go hand in hand with a drop in grades, loss of long-time friends, and isolation. **[This delves into some of the signs that a child is abusing drugs or alcohol.]** This chapter delves into the role of drug and alcohol abuse in depression. You also find a checklist of signs that they might be in play. **[Good: Parents need to know what the signs of abuse are, and it's important for the author to mention that they will be discussed here.]**

Chapter 6: Helping Your Teen Cope

Sixteen proven strategies will be provided to help your teen beat depression and have a rewarding high school and college experience. Depression may have no "cure," but it can be controlled, putting your teen back in control and giving the adolescent hope for an enjoyable and productive life. A checklist helps you select the strategies that are most likely to work for your teen. **[Yes! Closure, with an upbeat, can-do selection of strategies for success and a checklist so parents can narrow the selection to something more manageable.]**

Resources

Further Reading

Special Cases, Special Sections

Sometimes a book will include a foreword, dedication, acknowledgments, resources, glossary, endnotes, bibliography, recommended reading list, and/or appendixes. If any or all of these are suitable to your book, they should be noted and described in the Expanded TOC.

The Least You Need to Know

- An Expanded Table of Contents adds a brief descriptive paragraph to each part and chapter to give an agent or editor a better idea of your book's content.
- Make your Expanded TOC a short, narrative recap of the book's organization, providing two or three key descriptive sentences of the content in each chapter.

- Use the major points in each chapter in your chapter description to organize your book logically and informatively.

- Use the Expanded TOC to show the general organization, flow, originality of content, and need for the book, and to take the opportunity to showcase your writing style and qualifications to write the book.

- Pinpoint which chapter or text selection is included in the proposal as your writing sample.

The Nonfiction Writing Sample

In This Chapter

- Why the writing sample can seal the deal
- How to put together your writing sample
- Making your sample work for you
- Good and not-so-good writing samples

Finally! Your proposal is almost done. All that's left is the writing sample. Easy, right? Not necessarily. Your writing sample is the very last section an agent or editor reads, and it has to sing. This writing sample will show whether or not you can write, and whether or not you have what it takes to deliver a whole book. (This chapter deals with nonfiction proposals. For fiction proposals, where the rules are different, and for guidance on shaping a fiction writing sample, see Chapter 17.)

That is not a trivial concern, by the way. Many aspiring writers have never written anything longer than an article or a term paper. Can they really write a several-hundred-page book, and write it well and in a timely manner? The writing sample gives everyone who reads it a pretty good idea.

Nothing is more disappointing for an agent or acquiring editor than reading a compelling proposal for an original, exciting book idea, with strong support in the author's platform, and then discovering from the sample that the author simply can't write.

The Writing Sample Is Key

Agents and editors are always optimistic, looking for the "next big thing" every time they start reading a proposal. An editor we know once said that if she could picture the finished book while reading a proposal, she knew it would be a good addition to her list. But this optimism has to be supported by the writing sample—usually one to three chapters and any critical representative elements—or even the best proposal will end up in the reject pile.

> **PUBLISHING PITFALLS**
>
> In our experience, editors find the writing sample a key component of a proposal. And most writers we know are so passionate about their topics that they would write the entire book even if they didn't have a publisher. We don't recommend that approach, as a book can undergo a few transformations between its conception and publication. Agents and editors will have ideas for editing and shaping your book. But the passion behind it is something agents and editors look for in their authors. If you resent having to write even one chapter on "spec"—without prior compensation—you should ask yourself why you want to write the book at all. "Because I want to make money" is the wrong answer.

A writing sample must carry the enthusiasm and passion from the other components of the proposal to fruition. It's like the ending of a good novel, song, or movie: it leaves the audience wanting more. An editor or agent needs to know right from the start that an author is serious, that he can not only write a book, but *wants* to write it. A writing sample is especially important if you're a first-time author. An unknown author is an unproven author, and you must convince the agent or editor that you're not only an authority on your subject, but you can write about it in a compelling way.

Here's one more reason why a good writing sample is key: after the agent as gatekeeper, the next hurdle is the acquiring editor at the publishing house. As important as an acquiring editor is to your book's chances, never forget that she is just the first step in getting your book accepted by a publishing house. If the acquiring editor likes the book enough and chooses to present the book at an acquisitions review, the editorial and publishing boards and sales and marketing groups will be reading what you've written. That means your proposal needs to convince many types of experts who will be reading it critically: experts from the editorial, marketing, publicity, and special and foreign sales departments will all be weighing in on the decision to acquire or pass on your project. That's a lot of hoops to jump through, so a compelling writing sample is essential.

Putting Together Your Nonfiction Writing Sample

If you follow the guidelines in this section, you'll have an easier time selecting or creating a strong writing sample. Once you have a great writing sample to attach to your proposal, make sure your sample really is representative of the book—that you can deliver an entire manuscript that's up to the standards of your sample. Otherwise, you're in for trouble down the road. Typically, though, creating great sample text will excite and inspire you to live up to your own high standards when it's time to write the rest of the book.

AGENTS' ADVICE

If we think an idea is great, but the writing is weak, we may call up the author and try to work with them to improve their writing style. If we feel the writing still doesn't measure up to the rest of the proposal, a stellar concept, outline, and platform, we might recommend that the author collaborate with a freelance editor, co-author, or ghostwriter (see Chapter 9). We will make whatever appropriate suggestions it takes to get the book into print if we believe in its viability.

Now, let's look at what you need to do to pull that writing sample together:

- **Don't write the whole book.** The purpose of your proposal is to have it selected by an agent for representation or an editor for publication *before* you write your entire book. If you have already self-published the work and are now looking for a publishing house to pick it up and distribute it, then you would send a copy of the finished book. However, even if you've already written your whole book, an agent or editor may only want to see a proposal with a couple sample chapters at the outset, so a writing sample is all that is required. Different agencies have different requirements about what they will accept for review, so check out each agency's website for specifics.

Ideally, a writing sample should include one to three chapters. If chapters differ in style and content and length, such as text chapters and recipe or project chapters, you'll have to make a selection that is representative of the work. This will be enough to give the agent and acquiring editor a good sense of your writing style and how you handle your content.

- **Submit new text.** Including articles you've written previously, especially those that support your platform, is a great way to show your writing skills and experience. Even chapters from previously published books can be included, because they can show your skill. However, it's essential that you also provide a fresh, original writing sample that comes from the book you're proposing. Agents and acquiring editors want to see a sample of what you'll be saying in the book you are proposing to write so they can evaluate your intended tone, voice, and style.

- **Sweat the small stuff.** For the writing sample, correctness counts. Make sure you use spell-check before adding your writing sample to the proposal file and then ask a qualified friend or family member to critically review your text.

- **Think strong content.** Maybe it seems logical to use your book's introduction or Chapter 1 as your writing sample, but that's usually a mistake. That's because the introduction or first chapter is usually too general. You don't want to choose the final chapter, either, as it's the wrap-up. Instead, skip the appetizer and dessert and go for the meat and potatoes of your manuscript: a chapter (or chapters) that has really strong content, provides new information, and keeps the reader hungry for more.

Make sure you also include sample elements that showcase your content: photos, illustrations, recipes, maps, diagrams, tables, graphs, pull quotes, etc. (For example, a cookbook chapter may include a photo to accompany the recipe directions, or a memoir of your escape from an African rebellion will be enhanced with a selection of dramatic and skillful photographs.)

- **Try a bit of both.** If your chapters are long, but the format or content differs dramatically in different parts of the book, consider submitting excerpts from two chapters as your sample. If you believe you can make your strongest case for your book by using excerpts from more than one chapter, go ahead. Just make sure you label which chapters you are using in both the sample and the Expanded Table of Contents (see Chapter 15).

- **Take advice from someone you trust.** It might not take a village, but it could take one or two other people to make sure you're choosing your best sample. Of course, you need to trust your instincts, but it doesn't hurt to ask someone else what she thinks. A great way to do this is to present your writing sample at writers' conferences, workshops, programs, and the like, and seeing what presenters and attendees have to say. Unlike friends and family, they won't be tempted to spare your feelings by assuring you that it's fantastic when you really need to rethink and rewrite. (See Chapter 2 for more on getting feedback and writers' groups.)

HOT OFF THE PRESS

The "three P's" to keep in mind when choosing your sample chapter are these:

- *Provocative.* Does the chapter have a slant that's different and unique, that can draw the reader in?
- *Pertinent.* Does the chapter exemplify your book idea? Does it discuss one of the points you make in your proposal?
- *Promising.* Does the chapter display your writing talent? Does it showcase your style?

Getting Specific

Here are some book-idea examples of how to make your writing sample selection work for you:

- **Clutter:** You've developed a three-part system that will kick-start any decluttering effort. Make the chapter that presents an overview of your system your sample in the book proposal.

- **Beekeeping:** You're a beekeeper and your book is the first that covers raising organic hives. Use the chapter that showcases your organic methods as your writing sample.

- **Winemaking:** Your writing sample could follow a year in a vineyard, or showcase the trends with grapes that brought you the awards from a sommelier institute.

- **Travel:** Your book on the best small B&Bs in Europe could include breakaway Eastern European countries. Select the chapter that showcases the new countries and sets your travel book apart from everything currently on the market.

- **Reference:** Your college finance book includes a chapter that discusses the new laws on repaying student loans. This chapter would make a perfect writing sample, since it presents new data that hasn't yet been published in book form.

- **Business:** You are writing a book on investigating finance reform, and you have access to high-level bankers and politicians. Include a chapter that has an interview with the high-ranking person you have access to, someone who otherwise is unavailable to the press.

- **Cookbook:** You're writing a specialty book for gluten-free cooking and you have a pizza-dough recipe that doesn't use flour but still makes a great pizza. Build sample recipes on this innovative recipe. Include the basic recipe, variations (including various herb and spice combinations), and innovative toppings in your writing sample.

A Closer Look at Writing Samples

Presenting examples of good and bad writing is difficult because the terms "good" and "bad" are arbitrary. One person may love your writing sample, but another may hate it. But every good writing sample has two major elements: logic and readability. The sample should showcase your talent and your idea in the best possible light, and that means making it easy for a reader to navigate your text and a pleasure for him to read it.

For our example, we have two authors' hypothetical writing samples. They're both hoping to write books about attracting butterflies to your backyard.

The following sample is enthusiastic but rambling and uninformed. There is no logic to its narrative, which is all over the place, and no additional features to break up the text. It has a few typos and grammatical errors, which make it look as unprofessional as it sounds. It sounds as though anyone could have written it—there's no expertise demonstrated—but it would have to compete on the market with books written by experts. There's nothing here to tempt an agent, editor, or publisher to take a chance on this book.

Chapter 3: Bring On the Butterflies!

You remember how I talked earlier about falling in love with butterflies when I was six years old because I thought they looked like Tinkerbelle. Aren't they adorable? I know you'll want to get as many as possible to visit your yard.

Zebra swallowtails are my favorites, followed by monarchs. Have you ever seen a monarch butterfly emerge from its chrysalis? By the way, monarch chrysalises are the most beautiful shade of jade green. Won't you be lucky if a monarch makes a chrysalis in your yard?

In winter, most adult butterflies will have died or migrated to warmer climates. Monarch butterflies do this. I'll bet you've never seen a monarc in a snowstorm! But some butterflies may stay in your yard as pupas, so you need to provide shelter for them..

Butterflies like nectar. But that's not all they like! Did you know butterflies like mud, too? Yuck! But it turns out that mud is actually good for them because its full of minerals. Some people who are mineral-deprived eat mud, too, and so do macaws.

Lantana is a good butterfly plant. It's also really pretty and looks great in a pot on your deck. Butterflies also like daisy flowers. But they don't like sunflowers, even though sunflowers look like giant dasies.

You know how hummingbirds are attracted to red? Well, butterflies aren't that picky. They'll visit any flower if they can land on it.

Last week, I counted 20 different kinds of butterflies in my yard! It's oh so easy to attract these little fairies ...

Let's see how another author might handle the same chapter. This time, the text is clean, informative, and logical. It provides tips and action items to draw the reader in right away. An agent or editor looking at this version would see that the author has a mastery of his subject and knows how to attract an interested reader. The author didn't leave out that critical visual element, either. This book is on its way!

Chapter 3: Bring On the Butterflies!

Attracting butterflies to your backyard is easy, and it adds another dimension of beauty to your landscape. It can be as simple as setting out a shallow bowl with pebbles and water and planting a few containers of flowering annuals and perennials on your deck or patio. Or you can create an entire flower border designed to attract butterflies from spring through fall.

In this chapter, you'll discover how to make your backyard more welcoming to the butterflies that call your area home, whether you live in Washington State or Washington, D.C., Navajo country or Nashville, Tennessee. You'll also find in-depth profiles of two beloved North American butterflies, the zebra swallowtail and the monarch butterfly, as well as thumbnails of other butterflies by region, with photos of adults, caterpillars, eggs, and chrysalises for easy identification.

Tip: When you're creating a habitat for butterflies, make sure you give them the four essentials: food, shelter, water, and places to lay their eggs.

Butterfly-Attracting Basics

The more attractive you make your yard to butterflies, the more butterflies, and the more species of butterflies, you'll attract. And fortunately for you, the ways to attract them are all low-maintenance! No sterilizing messy nectar feeders or constantly refilling birdfeeders required. Get an overview of the options in "A Butterfly-Friendly Landscape" on page 000. You'll find more about great plants for butterflies on page 000, easy ways to add water on page 000, how to create a "Butterfly Spa" on page 000, and how to choose plants to feed butterfly larvae (a.k.a. caterpillars) on page 000. But first, let's take a quick tour of five butterfly-attracting essentials.

Five Fast Ways to Make Your Yard Butterfly-Friendly

Butterflies will flock—make that "float"—to your yard if you provide these proven butterfly magnets. They're all easy and inexpensive, and some add beauty on their own as well as drawing beauty in the form of butterflies. And did I say fast? You can add four of the five in an afternoon, and you probably already have the fifth and don't even know it. So let's get going!

1. **Provide trees and walls for shelter.** This one's the freebie; you almost certainly have both if you have a house and yard.

2. **Plant flowers and flowering shrubs to provide nectar for adult butterflies.** (Nectar is butterfly Gatorade, providing calories, nutrients, and fluid to sustain life with every sip.) Butterflies prefer large, flat flowers with many nectaries—coneflowers, yarrow (achillea), rudbeckias, lantana—because they provide an ample supply of nectar and a ready-made landing/launching pad. (See "Top Ten Butterfly Flowers" on page 000 and "Butterfly-Friendly Shrubs" on page 000 for details.)

3. **Add water.** Water is as necessary for butterflies as for all life. But you don't need an elaborate fountain, pond, stream, or even birdbath to supply butterflies' requirements. Instead, set the bowl of a birdbath or any shallow bowl on the ground. Add pebbles so the butterflies can perch without drowning, and then fill the bowl with water up to the level of the pebbles, leaving the pebble tops dry.

4. **Make a mud puddle.** Mud puddles give butterflies their equivalent of our vitamin and mineral tablets. Mud is mineral-rich, and butterflies flock to mud puddles to get the salts and minerals they need to survive.

5. **Don't forget the caterpillars.** Many butterflies are attracted to yards because they provide plants for the next generation. While butterflies typically drink nectar or, in some cases, don't eat at all, they instinctively lay their eggs on plants that their larvae (a.k.a. caterpillars) need to eat in order to grow. So if you plant these, you'll attract the gorgeous adults as well as have the satisfaction of knowing you're helping to perpetuate the species. Two examples: Zebra swallowtail larvae only feed on pawpaw leaves, and monarch caterpillars only eat leaves from plants in the milkweed family, including the ornamental butterfly weed.

A Butterfly-Friendly Landscape (sample illustration included)

The Least You Need to Know

- The writing sample provides essential proof that you can write and can deliver on your book's promise.

- Let your style, knowledge, and passion for your topic shine through in your writing sample.

- Choose a sample chapter, excerpt, or a combination of excerpts that provides strong content and an overview of the elements in your book.

- Keep it short and sweet: keep your writing sample to one to three chapters.

- Show what you know: impress your agent or editor with your style, logic, originality, content, and correct use of spelling and grammar.

Fiction Tips and the Process

In this part, you learn about what makes a strong fiction submission and what should be included in your proposal pitch. You also find what you need to know to make a clear-headed decision about whether to submit your proposal through an agent, submit it directly to a publisher, or self-publish—and in any of these cases, how to find a good fit for your personality, your needs, and your book. Finally, what should you do while you are waiting for a decision? We show you how to keep on building your platform and strengthening your writing career.

The Fiction Writing Sample

In This Chapter

- Write about a topic you know and love
- Research the competition
- Know your genre
- Presenting the structure, characters, and action
- Honing your work
- What you need to send to the agent

You love to read, you love to write. What could be more natural than trying your hand at a novel? We say, by all means go ahead! Unlike nonfiction, where you need to thoroughly research and develop your idea but may not need to write more than a sample chapter or two before pitching it to an agent, when you're writing fiction, you need to write the entire novel or a substantial portion of it *before* you pitch it. You need to make sure it's strong enough to publish before you submit it.

In Chapter 7, we discussed how to write a fiction query letter. Here we'll talk about how to go about getting your novel into its best shape; how to be objective, analytical, and critical about your own work; what to send the agent who requests to see book material; and, finally, what to expect when you do submit that query and then the proposal. Because fiction is an individual and artistic act, we're not including "good and bad" examples in this chapter. It's up to you to realistically assess your work.

Write About What You Know and Love

This may seem obvious, but we want to say it anyway: if you live in Minnesota and your favorite escapist fiction is Regency romance novels, please don't suddenly decide to write a gritty novel about the drug wars in the seamy underside of Miami just because you've noticed that novels about drug lords and drug traffic keep showing up on bestseller lists. Your best shot at getting a novel published is to write about what you know and love, whether you base your historical novel on your grandmother who grew up in the Depression era or your passion for space travel in your work of science fiction.

Think about what you can bring to a novel that will give it that authentic level of detail and credibility. At its most basic, a novel is a story, and like Scheherazade of *Arabian Nights* fame, your job as the storyteller is to entice readers into the world of your creation. While they're turning your pages, you want them to be transported to your fictional world. You want them to fall under your spell.

Hit the Shelves

You want your novel to be unique, a story that is busting to come out, one that you can tell with authenticity, skill, and passion. But that doesn't mean you should be unaware of what else is out there in your category. Like nonfiction, you want to be educated about your genre. It's important to try to read everything that is germane to your concept. If you love Sherlock Holmes and you are writing a mystery with a Holmes-like character as your detective, you should read the entire canon of Sir Arthur Conan Doyle stories and novels, and you should be familiar with how other modern writers have treated the great detective. Otherwise, you might spend months writing a certain type of mystery novel, only to discover that there was already a hit series on that very theme and a publisher might think your work is derivative and pass on it. If you're writing a novel that's based on personal history—yours or another's—see how other authors have drawn readers into their experiences; see how they've set up their novels and how they've combined fact and imagination to create fiction.

It's also helpful to familiarize yourself with works that differ from yours but are related, as they can add synergy to your thinking as you work through your material. If you want to write mysteries that feature a sleuthing chef, of course you should read the other cooking-related mysteries that are published. But you should also read some quilting and gardening or other special-interest mysteries to see how the authors treat their detectives. They may give you ideas on how to present your characters that are new to cooking-related mysteries. This research will give you some guidance on how another writer might integrate the background into his story. Some of these subcategories represent excellent marketing opportunities at publication. For example, culinary mysteries might be suitable for placement at cooking stores, or be promoted on culinary blogs and websites. Fiction authors have to think about marketing their books and be prepared to share ideas on their marketing platform page. Some fiction books have nonfiction elements that lend themselves to marketing opportunities.

Aim to see what's selling in *genre fiction* and what's not selling and why. If you can't determine from reading why one book shot to the top of the bestseller lists in your category while another languished, spend some time trying to deconstruct success in your given market. Talking to fellow writers in the genre can often shed some light. Joining an organization in your topic area and becoming an active participant can be hugely helpful as well.

 DEFINITION

Genre fiction is fiction that falls into a specific category, such as mysteries, romance novels, science fiction, fantasy, young adult, or historical fiction. There are also subgenres, such as tea-cozy mysteries, police procedural, and detective novels or Regency, paranormal, or Christian-themed romances.

Genre Mastery

Genre research and mastery is an ongoing process. Always do your homework. It's important to know what your readers will be looking for in your novel and will expect from you as the author. If you're writing a contemporary romance set in your hometown, you have the familiarity with the setting, local dialogue, dialect, and characteristics of the area to get you started. But if you're writing genre historical fiction, you must steep yourself in the conventions of the period. You need authentic details to add substance and realism to your story. To achieve this, you need to do your research.

The following sections discuss some of the most common genre categories. For a discussion on children's books, young adult, and humor genres, see Chapter 7.

Romance

Romance novels are huge sellers and a significant portion of mass market paperbacks sold each year are romances. Your romance can be set in almost any time period, be it historical, contemporary, or fantasy. There is romantic suspense, paranormal, and general chick lit. Each has its own distinctive characteristics. For example, if you're writing a Regency romance, these are set from 1811 to 1820. Your Regency must comply with the conventions of the period, from the clothing to the politics, from the decorations to the actual historic figures.

You should read Jane Austen and Georgette Heyer. Heyer is the twentieth-century British author who was inspired by Jane Austen to create the Regency romance genre. Unlike Miss Austen, who lived in her world and assumed everyone would understand her references to fashion, transport, class, and manners, Miss Heyer researched the period extensively and incorporated popular expressions and definitions into her novels. You should watch films based on Jane Austen's novels, absorbing period detail and mannerisms. Documentaries and books of Jane Austen's life, her era, fashions of the time (don't forget male fashions), even cooking in the Regency era, are all sources of background information that will make your book richer and a more satisfying, and accurate, reading experience. If possible, take your research to the actual settings. You can visit London, Bath, Brighton Beach, and other key Regency sites, visit museums, tour Regency-era houses and landmarks, and the like. We advise you to join a local branch and attend a national conference of the Romance Writers of America.

Historical Fiction

Writing historical fiction? Read Mary Stewart's Arthurian novels and Sir Walter Scott's *Ivanhoe*. Watch movies about Arthur, Ivanhoe, the Knights Templar, and Robin Hood. Delve as deeply into your period as you can: How did they live? How did different classes interact? What was grown, what was eaten, what was worn? Were there catastrophic diseases like smallpox or the plague ravaging the area at the time in which you want your novel to be set? What did people do for entertainment, what was their education, how did religion affect their lives? If you're writing about life on the prairie, read *Little House on the Prairie*, nonfiction books about prairies, and pioneer women's diaries. If you're writing about Mary, Queen of Scots, make sure you read and watch every book and movie and TV series about Mary and her era, including the Showtime hit *The Tudors*.

Sci-Fi, Fantasy, and Horror

Writing science fiction? Read Herbert and Heinlein. Watch TV shows and films like the *Star Trek* series, *Star Wars*, *Independence Day*, and *Avatar*. Attend a Star Trek convention and see what's hot. Brush up on your astronomy, astrophysics, engineering, and quantum physics. Keep up with NASA and the current state of space technology. Good science fiction gets the tech aspect right.

Are you writing fantasy, a novel set on another world but ultimately providing a moral lesson for our own? Read the greats: Sheri Tepper, Joan Vinge, and Mary Gentle. What about epic fantasy in the tradition of J. R. R. Tolkien's *Lord of the Rings* trilogy? Try Guy Gavriel Kay and Stephen Donaldson, the *Harry Potter* series, and Stephen King's *Dark Tower* series. Read the classic fairy tales by Grimm and Andersen and their more recent interpretations. Read Steven Brust's

Vlad Taltos novels to see how one fantasy novelist added humor and biting wit to his fantasies to turn them into something completely original, despite the usual dragons and wizards. Watch the *Lord of the Rings* trilogy and the *Conan* movies.

Horror can be set in the past, present, or future, in this world or any other. Whether you're writing about Jack the Ripper or vampires, Satanic possession or killer sharks, as long as fear, terror, and the prospect of whatever-it-is turning up and wreaking destruction at any moment is present, you're writing a horror novel. Again, read the classics, including *Dracula, Frankenstein, The Strange Case of Dr. Jekyll and Mr. Hyde,* and the stories of Edgar Allan Poe and H. P. Lovecraft. Read the modern master of the genre, Stephen King. Watch films like *The Mummy, Children of the Corn, Alien, Dawn of the Dead, The Blair Witch Project, The Exorcist,* and *Rosemary's Baby.*

AGENTS' ADVICE

Whether your passion is for science fiction or fantasy, consider joining the Science Fiction & Fantasy Writers of America, Inc., and attending their conferences. Check out the Science Fiction Writing Resources website (www.ebookcrossroads.com/science-fiction-writing.html) for upcoming workshops, such as the preeminent Clarion Science Fiction & Fantasy Writers' Workshop, held at UC San Diego since 1968.

Mysteries and Thrillers

Writing a murder mystery? You may not be able to bring P.D. James's and Patricia Cornwall's knowledge as a coroner and their fantastically realistic descriptions of murders, motives, and victims to your novel, but you can still bring realism and excitement to your work. Like all genre fiction, there's a set pattern to mysteries, and readers will be deeply disappointed if you stray from the pattern: the motive; the deed is done and discovered; the good guys are on the case; they end up following false trails while the bad guy is still on the loose and taunting them for their incompetence while continuing his rampage; the good guys finally figure it out and catch, kill, or watch in impotent horror as the bad guy escapes, promising sequels.

The key is to consider how bestselling mystery writers who lacked technical knowledge, from Edgar Allan Poe and Sir Arthur Conan Doyle through Dame Agatha Christie and Tony Hillerman, used their police connections to learn what makes a strong sense of place and plot that properly showcases their compelling detectives. Read, watch, interview the experts and learn. Watch classic movies in the genre, from *In Cold Blood* to *The Silence of the Lambs* to *Coyote Waits*. See how bestselling mystery writers created their unforgettable characters, from Thomas Harris's Hannibal Lecter and Agatha Christie's Hercule Poirot and Miss Marple to Tony Hillerman's Jim Chee and Joe and Emma Leaphorn, to Mr. Frost. Like Lecter and Frost, sometimes the creepy bad guys are the most memorable; and like Sherlock Holmes, Nero Wolfe, Adam Dalgliesh, Columbo, and Monk, sometimes it's the good guys.

Hone your work by joining the local and national chapters of the Mystery Writers of America, based in New York, and attending their conferences. Read mysteries that have won their Edgar Awards.

For a thriller, where there may or may not be a mystery, but a fast pace, excitement, and a villain-dominated plot are hallmarks, you need to spend time with the classics: the novels of John le Carré, Robert Ludlum, John Grisham, and Michael Crichton, and the Hitchcock and James Bond movies. Some films of the genre include *The Silence of the Lambs*, *Rising Sun*, *The Da Vinci Code*, *Jurassic Park*, *Day of the Jackal*, *The Manchurian Candidate*, *Marathon Man*, *The Perfect Storm*, and *Seven*. Thrillers simply *must* have that edge-of-your-seat quality, unlike mysteries, where detection and logical deduction are key, so learn from the best and pace your work accordingly.

Western

Writing a Western? Not only should you know the evolution of your genre, from Zane Grey to Louis L'Amour, you should make sure you know what modern writers of Westerns are doing to give their novels relevance. You should try to spend a vacation on a working ranch, visit Santa Fe, Albuquerque, Baja California, Utah, the

Sonoran Desert, Mexico—wherever you plan to set your novel. Visit a silver mine, pan for gold, attend a Pueblo ceremony or festival. Check out authentic area crafts and furniture in museums and shops and buy books that feature them and tell their history. Stay in a hacienda. Tour one of the old Franciscan adobe churches. Immerse yourself in regional cuisines—frybread, beans, nopalitos, salsas, hot peppers. Buy field guides to the region's flora and fauna. Go to a gun show and/ or firearms museum to familiarize yourself intimately with the era's weaponry of choice. And, of course, watch the great Western classic movies, from John Wayne to the Spaghetti Westerns, and rent shows like *Wagon Train* and *Bonanza* so you know what created the genre's structure and expectations to begin with.

Presenting Your Story in Three Documents

Your novel should demonstrate a mastery of your genre and offer convincing evidence that your work has the right elements to appeal to the market. Novels may seem like spontaneous outpourings of writing, but good novels, and good short stories, are built on strong underlying structure. As the author, it's your job to present the structure, the characters, the dialogue, and the action. You have to show the agent that these pieces are in place in your novel. An easy way for an agent to see what your novel accomplishes is for you to provide three documents that detail your novel: a short synopsis, a cast of characters, and an expanded synopsis. Together, these documents will show if your plot is strong or weak and if the action is believable and logical; it will introduce your characters and the conflict; it will demonstrate if the plotline is sustained or interesting and if scenes are redundant or key scenes are missing; and so on. All these elements, professionally crafted, may become the basis of your fiction proposal presentation. These may be the most effective way to introduce your work to an agent. Let's take a closer look at all three documents.

Short Synopsis

This condensed treatment gets to the essence of what you write about in your novel. Look to outline your novel in 125 to 200 words. Here's an example:

> *Anne of Hever Castle* is a fictionalized love story loosely based on the early life of Anne Boleyn before she met Henry VIII. It shows Anne growing up at Hever Castle, Anne as an accomplished young lady at the court of France, and Anne returning to England and falling in love with Henry Percy, leading to their secret engagement and marriage. The novel ends as Anne's father and uncle, the Duke of Norfolk, discover and destroy the engagement, leaving Anne heartbroken, cynical, and bitter. She sees Henry VIII for the first time in the final chapter, setting the stage for a possible sequel. The novel also explores Anne's complex and sometimes-explosive relationships with her scandalous siblings and power-mad uncle, the Duke of Norfolk, who would send Anne and a second niece to her death at Henry's hands before his grab for power was over.

If you can't summarize your novel in this brief format, you might not have a clear idea of what you want to write or be able to give the agent a quick snapshot of the story.

AGENTS' ADVICE

A publishing house maxim is that you should be able to capture a book idea in 25 words or less. Thank goodness you have up to 200 words to work with in your short synopsis!

Cast of Characters

Rather than head from the brief synopsis directly into the expanded synopsis, the second step is to flesh out your major characters. Who are your characters? What do they contribute to the story? What are their personalities and characteristics? What are their unique physical descriptions? What are their professions and interests? Write a thumbnail description for each character—no more than a short paragraph for each. The entire section should be no more than a page.

Here's an example of a character description for a female main character in an historical novel:

> Anne Boleyn is the intelligent and indulged daughter of nobility, part of the great Howard family headed by her uncle, the Duke of Norfolk. Raised in the courts of France, the Netherlands, and England, Anne is multilingual, highly educated, and idealistic. She turns heads and wins hearts with her wit, talent, sophistication, and sense of style. Petite, dark-haired, and dark-complected, Anne's looks are more Gaellic than English, but her mesmerizing black eyes and exuberant personality are bewitching.

Expanded Synopsis

Now that you have a thumbnail overview of what your novel is about and the key characters in it, it's time to craft a more detailed and nuanced account. The expanded synopsis is generally about 250 to 750 words in paragraph form that outlines the storyline in dramatic fashion, touching on key plot events and main characters.

The documents should hold interest, paint a fairly complete picture of your novel, and, as always, showcase your writing ability. The goal is to get an agent to read the novel, so it's important to put your best effort into this process.

> *Anne of Hever Castle* opens as Anne Boleyn, a brilliant and seductive 20-year-old, is about to set foot in the court of Henry VIII for the first time to take up her duties as lady-in-waiting to Queen Catherine of Aragon.
>
> The action then flashes back to the story of Anne's happy childhood growing up at her family seat, Hever Castle, where we meet her parents, brother, sister, and powerful uncle, the Duke of Norfolk, all of whom will play large, ongoing, and dramatic roles in Anne's life. Contrasting with Anne's happy

childhood is a glimpse into the miserable childhood of Henry Percy, the future Duke of Northumberland, as he grows up under the cold, ambitious eyes of his father, the present Duke.

The reader travels with the adolescent Anne to the royal court of the Netherlands and ultimately to the great court of France, where she joins her sister Mary, now one of the numerous mistresses of King Francis I. Anne vows that she will never follow in her sister's footsteps as a king's mistress. Returning to Northumberland, we see Henry Percy being forced by his father into an engagement to his cousin Mary, whom he loathes, to further his father's dynastic ambitions.

We then return with Anne to England, where her father hopes to engage her to her own cousin, the future Duke of Ormonde. But when the engagement falls through, Anne is sent to the English court to serve Queen Catherine. There, she meets Henry Percy, the two fall in love, and Henry dares to defy his father by becoming secretly engaged to and marrying Anne.

However, Anne's father and her uncle, the Duke of Norfolk, now have dynastic plans of their own. They perceive that King Henry is tiring of Anne's sister Mary and want to replace her with Anne. Furious at Anne's defiance and announcement of her marriage to Percy, they inform Percy's father, who descends upon the hapless pair and drags his son back to Northumberland and a loveless marriage to his cousin. (Because the marriage was secret, known only to the families and the priest who performed it, Percy's father is able to pay off the priest and send him out of the country, leaving no one the wiser.)

A shattered Anne is left to pick up the pieces of her life, which will prove to be far more ambitious than even her uncle could have imagined.

Polishing Your Work

Perhaps you have finished writing the novel. You're exhilarated, euphoric, and eager to print it out and send it off. But wait, you're still not ready. A first draft is only the beginning.

Authors really need thick skins to succeed in the publishing world, and that's as true of fiction writers as of nonfiction writers. Before your novel sees the light of publication, it will be viewed and criticized by many levels of reviewers: your agent, one or more acquiring editors, marketing committees, publishing execs, developmental editors, and bookstore buyers. Everyone will have suggestions.

You may end up feeling like a fly constantly dodging the swatter as you try to make everyone happy. Through it all, bear in mind that the purpose of all these comments is to get your novel read. Take criticism from worthy sources—your writing partner, writing group, or agent—and make your writing the best possible work you can create.

PUBLISHING PITFALLS

Writing a novel is a major undertaking that can take years and many drafts and revisions. When you leave the writing world for the publishing world, your novel has to be perfect. Most of the novels we see simply are not ready for final consideration. You get one shot with busy agents, so don't rush to decide your work is completed when, in fact, the novel still needs to be revised.

Be Your Own Critic

Before you even think about submitting your novel to an agent, read it again as if you were an agent who is reading it for the first time. As you read, ask yourself these questions:

- How does my work compare to popular works in the genre?

- Is the dialogue realistic, i.e., could I imagine real people saying the words?

- Are the characters compelling and realistic? Do I like (or hate) them, and most especially, want to read more about them?

- Is the action logical and believable?

- Are the setting and details convincing and accurate?

- What unique aspects have I brought to the story?

- Has the story and have the characters provoked an emotional response? Have I laughed, cried, cheered, shouted, or sworn as I've read the work?

- Have I been drawn into the story, losing track of time and/or staying up late to finish reading it?

Your honest answers to these questions can show you the strengths and weaknesses of your novel. Where you see a weakness, go back and rework your text.

Now What?

If you're struggling to perfect your novel and you can't bring yourself to rewrite, or you don't know where to begin, there are options. Other people can help you. If you have friends or colleagues who love your genre, ask them to honestly review your novel. (And please, don't hold their comments against them.)

Attend local and national writers' workshops and conferences and give strangers a chance to read and critique your work (see Chapter 2). Search for these online; there are many brick-and-mortar and online workshops. Also check with area colleges, which often sponsor local writers' workshops. This may also offer you an opportunity to hook up with agents.

Consider hiring a freelance editor (see Chapter 9) to give your novel the once-over and make suggestions. You can search for "freelance editors" and "freelance book editors" to find some associations and individuals who can help you. Remember, this is the stage where you are taking your novel from an idea to a finished book. And with picky publishers only taking a tiny fraction of the novels that are submitted, you need every advantage you can get.

Yes, you'll have to step back from your role as author/creator and join your readers/reviewers as a self-critical reader in order to appreciate their comments on your work. Yes, you may discover that your first novel is a training ground for your subsequent efforts. But remember, writing is a craft, and you're trying to hone your skills. If you have what it takes to write one novel, you have what it takes to write more. Don't be discouraged. Just do whatever you have to do to make this novel—or the next one—better.

What to Send to the Agent

You've done your homework; your novel is in perfect shape; you have written the three essential documents (short synopsis, cast of characters, and expanded synopsis); and your proposal package is complete (see Part 4). You need to assemble these core proposal materials along with a writing sample. What size writing sample should you send? We suggest three sequential chapters that show the characters, action, and details in the strongest light. It's a mistake to ignore an agent's request and send more text than they ask for. They're very busy, and they don't want to read 320 pages when they've asked for 50.

Now for the good part. Recheck the agency's e-mail requesting more material, review the agency's guidelines for submission, and be sure to comply. Then craft a letter addressed to the agent, reminding him of the request, and detail what is attached or enclosed. Send the letter, and you're on your way!

HOT OFF THE PRESS

It may take a while to hear back from an agent. Agents are very busy and receive many queries coming over the real or virtual transom, so give them at least a month to six weeks before you send a follow-up e-mail. It also takes an agent longer to read fiction than to review a nonfiction proposal, so don't get discouraged if you don't hear back right away.

The Least You Need to Know

- Write and polish your novel before you even send out a query letter, much less a proposal.

- Write your novel about a topic you're familiar with and passionate about.

- Check your local bookstores, online bookstores, and, if applicable, specialty shops and websites to see what's hot and what's selling in your chosen genre. Keep up with the competition and make sure to read it!

- Know the conventions of your chosen genre and make sure your novel satisfies them, while still contributing something fresh.

- Include a short synopsis, cast of characters, and expanded synopsis of your novel with your proposal.

- Be sure your submission packet includes all the key proposal components, and pick a writing sample that best reflects your novel.

Using an Agent or Not

18

In This Chapter

- Deciding whether you need an agent
- The benefits of having an agent
- How to find the right agent
- When it makes sense to go it alone
- When you choose to self-publish

Editors tell us this is the most frequent question they get from would-be authors: should we go with an agent or just send you our material? As agents, of course we think you'll get better professional advice and have a stalwart advocate throughout the publishing process if you choose to go with an agent. And there are cases when you *must* go with an agent, as some publishers will only work with agents. Further, a work of fiction is very difficult to place on your own. To be sure, though, there are some writers who possess the skill, contacts, background, or credentials to pitch a proposal on their own.

In this chapter, we'll review your options so you can make your own decisions. And we'll give you tips on how to find a congenial agent if you choose to take that route.

Do You Really Need an Agent?

The answer is yes, no, or maybe. If you're writing fiction and aren't self-publishing (discussed later in the chapter), you increase your chances of getting your proposal read if you have a *literary agent*. Some publishing houses will consider proposals sent directly from an author if the work is nonfiction. But every publishing house will accept agented proposals for nonfiction, so you up your chances of getting published if you go through an agency.

> **DEFINITION**
>
> A **literary agent** represents authors and their works to publishing houses. Literary agents assist the author in preparing their book materials; identify the publishing houses and editors that are the best fit for the book for submission; and negotiate contracts, acting as an advocate for the writer throughout the publishing process. Agents are paid on a commission basis of all income earned on the project.

As long-time industry professionals who have experience on both sides of the publishing desk, both as in-house publishing executives and independent agents, it is our opinion that writers are best served in their interests by being represented by an agent. Your task is to find the right agent for you and your work. Finding an agent can be a tough and time-consuming process, but it's usually worth the effort. However, if you are reluctant to pay the agent the commission, concerned about being one of many clients on an agency roster, or questioning the ethical behavior of someone, you should assess your personal goals and needs to make an educated selection about what works best for you.

Another option is self-publishing, which we'll discuss in detail later in this chapter. You may elect this option if you've not been able to elicit interest from a publisher previously or if you want total control over the look, content, packaging, pricing, and distribution of your project; if you want to condense the publishing timeline and achieve speed to market; or if you want to make more money on each copy sold.

Let's say you're an expert in your field with a ready-made audience: you're the beauty expert who speaks at every beauty and spa convention; you're the self-help guru who draws thousands to every seminar; you're the celebrity chef whose audiences scream and swoon at your live appearances. So you write and self-publish a book to sell at your appearances, and before you know it, you've sold 50,000 copies at your seminars and to your client base. The irony is, this level of sale will capture a publisher's attention. So you ask yourself, "Is there any advantage to going with a publishing house at this point in the publishing cycle rather than reprinting the book on my own? And if I opt for a publisher because doing so adds a dimension to my marketing and sales that cannot be achieved on my own, do I need an agent at this point to stand in my corner and broker the deal?"

What an Agent Can Offer

An agent is your advocate, your point of entry to the proper publisher, and she fills the roles of negotiator, sales rep, and advisor about your books and career. Let's take a closer look at the advantages of going with an agent:

- **Agents know the publishing world.** Agents have relationships with acquisitions editors at publishing houses. They know editors' areas of interests and publishers' needs and requirements. With their established access, it's much easier for the agent to get a proposal read than it would be for an unagented or unsolicited work that arrives on an editor's desk over the transom. After all, the editor knows and trusts the agent to present quality proposals in the subject areas she is interested in pursuing, while on your own, you are an unknown quantity. With the Internet, the volume of submissions can be overwhelming. Agents act as the first level of filter and evaluation.

- **Agents know the market.** It's a critical part of an agent's job to stay on top of publishing trends, to know what's hot and what's not. If the market seems saturated with vegan books this year, for example, he'll be able to help you position your book in a fresh way so as to reach the existing audience and appeal to the acquiring editors. He may suggest that you reposition your general vegan concept as a vegan book for toddlers or, perhaps, *The 30-Minute Vegan*. The agent frequently knows what publishers are looking for to fill a hole in their publications' list for the upcoming season and will be able to advise you that submitting your recast proposal to that house would be a smart and timely move.

- **Agents work for *you*.** They're your advocate as you navigate the publishing process, working with you every step of the way from polishing the proposal to sitting in on conference calls and meetings with the publisher to seeing the book into print. It's in their best interest to help you succeed, and to see your book succeed, as they share in your success both in financial participation and professional growth. Agents will want to work with successful, professional writers on an ongoing basis and develop a working relationship that continues for years.

- **Agents know how to sell.** Because of an agent's thorough grasp of the market and familiarity with publishing houses and their quirks and specialties, he knows where and how to pitch your book. If you're lucky, he might even be able to start a bidding war for your book by pitching it to a number of publishers and getting interest from several of them. In doing so, this may increase the financial offer for your work. Agents can guide you in evaluating multiple offers. Ask yourself, "Could I do this on my own?"

- **Agents can negotiate.** Most people find it difficult to negotiate for themselves, to represent themselves objectively and with a certain toughness that may be required. Negotiating a book deal is, frankly, an ordeal for most authors, but agents are pros at it. They're not afraid to put pressure on the publisher to get better terms for the author. By letting the agent play the heavy on your behalf, you can maintain a cheerful, cordial relationship with your editor and publisher.

- **Agents know contracts inside and out.** If you've never seen a book contract before, you'd be stunned at the intricacies and complexities of terms. An agent can quickly tell if the payout of advance and royalty rates on all formats on offer are standard or substandard; if subsidiary rights are appropriately divided and accounted for; if certain rights are better retained by the author; if the author is given appropriate control over the publishing process; and if the author's work, both the current project and future works, are protected. Contract negotiations, which can drag on for months, are one reason why most authors are really grateful to have an agent in their corner.

- **Agents are in it for the long haul.** Publishing can be a slow-moving business; editors have a lot on their plates, and the submission process can take many months, especially if you're submitting the proposal on your own. Agents try to put together a timeline and submission strategy for you, which may take your work from an A list of choice publishers to a B list and so on, if necessary. It can be discouraging for you as an author to receive rejections from publishers; after a while, you may be frustrated, doubting yourself and the value of your work. The agent handles any rejections and requests for revisions. The agent has been there and knows that the process usually takes time, so she's not crushed or discouraged by bad news. She'll keep on fighting for your book.

How to Find an Agent

Once you decide to go with an agent, you need to find the right agent for you. But how do you choose from the thousands of agents and hundreds of agencies out there? Do you go with an agent who works alone, a small boutique agency like our own that can give you personalized attention, or a large agency like ICM (International Creative Management), William Morris, or Writers' House? Following are some helpful tips.

- **Go online.** You can find agents and agencies online at sites like Publishersmarketplace.com, WritersMarket.com, or WritersNet (www.writers.net/agents.html).

- **Go to writers' workshops, conferences, and book fairs.** Often, agents attend these events and interview authors. From a writer's perspective, this is one of the highlights of the event.

- **Look in the books.** There are several resource books you can review, such as *The Literary Marketplace* and *Jeff Herman's Guide to Book Publishers, Editors, and Literary Agents*. Check Amazon.com or your local library.

- **Get a recommendation.** As agents, our favorite way of getting new authors is through recommendations from our clients, the authors we already know and love. If you know any authors who are happy with their agents, see if they'll recommend you and your project.

PUBLISHING PITFALLS

One reason agents work so hard to get you the best possible deal is that the more you get, the more they get. Agents typically receive 15 percent of an author's earnings. Most reputable agents only get paid when an author's book is sold to a publisher, so they only take on projects they think they can sell. Be wary of people who charge big fees upfront or make ridiculous promises.

Making a Good Match

When you choose an agent, you're starting a relationship that may continue for years or even decades. So you want to take your time and find a good fit. Start with agencies that focus on your category, because they will have the best editorial relationships. Keep in mind that if you're a laid-back type who hates deadlines and wants to write when you feel like it, an aggressive, Type-A agent is probably a bad fit. If you need a lot of hand-holding and encouragement, a small agency or individual agent is probably a better choice than a large agency. If you're already a successful, driven type, you're better off with a bustling, high-octane agency that reflects your own relentless drive.

Take your time and choose carefully, because you have to choose just one. It's unprofessional and inappropriate to try to sell the same work through multiple agents. Neither the agents nor the publishers will appreciate it, and trust us, publishing's a small world and word gets around fast. Don't blow your chances by shopping your book through several agents at once.

Most agencies formalize the relationship with the clients by having their authors sign an agency agreement. The agreement spells out the terms of the author/agent relationship, including the agent's commission, handling of future works, and term of the agreement and renewal issues. This will clarify issues of exclusivity upfront, and an agency agreement puts the relationship on a professional basis, clearing up any potential confusion from the start of the relationship.

That isn't to say that the agent/author relationship isn't fluid. If you're not happy with your agent or your agent isn't happy with you, and you can't work out your differences, of course you can dissolve your relationship based on the terms of your agency agreement, say goodbye, and find a better fit.

Going It Alone

Given the advantages of using an agent, why would you want to try to go it alone? There are several reasons:

- You have a preexisting relationship with a publisher or editorial contacts.
- Your work is appropriate to a very specialized and identifiable publisher.
- You have a scholarly or academic work.
- Your work is of specific regional interest to a local publisher.

But remember, you need to be a strong negotiator, be savvy about the contract, and be willing to stand up and fight for yourself. This isn't a simple process, and insiders have the advantage.

Here are a few pitfalls to watch out for:

- It's hard to negotiate money and entitlements for yourself.

- You may find that you've irrevocably tied yourself, your project, and future projects to a specific publishing house. There are good reasons you may want to get out: the publisher is bankrupt, your payments aren't made, or there are inventory and stock issues. An agent might have been able to help you resolve all these issues.

- You may have a disappointing experience with a publisher, and have little clout and no advocate to resolve disputes.

- You don't know the industry standards on royalty rates, e-book rates, and so on, and you may undersell your work. An industry-savvy agent would keep you from settling for less than you're worth and what the market may in fact be willing to pay.

If You Opt for Self-Publishing

Self-publishing can be a great move or a disaster. It's a great move if you have a ready-made audience to buy your book. For example, it may make sense to self-publish if you are selling at seminars or conferences as an outgrowth of your business and you don't need a bookstore machine. But it can be a disaster if you're competing with at least 764,448 other self-published books (the stats for 2009 according to *Publishers Weekly*) with limited access to bookstores or other book-sales venues.

DEFINITION

Self-publishing is when an author undertakes the publishing of his own book at his own expense. With a self-published book, the author pays for all costs; writes the book or hires someone to write it; designs the book or hires a designer; handles printing and shipping the book; and self-markets, sells, bills, and collects payment on the work. These books are typically undertaken to support a successful business or a successful personality who sells books via seminars, conferences, workshops, and the like.

If you do self-publish and find that your book and/or business have grown into a phenomenon, like Carla Emery's *The Encyclopedia of Country Living*, Amy Dacyczyn's *The Tightwad Gazette*, or the *Gooseberry Patch* series, in the future you may wish to parlay your sales figures into a lucrative publishing contract with a legitimate publishing house. But if you take this route, you'll definitely need the sales numbers and marketing and self-promotional savvy to back up your claims.

One caveat to be aware of: you are now responsible for every aspect of your book—from the writing to editing, from design to fulfillment—including the financing of the process. Quality shows, and therefore such wide-sweeping responsibility for creating your project may be too much for some. An upside is that potentially you could make a lot more money on every copy sold because there is no publisher involved to share revenues or an agent to pay commission.

The Least You Need to Know

- Agents offer authors many advantages and are usually the best choice.
- Working with an agent, like working with a publisher, is all about building a relationship. Choose carefully and with the long term in mind.
- If you think you can go it alone without an agent, do your homework and make sure you are up on the latest trends in publishing and publishing houses.
- Self-publishing can make sense for authors with established sales outlets and the ability to underwrite the costs. Make sure you calculate the odds carefully before choosing this option.

While You Are Waiting to Hear

In This Chapter

- Understanding a typical publishing timeline
- Why you should continue to work while you are waiting
- Continuing to build your platform

You've found a great agent. You've written and polished your book proposal. You've written and rewritten your sample chapters or, in the case of a novel, perhaps you've completed the entire book. You've sent off your proposal to the appropriate agents and/or acquiring editors. Your work is done. Or is it?

Maybe not. That's because the publishing process takes time. This is a business that requires patience at all steps of the process, and that means waiting. This can be aggravating if you think you're the next Martha Stewart or John Grisham, or have written the next *Lord of the Rings* or *The Tipping Point* or *The Da Vinci Code* or *The Nanny Diaries*. It can also be frustrating not to have any news if you're trying to publish a book to help take your business to the next level or set yourself apart from the competition. You wonder: will I *ever* get a publishing contract?

The Publishing Timeline

There are stories throughout the industry about projects bought quickly on a few slim pages. This is a rarity. It has taken you months to find your agent, more months to polish your proposal, and finally the submission process is underway. Most authors wait for many weeks, even months, to get interest from a publisher. From editorial interest to pub board approval, and finally to an offer, can be another lengthy step in the process. In fact, once you receive the long-awaited offer to publish, it may take additional months for the terms of the contract to be finalized and signed.

Let's look at a probable timeline to put the publishing process in perspective. Many of these time ranges are best-case scenarios:

- **Sending the query letter.** It may take up to six weeks for a response from an agent for a nonclient. Keep a log of your submissions; you may send courteous follow-ups if needed. If you're not getting a response, think about reworking your query letter; be advised that no response sometimes means you should move on to other agents.

- **When an agent asks for more materials.** Send the materials promptly, clearly identify the project as requested material, and make sure your contact information is included, especially your e-mail address. Agents are busy with numerous other proposals, book deals, and managing their businesses. It may take two to six weeks before you get a response to your proposal materials.

- **Signing to work with a specific agent.** The agency agreement will be drafted. Once an agent agrees to take you and your project on, it may take one to two weeks to conclude the terms of the agency agreement.

- **Final shaping of proposal and/or manuscript to submit to publishers.** Because it's critical to get this material into perfect shape, this step may take two weeks to three months as you work under the direction of your agent. A novel may take longer.

- **When the proposal is submitted to publishers.** This step could take weeks to several months because there are many layers of decision-makers along the way. Some editors take two months just to read a proposal, and they're only the first step. The submission goes to the editor; then the editorial board; then to the marketing review committee, publications board, or acquisition board, all of which need time to review and confer. And that's just one publishing house; your proposal is most likely circulating among several. If your proposal gets interest from one publisher, your savvy agent may be able to turn that into interest from others, which could speed up the process.

- **Contract negotiations.** Once a publisher has made an offer for the work, there may be days, even weeks, of back-and-forth negotiations, before your agent accepts the deal on your behalf. Then there is still the complex contract to review. Negotiations can go on for one week to two months.

- **You have a fully executed publishing contract.** The typical term to write the work is nine months to one year. Frequently publishers want to schedule works for publication quickly, and your time to complete the work will be a negotiating point in the contract. In some cases you may be given about three to six months to complete the work.

- **Your book is finally in print.** Publishers' contracts typically request 18 to 24 months to publish the book. This term begins when you deliver a complete and acceptable work to the publisher. During this period, the work is edited, copy-edited, and proofread; the cover is created; the pages are designed; and the final book is printed. Publicity and marketing teams develop campaigns and begin to pitch the book to the media. Meanwhile, sales materials are prepared, and sales executives sell to retailers, foreign publishers, and special markets months in advance of finished copies being available. Then the book still needs to be shipped from the printer and delivered to stores.

The bottom line: this is a slow-moving business. It may take up to several years between submitting your query letter and seeing your book on the shelves. The industry is trying to condense the process, so there are some cases in which a query letter to the finished book can happen inside of a year. This is especially true if the project has been put on the fast track if the subject is hot, the publisher needs the book to publish in a particular season, or the author is suddenly in the public eye.

What to Do While You're Waiting

Instead of pulling your hair out, biting your nails, or calling your agent every five minutes, there are plenty of things you can do while you're waiting to hear if a publisher has an interest in your proposal. This waiting period is a hard time for a writer, but you should put the time to good use. What can you do to advance your project while you wait?

Fiction

If it's a novel and you've finished it before submitting the proposal, you can reread; continue researching, revising, and sending it to contacts for their opinions; and/or share it at writers' conferences, seminars, and workshops. You can plot out the sequel or sequels and start writing the follow-up. If you didn't plan on sequels, you can think about what you'd like to write next. You don't have to consider your novel done just because it's on submission; writing is an on-going process. Keep writing.

Keep working on your marketing. If you're writing genre fiction (see Chapter 17), make sure you join relevant associations and attend conferences and conventions. Network. Make connections. Make yourself visible in the community. Try to connect with illustrators who are well known in your genre. Socialize with published authors while you're conferencing and see if you can learn something. Be as personable as possible; you want other writers and people connected with your genre to remember you in a positive way. If you're lucky, this could lead to cover endorsements.

Nonfiction

If you're writing nonfiction, such as a history or how-to book, you can spend the time between submission and acceptance working on the book, researching, and amassing statistics if appropriate. If it's a book on making furniture, you can complete more projects and take step-by-step photos to support each project. If it's a diet book, you can put more people on your diet and collect more first-person testimonials, with before-and-after photos. If it's a biography of Louis XIV, you can continue to research, read, and travel to dig up little-known facts about the Sun King to enrich your book. If it's a cookbook, work on those recipes, capturing every detail in your directions, getting a friend who's great with photos or a professional photographer to capture gorgeous images of your food.

Keep Building Your Platform

The other important—we'd say vital—step to work on while you're waiting is to continue building your platform. This will not only strengthen your case with a potential publisher, but it will guarantee sales once the book is in print. Review Chapter 14 on the platform and see how you can put some of these suggestions into practice. Every little bit helps! Here are a few suggestions to keep you busy while you wait to hear:

- **Build your market.** Create a website, build your e-mail list, write a blog on your book's topic, and join other suitable blogs. Find like-minded people and connect with them.

- **Try to write for publication.** Submit newspaper, magazine, and online articles on your book's topic. Pitch op-ed articles from local to national publications. Publishing credits can help your agent to sell your book.

- **Look for opportunities that your agent can use to go back to publishers.** Receiving major speaking opportunities, receiving awards, winning competitions, teaching classes, or speaking at seminars all help build your platform.

- **Continue to expand your business and investigate opportunities for special sales.** Every advance in your business—assuming it's related to your book topic—and every deal you can make for special sales of your book will strengthen your platform and help convince publishers to take a chance on you.

You're On Your Way

Congratulations! You've made it to the end of this book, and you're ready to start applying the advice and tips in these chapters to your own query letter and book proposal. Now you know that creating an original book idea and writing the manuscript are just the first steps in the publishing process. The rest involves crafting a great query letter and book proposal that will convince an agent, acquiring editor, and publishing house to take you on. With the tools in this book, we're confident that you can take your book idea all the way from concept to publication.

The Least You Need to Know

- It may take months or even years to get a book deal, and you may have to deal with many rejections before you get to "yes." Be prepared and be patient.
- While you wait, continue to develop and polish your work. Share your work with objective readers and keep writing.
- Help your agent sell your book by strengthening your platform. Work on your website, your blog, and your e-mail list, and continue to build your business.

Glossary

About the Author A section of a book proposal that succinctly introduces the author. It conveys the author's appropriate credentials, detailing why the author is qualified to write the book; provides previous publishing and/or media history; and supports the author's platform. *See also* platform marketing section.

advance The amount of money a publisher pays an author for the right to publish the book. The advance is most often divided and paid in parts with some likely payment thresholds on signing, manuscript delivery and acceptance, and even publication. The advance must be earned out in profits from sales of the book and related book rights before an author will begin receiving royalties. *See also* royalties.

advance against royalties *See* advance.

agency agreement The contract between a literary agency and client detailing terms and responsibilities for both parties.

agent *See* literary agent.

art publisher A publishing house that specializes in books that are often oversized with exceptional attention to visuals and production values, also known as coffee table books.

audio books Books read aloud on tape or CDs or downloads. A book may be read in its entirety, in an abridged version, or in an enhanced version and it may be read by the author, an actor, or a professional reader.

autobiography A history of a person's life written by that person. *See also* biography, memoir.

back matter   The sections of a book that follow the main text. Back matter can include appendixes, a resource section, a bibliography, an index, and an About the Author section.

bestseller lists   The compilations of books that are selling at the top of their markets in a given week or time period. The best-known lists are *The New York Times* bestseller lists, which are divided into these categories: hardcover fiction, hardcover nonfiction, paperback trade fiction, paperback nonfiction, paperback mass-market fiction, hardcover advice, paperback advice, children's books, graphic books, and business bestsellers.

bibliography   A list of references at the end of a book, preceding the index. A bibliography typically includes books and other references used during the research and writing of the book, and may also include books and other materials (articles, DVDs, etc.) on the topic that the author thinks readers of the book would find useful.

biography   The written history of a person's life authored by another writer. *See also* autobiography, memoir.

blog   Short for "web log." An online diary or series of essays, short articles, recipes, observations, poems, short stories, etc. A blog can be written by one person, called a blogger, or have a number of contributors. It can be topical or personal, it can express a point of view, or it can be instructional. Blogs can be simply or elaborately designed and incorporate photos, music, videos, and other links, such as to websites that carry the blogger's books or crafts. A blogger can have multiple blogs, such as one for each of his or her books. Blogs are stored and maintained by blog hosts; the two biggest are Blogger (operated by Google) and WordPress.

blurb   A quote that appears on the front cover, back cover, or page of a book praising the book and/or the author or the author's earlier works.

book proposal   The detailed presentation of a book in development with the intent to get an agent and/or sell the project to a publisher for publication. Components of a book proposal include a cover letter, title page, overview, About the Author section, platform and promotion plans, review of the market and audience for the book, overview of the competition, Table of Contents and Expanded Table of Contents, and sample text.

Books in Print   An essential reference to all books currently in print, as well as audio books and videos. You can view new nonfiction and fiction books in print on the website (www.booksinprint.com).

cast of characters   The characters who are featured in a book. These may be invented (in the case of fiction), historical (in the case of history, biography, true crime, case studies, etc.), or a combination of both (as in historical fiction).

chick lit   A genre of fiction revolving around the interests of 20-something women ("chicks"). Originating with Jane Austen's novels, but defined with the advent of *Sex and the City* and Helen Fielding's *Bridget Jones* series and popularized by authors such as Sophia Kinsella.

children's books   Books for children of many ages and reading levels. Categories range from picture books, books for toddlers and pre-schoolers, easy readers, and books for middle grades up to young adult. *See also* young adult fiction, young adult nonfiction.

co-author or **co-writer**   A full partner in the book's conception, writing, and promotion process. Indicated as such by an author credit of "By XXX *and* XXX" as opposed to "By XXX *with* XXX."

collaboration   Typically, when an expert teams with a writer who receives cover credit ("By XXX *with* XXX"). In a collaboration, the author provides the authority and is the public/promotional face of the book, while the co-writer is the one who does the actual writing.

commercial fiction   Fiction that capitalizes on popular trends, fears, or dreams with an accessible writing style, characters, and plotline. Distinguished from literary fiction. *See also* literary fiction.

Competitive Review   A section of the book proposal in which you discuss differences and similarities between your proposed project and books on the topic that are already published.

contract   In publishing, a contract refers to the legal document between a publisher and author stipulating the terms of publishing the author's proposed book. The contract typically covers the author's obligations in terms of length and content of the manuscript, delivery schedule, provision of supporting materials (such as references), visuals and permissions, legal obligations, and promotional obligations. It also covers the publisher's obligations in terms of timely publication, advance and royalty payments, and many other matters.

copyright   The legal right to ownership of the content of a work and registered at the U.S. Copyright Office. Normally, an author holds the copyright to a royalty book, and the publisher holds the copyright to a work-for-hire book. *See also* royalties, flat fee, work-for-hire.

cover letter   The author's introductory letter that accompanies a book proposal. It should recap the author's name and book title, and give a brief description of the book theme and platform to set the stage for the proposal.

CV   Short for curriculum vitae. Usually used only in academic circles in the United States and Canada, a synonym for resumé in Europe. *See also* resumé.

deal memo   An agreement between an author and publisher about the basic terms of the deal that grants approval to proceed to drafting a publishing contract.

demographics   Population-related statistics, from broad-brush figures such as gender, age, nationality, economic status, level of education, religion, geographic location, and political leanings to specifics such as the number of Boomer women who ride Harleys or the number of Cordon Bleu graduates in 2010. Used to support the market and audience portion of a book proposal.

dust jacket   A laminated paper cover that protects a hardcover book. The dust jacket can show more dramatic images than the underlying cover, or reproduce it.

eBook   An electronic version of a book. The book may be sold through an eBook outlet like Amazon's Kindle, iPad, or Barnes & Noble's NOOK, or it may be offered for sale on the author's own website or the eBook publisher's website, such as Safari Books.

editor   A publishing professional who works with the author to shape a book so that it will sell in the book market. An *acquisitions editor* is responsible for bringing in new books to fill a publisher's list. The acquisitions editor works with an agent or author to make the work suitable for the publisher's program. A *developmental editor* works with the author to shape the book and make sure it's logical, well written, and conforms to the publisher's guidelines. A *technical editor* makes sure technical information such as engineering, mathematical, or software data is accurate. A *copy editor* makes sure the manuscript is grammatically correct and contains no logical or other errors.

Expanded Table of Contents   The Expanded Table of Contents includes detailed part and chapter summaries, each with a heading or title. This provides an overview or synopsis of each section's content. An element of the book proposal, the Expanded Table of Contents gives the agent and publisher the opportunity to evaluate the content and organization of the book. *See also* Table of Contents.

fantasy   A novel set in an alternate world or alternate reality. J. R. R. Tolkien's *Lord of the Rings* trilogy defined this genre, and the *Harry Potter* series and *Avatar* exemplify it for today's audiences. Distinguished from science fiction because the various cultures are the focus rather than the technology. *See also* science fiction.

fiction   A work of creative writing—typically a novel, short story, or collection of short stories.

flat fee   A one-time payment for a freelance writing assignment. Any subsequent profits go to the other parties of the agreement: the author and/or the publisher. A flat fee is typically paid in the manner of an advance, but there are no subsequent royalties. *See also* advance, royalties.

foreign rights   A book is published in its native country and language, and foreign language licenses (the right to publish the work in a foreign country in the language of that country) can be placed by whichever party retains those rights, either the author as represented by the agent, or the publisher.

format   The manner in which a publisher brings out a given book. This can be hardcover, trade paperback, mass market, eBook, or audio. *See also* audio book, eBook, hardcover, mass market, trade paperback.

freelance editor   A professional self-employed editor who takes on a variety of editing assignments. A freelance editor can review and polish written book material to ensure consistency and style in content and presentation.

freelance writer   A professional self-employed writer who takes on a variety of writing assignments. A freelance writer could create original material for a book or publication, or work as a collaborator or ghostwriter for another author.

front matter   The title and half-title page, book blurbs, copyright page, dedication, acknowledgments, and Table of Contents that precede a book's actual running text.

genre   The category your novel falls into so that agents, editors, and book sellers know who the reader is, how to package the book for that audience, and how to sell and market for these readers.

genre fiction   Fiction that falls into a specific and definable category, such as mystery, romance novel, science fiction, fantasy, vampire novel, western, horror, young adult, or historical fiction.

ghostwriter   A "writer-for-hire" who works anonymously with an expert to write a readable book. Unlike a co-author or collaborator, the ghostwriter's name is not credited on the cover or in the book, so he or she is invisible—thus the name *ghost*writer.

hardcover   A rigid book binding with a cardboard base, either laminated or covered with cloth (cloth-bound). A publisher will typically release a book in hardcover before following with a trade paperback and/or a mass market edition. *See also* mass market, trade paperback.

hook   The unique feature that immediately pulls in the reader. The hook can be storyline, statistics, marketing information, or a distinctive author credential.

horror   A genre of fiction involving the supernatural or paranormal, where the protagonists and other characters are threatened by evil beings intent on their destruction. This genre was spawned by Mary Shelley's *Frankenstein*, Bram Stoker's *Dracula*, Herman Melville's *Moby Dick*, and the Gothic novels of such authors as Horace Walpole and Ann Radcliffe.

imprints   Trade names under which publishers publish books, using imprints to distinguish the type and content of various books they bring out. For example, a publisher might bring out practical nonfiction under one imprint and romance novels under another.

ISBN   Short for International Standard Book Number, a numerical code that is used for cataloguing and inventorying a specific book. In this series of numbers, the first number details if the book was produced in the United States, the next three to five numbers pinpoint the publishing house, and the last set of numbers signifies that particular book. Each book is assigned its unique number. For each edition of a book, hardcover or paperback, a new ISBN is assigned.

juvenile books   Books aimed at young readers from second through sixth grade. The *Harry Potter* and *A Series of Unfortunate Events* series are good examples of juvenile books. *See also* genre fiction, young adult fiction, young adult nonfiction.

keyword   Words that match the words in a browser search to help potential readers find your book.

letterhead   The printed or engraved address, which also may include e-mail address and website, at the top of a letter. Business letterhead will usually have a logo design along with the address.

literary agent   A publishing-industry professional who represents authors and their works to publishers, presenting proposals and negotiating contracts and acting as the liaison between author and the publishing company.

literary fiction   Fiction that offers a developed and polished writing style that explores beautifully crafted styles of writing, elegant language, and insightful storytelling qualities.

marketing plan   The all-inclusive strategy devised by a publisher to sell a given title. This can involve publicity; public appearances, radio and newspaper interviews, book signings, and TV appearances by the author; viral campaigns; a website devoted to the book; an author tour to promote the book; special sales; hardcover, trade paper, and mass market releases; and sales to foreign, subsidiary rights, audio, and other markets. *See also* platform marketing section.

mass market   The small-format, inexpensive paperbacks sold in bookstores as well as airports, supermarkets, pharmacies, newsstands, and other nonbookstore locations. Many books are sold in mass market format after they appear in hardcover and trade paperback; others, especially genre novels such as romances and mysteries, may be released only in mass market format.

memoir   A narrative that focuses on a personal time, experiences, and/or people in the author's life that has universal appeal. *See also* autobiography, biography.

mystery   A whodunit or puzzle-based novel with a plot that revolves around the main character's ability to solve a crime. The hero can be an amateur sleuth (such as Nero Wolfe, Miss Marple, and Rita Mae Brown's cat sleuth, Mrs. Murphy) or a professional detective (such as Sherlock Holmes, Adam Dalgliesh, and Joe Leaphorn). There are many specializations within the mystery genre, in which the author focuses on a particular subject or a specific time period. *See also* thriller.

nonfiction   Writing that centers on a skill, craft, biography, science, history, how-to, or any topic that is factual rather than imaginative.

option clause   In a book contract, a clause stating that an author must exclusively offer his next book to the publisher of the book under contract. If the publisher and author can't reach an agreement on the subsequent book, or if the publisher has no interest in the book, then the author has the right to offer it to other publishers.

overview   *See* proposal overview.

pages or page proofs   Once a manuscript goes to the printer, the printer sends back an advance set of pages or proofs for the author and publisher to review prior to printing. This is the final check before a manuscript goes into print as a finished book.

paranormal romance   A romance novel involving a contemporary protagonist and an otherworldly love interest. This love interest can be a vampire, werewolf or other shapeshifter, alien, witch or wizard, or ghost. Paranormal romances can also involve time travel or people with psychic abilities. The roots of this genre lie with Bram Stoker's *Dracula*, where the vampire preyed on lovely and vulnerable young women.

platform   *See* platform marketing section.

platform marketing section   An author's ready-made market. It gives an overview of an author's existing media outlets and speaking experience, contacts, the size of an author's current audience, the success of previous publications, and any related spin-offs, such as a product that could be author-branded or endorsed and used to promote and sell the book.

plot   The story, the dramatic conflict central to the novel, and the way the writer makes a universal theme unique. There may be many subplots running through the work.

point-of-purchase racks   The racks of books placed prominently in bookstores and other locations where books are sold, positioned for customer traffic and impulse purchase.

positioning   Strategically defining and shaping a book so it can sell in a given market. This is done by first differentiating the book from the competitors and demonstrating the need it fills. An essential component of a book proposal.

primary markets   Brick-and-mortar bookstores and online bookstores like Amazon.com and barnesandnoble.com.

proofs   *See* pages or page proofs.

proposal   *See* book proposal.

proposal overview   The summary of the entire book, including a review of pertinent selling points, the author's platform, competitive titles, and details about the potential audience.

query letter   A brief presentation of your book concept that invites the interest of an agent or editor in seeing more material, with the ultimate goal of introducing your book to the publishing community.

Regency romance   A work of romantic fiction set in the Regency period of England, 1811–1820. Regency romances owe their popularity to Jane Austen, whose romantic novels were set during the Regency period, when she lived and wrote. *See also* romance novel.

resumé   A summary document that focuses on a person's work experience, education, awards and honors, publications, membership in professional organizations, and related experience. As such, it can be an excellent jumping-off point for an About the Author section or a supporting attachment to a book proposal. *See also* CV.

romance novel   A work of fiction centering on a romantic relationship. In a romance novel, a couple meet, then are separated by misconceptions, circumstances, prejudice, class distinctions, previous entanglements, etc. Eventually, after overcoming many obstacles, they get together. The romance novel originated with Jane Austen's "novels of manners" in Regency England. Today, many sub-genres exist, including gay and lesbian romances, young adult romances, and Christian romances. *See also* Regency romance.

royalties   A negotiated percentage paid to the author on each copy of the book sold, typically based on cover price or net receipts. Percentage of royalty rates depend upon the format of the work. They are paid after the advance is recouped and are typically paid out twice a year, accompanied by a report detailing sales.

sample   *See* writing sample.

science fiction   Works of fiction set in the future, using technology not currently available on Earth. These books usually involve space and/or time travel, focusing on human interaction with alien worlds and cultures. The *Star Trek* and *Star Wars* series are both examples of science fiction, as are Frank Herbert's *Dune* series and Robert Heinlein's novels. The focus on the technology—the workings of the spaceships, gear needed to survive in alien climates, weaponry, etc.—is what sets science fiction apart from science fantasy, which may also be set in the future in alien worlds but focuses on the culture and human-alien interactions rather than the tech aspects. *See also* fantasy.

search engine   An online research tool to help an author find information and statistics to support a topic and book proposal. Google is probably the best-known search engine, but Dogpile, Yahoo!, Bing, Ask, and the like present viable alternatives.

secondary markets   Nontraditional outlets for book sales such as catalogs, specialty stores, boutiques, corporations, seminars, schools, associations, websites, and nonbookstores. Secondary markets may be even more lucrative for special-interest authors. Sales to these outlets are called special sales. *See also* special sales.

self-publishing   An author undertaking the publishing of his own book at his own expense, typically to support a successful business or a successful personality who sells books via seminars, conferences, workshops, and the like.

serial rights   The licensed right to publish a part of a work in another publication. First serial rights give a magazine, newspaper, or other outlet the exclusive chance to publish the excerpt, a selection of the work, before initial publication. Second serial rights give others the right to publish part of the book after the official publication date.

social media marketing   Constructing your platform through an online presence, such as a website, blog, Facebook, Twitter, LinkedIn, e-newsletter, or extensive e-mail list that relates to your topic. It provides an instantaneous way to reach your audience and promote your book.

social networks   Online networks that link people together, such as YouTube, Facebook, LinkedIn, and MySpace.

special sales   Sales of a book to outlets other than bookstores and online bookstores such as Amazon, such as from catalogs to corporations, from QVC to specialty stores. *See also* secondary markets.

subsidiary rights or **sub rights**   Sales made (and rights assigned) to venues other than the originating publisher, such as print periodicals, electronic magazines, and/or eBook companies; content for websites, audio books, movie, and/or TV companies; foreign publishers; and merchandise, such as calendars, gift cards, and games developed from the book. All of these rights are separate terms and negotiations. In some cases, authors retain certain rights, and in others they are shared with the publisher.

suspense *See* thriller.

synopsis A brief summary of a book's content; an important part of a book proposal.

Table of Contents The chapter listing of a book's content, providing an at-a-glance overview of the topics and flow of the book, including chapters, parts, resources and other appendixes, bibliography, and index(es), where appropriate. *See also* Expanded Table of Contents.

tagline *See* keyword.

theme What your novel is about.

thriller A suspense novel pitting a hero or heroine against a villain. Usually fast-paced and hair-raising, with lots of drama, action, and plot twists and turns. The James Bond series and the Hannibal Lecter series would both qualify as thrillers, as would Dan Brown's and many of Michael Crichton's books. *See also* horror, mystery, science fiction.

title page In a book proposal, the title page lists the title, subtitle, and possibly a key selling line of the book, along with the author's name and key credentials (educational or significant business title), if applicable. Author contact information including name, address, phone number, fax, e-mail address, and website should appear.

trade paperback An oversized paperback book. *See also* hardcover, mass market.

work-for-hire A specific assignment, typically assigned to a freelance writer, editor, copyeditor, proofreader, or indexer who works on a per-assignment basis for a flat fee, eschewing book credits. Writers who take on work-for-hire assignments receive an upfront payment as opposed to an advance and royalties, and copyright credit. *See also* flat fee.

writers' conference An organized series of seminars and workshops where established authors, editors, agents, and other publishing professionals meet to network.

writers' group   A group that has clearly defined goals to provide constructive critiques of group members' writing.

writing sample   The chapter(s) or representative work an author submits with a book proposal.

young adult fiction   Sometimes called coming-of-age fiction, books in this market are aimed at adolescents and young adults typically between the ages of 12 and 17. Young adult fiction typically features a teenaged protagonist and approaches the novel's subject from a teen's perspective. *See also* genre fiction, juvenile books, young adult nonfiction.

young adult nonfiction   Any nonfiction book aimed specifically at the young adult market, from books on safe sex to cookbooks, science books, and fashion books.

Online Resources for Writers

Industry Resources

Agent Research and Evaluation: www.agentresearch.com

AgentQuery: www.agentquery.com

Agents' E-mail Addresses: www.writers-free-reference.com/agents/index.html

Authorlink: www.authorlink.com

Go Publish Yourself: www.go-publish-yourself.com

Literary Marketplace: www.literarymarketplace.com

Media Bistro: www.mediabistro.com

Predators and Editors: www.anotherrealm.com/prededitors

Publishers Lunch: www.publisherslunch.com

Publishers Marketplace: www.publishersmarketplace.com

Publishers Weekly: www.publishersweekly.com

Writer's Break: www.writersbreak.com

Writers Manual: www.writersmanual.com

Writers Market: www.writersmarket.com

Writing World: www.writing-world.com

General Associations and Organizations

American Booksellers Association: www.bookweb.org

American Journalism Review: www.ajr.org

American Library Association/Booklist: www.ala.org

Association of American Publishers (AAP): www.publishers.org

Association of American University Presses: www.aaupnet.org

Association of Authors' Representatives, Inc.: www.aaronline.org

The Authors Guild: www.authorsguild.org

Independent Book Publishers Association: www.pma-online.org

National Association of Independent Publishers Representatives: www.naipr.org

National Writers of America: www.nationalwriters.com/page/page/1963103.htm

National Writers Union: www.nwu.org

PEN American Center: www.pen.org

Writers Guild of America: www.wga.org

Genre and Topic-Specific Associations and Organizations

Academy of American Poets: www.poets.org

American Christian Fiction Writers: www.acfw.org

American Crime Writers League: www.acwl.org

American Society of Journalists and Authors: www.asja.org

Electronic Literature Organization: www.eliterature.org

Electronically Published Internet Organization (EPIC): www.epicauthors.com

Historical Novel Society: www.historicalnovelsociety.com

Horror Writers Association: www.horror.org

HTML Writers Guild: www.hwg.org

Mystery Writers of America: www.mysterywriters.org

National Society of Science Writers: www.nasw.org

Novelists, Inc.: www.ninc.com

Romance Writers of America: www.rwanational.org

Science Fiction & Fantasy Writers of America: www.sfwa.org

Society of Children's Book Writers & Illustrators: www.scbwi.org

Writers' Conferences, Workshops, and Residencies

Absolute Write University: www.absoluteclasses.com

Association of Writers and Writing Programs: www.awpwriter.org

Corporation of Yaddo: www.yaddo.org

Gotham Writers' Workshop: www.writingclasses.com

Internet Writing Workshop: www.internetwritingworkshop.org

MacDowell Colony: www.macdowellcolony.org

Vermont Studio Center: www.vermontstudiocenter.org

Write 101: www.write101.com

Writers' Conferences and Centers: www.writersconf.org/#

The Writers' Croft: www.writerscroft.com

Writers Online Workshops: www.writersonlineworkshops.com/retail

Writers' Groups

Blue Oasis Online Support Teams (BOOST): www.boost4writers.com

Book Industry Study Group: www.bisg.org

Coffeehouse for Writers: www.coffeehouseforwriters.com

Writer's BBS International Writers Community: www.writersbbs.com

Writers on the Net: www.writers.com

Writers Write: www.writerswrite.com

Industry Magazines

Booktalk: www.booktalk.com

Midwest Book Review: www.midwestbookreview.com

Poets & Writers Magazine: www.pw.org/magazine

R.R. Bowker (for *Books in Print*): www.rrbowker.com

The Writer Magazine: www.writermag.com

Writer's Digest: www.writersdigest.com

Writers' Journal: The Complete Writer's Magazine: www.writersjournal.com

Index

A

About the Author section, 12, 153
  curriculum vitae, 154
  definition, 154
  example, 165
  introduction, 153-155
  qualifications, 157
    career, 157
    education, 158
    geography, 161
    personal experience, 161
    prizes and awards, 160
    publications, 159
    relevant hobby, 159
    research, 161
  strengths, 162
    business, 162
    children's books, 165
    cooking, lifestyle, and crafts, 163
    fiction, 164
    health and nutrition, 162
    history and science, 164
    parenting, 163
    pop culture, 163
  too much information trap, 158

About the Market section, 12, 169
  Competitive Review, 179
    book summary, 182
    book uniqueness, 182
    format and price, 182
    general rule, 181
    identification of competition, 180
    niche title, 181
    sales information, 183
    sales statistics, 181
    topic rebounding, 182
    versions, 184
    writing, 181
  enthusiasm, 187
  expertise, 171
  help, 172
  importance, 170
  questions, 169
  research, 170
    audience definition, 173-174
    claims, 175
    conferences, seminars, or lectures, 178
    demographics, 176
    goal, 173
    institutions, 178
    primary market, 173
    qualitative component, 177

secondary markets, 178
statistics, 176
acquiring editor, 215, 230
Adam Dalgliesh, 249
advances, 122-123
agency agreement, 265, 270
agency requirements, 232
agent, 10, 259
    advantages, 261
        advocacy, 262
        commitment, 263
        contract knowledge, 263
        market knowledge, 261
        negotiation skills, 262
        publishing knowledge, 261
        selling ability, 262
    areas of expertise, 93
    Expanded Table of Contents, 215
    fees, 264
    as gatekeeper, 230
    going without, 260, 265-266
    image, 118
    locating, 263-264
    looking for next big thing, 230
    need for, 260
    opportunities, platform building, 273
    query letters received by, 30
    relationship, 264-265
    request for materials, 270
    self-publishing, 260, 266-267
    snail mail preference, 57
    Type-A, 264
Alien, 248
Amazon, 164
American Medical Writers Association, 26
Arabian Nights, 244
art publishers, 83
audience, 139, 173
Austen, Jane, 246

author. *See also* About the Author section
    handling criticism, 254
    market research, 172
    praise, 205
    socializing with, 272
Author's Guild, 26
Avatar, 247

B

beekeeping book, writing sample, 234
Bell Jar, The, 90
Benchley, Peter, 15
Berkowitz, Bernard, 80
big book retailers, 135
biography
    About the Author section, 155
    checklist, 155
    query letter, 76
BIP. *See Books in Print*
Blair Witch Project, The, 248
Blink, 16
Blogger, 201
blogs, 201
    followers, 204
    hosts, 201
    platform building, 273
Bonanza, 250
book doctor, 7
book proposal, 11
    About the Author, 12
    About the Market section, 12
    agents, 261
    components, 12
    contents, 117
    definition, 131
    description, 11
    difficulty writing, 12

Expanded Table of Contents, 12

nonfiction writing sample, 12, 231

overview, 12

platform marketing, 12

purpose, 231

resumé, 155

submission, 270

writing sample, 230

book proposal, basics, 117

About the Market, 12, 125

advance, 123

collaboration, 120-122

advances and royalty splits, 122

co-writer, 120

freelance writer or editor, 122

ghostwriter, 121

literary agent commission, 123

writer's credit, 123

development, 118-119

getting started, 126-128

guidelines, 129

parts, 124

About the Author, 125

Competitive Review, 125

cover letter, 124

Expanded Table of Contents, 125

Overview, 125

platform marketing section, 125

Proposal Table of Contents, 124

title page, 124

writing sample, 126

purpose, 117

royalties, 123

subsidiary rights, 123

book proposal, overview, 143

book structure, 149

competition, 148

credentials of author, 146

delivery dates, 150

do's and don'ts, 151

elements, 144

enthusiasm, 150

hook, 146

importance, 143

introduction, 143

longer hook, 146

positioning, 147

potential markets, 147

quick hook, 144-145

relevant information, 150

success, 152

Books in Print (BIP), 136, 180

branding, 13, 197, 205

Buffett, Jimmy, 197

business book, 80, 234

business expansion, 274

business letterhead, 67

C

Card, Orson Scott, 99

Catcher in the Rye, 90

characters, 91, 252

Child, Julia, 15

Children of the Corn, 248

children's books, 98, 165

Christian-themed romances, 245

Christie, Agatha, 249

Churchill, Winston, 99

clutter book, writing sample, 234

co-writer, 120

competition, 74

addressing in query letter, 61, 65

book idea, 8

book proposal, 118, 148
bookstore browsing, 137
Expanded Table of Contents, 214, 217
feedback, 19
identification of, 180
market, 10, 170
pre-proposal marketing, 131
query letters, 35
research, 132-134
sabotage, 22
vagueness, 36
Competitive Review, 179-180
book summary, 182
book uniqueness, 182
compelling outline, 213
definition of, 179
format and price, 182
general rule, 181
market research, 180
niche title, 181
sales information, 183
sales statistics, 181
topic rebounding, 182
versions, 184
writing, 181
conferences. *See* writers' conferences
contact information, 37
continuing education classes, 203
contracts, 263, 271
cookbook, 163
e-mail query letter subject line, 46
query letter samples, 74
writing sample, 234
copyright credit, 7
Cornwall, Patricia, 248
cover letter, book proposals, 124
Coyote Waits, 249
craft books, 80, 163

Craigslist, 21
credentials of author, 34, 146
credibility of author, 9-10
Crichton, Michael, 249
culinary mysteries, 245
curriculum vitae, 154
Curves platform example, 197

D

Dacyczyn, Amy, 267
Dark Tower series, 247
Dawn of the Dead, 248
definitions
About the Author section, 154
advance, 123
art publisher, 83
book proposal, 12
Competitive Review, 179
Expanded Table of Contents, 214
genre fiction, 245
ghostwriter, 7
letterhead, 67
literary agent, 260
memoir, 71
platform marketing section, 190
point-of-purchase racks, 100
query letter, 6
royalties, 123
self-publishing, 266
subsidiary rights, 123
demographics, market research, 176
detective novels, 245
Doyle, Arthur Conan, 249
Dr. Phil, 174
Dracula, 248

E

e-mail
  address, 270
  contacts, 204
  stranger's versus strange, 44
e-mail query letter, 43
  content, 49
  do's and don'ts, 52
    consistency, 53
    guidelines, 54
    honesty, 54
    typos and grammatical
      errors, 53
  first impressions, 43
  professionalism, 47-49
  samples, 50
  sign of mass submission, 48
  subject line, 44-46
eBay, 164
editor
  freelance, 122, 255
  frequent question for, 259
  image of, 118
  looking for next big thing,
    230
  query letters received by, 30
  writing sample, 230
elevator ride test, 5
Emery, Carla, 267
*Encyclopedia of Country Living,
  The*, 267
entrepreneur, 158
escapist fiction, 244
Etsy, 164
Evanovich, Janet, 92
Exorcist, The, 248
Expanded Table of Contents, 12,
  213
  agent view of, 215
  book organization, 218-219
  book quality, 215

bullets, 219
business sense, 217
chapter descriptions, 219
chapter key points, 215
chapter titles, 217
confidence, 218
creation, 215
definition, 214
description, 214
difficulty, 215
examples, 220
flexibility, 216
lack of substance, 213
length, 216
logic, 217
narrative content, 219
objectivity, 215
opportunity, 214
organization, 216
purpose, 214
revelation, 214
special cases, 226
trap, 220
typeface, 217
variety, 217
vision, 214
writing sample, 218
expertise, claims checked, 34

F

fabric design, 164
fantasy novels, 99
Fat Flush Plan, The, 16
feedback, 19
  nonfiction writing sample, 233
  reason for, 19
  writers' conferences, 24
    American Medical Writers
      Association, 26

Author's Guild, 26
Google, 26
locating, 25
networking, 24
researching, 26
rules, 24
search engines, 26
skills, 24
trade magazines, 26
writers' group, 20
compatibility, 20
critiques, 22
goals and procedures, 20
leaving, 23
location, 21
rules, 22
work, 21
fiction query letter, 89
basics, 91
agent areas of expertise, 93
agent connection, 92
closing, 95
hook, 94
length, 91
name, 92
platform, 95
proofreading, 94
research, 91
submission guidelines, 92
elements, 90
examples, 100
genre, 98
children's books, 98
historical novels, 99
humor books, 99
mysteries and thrillers, 100
romance novels, 98
science fiction/fantasy/
horror novels, 99
young adult books, 98
pre-query musts, 6

rules, 95
expert, 96
hook, 96
sample, 97
synopsis, 97
fiction writing sample, 243
credibility, 244
documents, 250-252
drafts, 254
expanded synopsis, 250
familiarity with related works,
245
genre fiction, 245
genre knowledge, 244
genre mastery, 246
historical fiction, 247
mysteries and thrillers, 248
romance, 246
sci-fi/fantasy/horror, 247
Western, 249
materials assembled, 256
refinement, 254-255
topic, 244
first impressions, e-mail, 44
Fortune 500 company, 162
Frankenstein, 248
Freakonomics, 16
freelance editors, 122, 255

G

gatekeeper, agent as, 230
genre, 90, 244-245
ghostwriter, 7, 121
Google, 26, 200
Gooseberry Patch series, 267
Gray, Robert, 139
Grey, Zane, 249
Grisham, John, 249
Grogan, John, 16

H

Harris, Thomas, 249
Harry Potter series, 91, 247
health issues, journalist
  specializing in, 162
Heavin, Gary, 197
Heinlein, Robert, 99
Heyer, Georgette, 246
Hillerman, Tony, 249
historical fiction, writing sample,
  247
historical novels, 99
Hitchcock, Alfred, 249
hook
  anecdote, 32
  e-mail query letter, 49
  fascinating fact, 31
  longer, 146
  nonfiction query letter, 69
  opening line, 32
  question, 32
  quick, 144-145
horror novels, 99
How to Be Your Own Best Friend,
  80
humor books, 99

I

ICM. *See* International Creative
  Management
illustrations, pre-proposal
  marketing, 139
illustrators, 272
In Cold Blood, 85, 249
inappropriate intimacy, 62
Independence Day, 247
interior decorating, 164

International Creative
  Management (ICM), 263
Internet booksellers, 93
Iron Chef America, 193
ISBN (International Standard
  Book Number), 133
Ivanhoe, 247
iVillage, 163

J-K

James, P. D., 248
James Bond movies, 249
Jaws, 15
*Jeff Herman's Guide to Book
  Publishers, Editors, and Literary
  Agents*, 264

King, Stephen, 247-248
Kirkus Reviews, 136
Knights Templar, 247

L

L'Amour, Louis, 249
le Carré, John, 249
Library Journal, 136
lifestyle books, 80, 163
literary agent, 123, 260. *See also*
  agent
Literary Marketplace, 38, 49, 54,
  92, 264
Little House on the Prairie, 247
local bookstore, 135
Lord of the Rings trilogy, 247
Ludlum, Robert, 249

M

Making Peace with Your Past, 16
market. *See* About the Market
   section
marketing, 272. *See also* platform
   marketing section
   campaigns, 271
   component, solidity, 132
   mantra, 193
   networking, 272
   pitch, 171
   platform, 70, 273
   potential audience, 10
   social media, 14, 191
   supporting statistics, 10
marketing, pre-proposal, 131
   bookstore browsing, 134-135
      Books in Print, 136
      competition, 137
      local bookstore, 135
      media outlets, 137
      newspaper book review
         section, 135
      professional magazines, 136
   competition, 132-134
   expertise, 137
      authorship, 138
      illustrations, 139
      scope, 138
      style, 138
      wording, 138
   organization, 139
      audience consideration, 139
      focus, 139
      passion, 139
      presentation, 139
Marley and Me, 16
Martha Stewart Living, 193
*Mastering the Art of French
   Cooking*, 15

Mayles, Peter, 72
media, 14, 190-191
memoir, 45, 71-72
Microsoft Word, 59
military service, 158
Mummy, The, 248
mysteries and thrillers, 46, 100,
   248

N

name dropping, 99
national media programs, 160
negotiation skills, agent, 262
Nero Wolfe, 249
networking, 24, 272
New York Times, The, 193
Newman, Mildred, 80
niche audience, 10, 181
Nielsen BookScan, 172-173
Noble House, 91
nonfiction query letter, 69
   category, 71
      biography, 76
      business book, 80
      coffee table book, 83
      cookbook, 74
      crafts, 80
      current event or true crime
         query, 85
      decorating, 80
      diet and health, 80
      financial book, 80
      gardening, 80
      history book, 76
      how-to or self-help book,
         79
      lifestyle, 80
      memoir, 71
      sports and fitness, 80
      travel book, 78

fundamentals, 69
highlights, 70
hook, 69
memoir, 72
pre-query musts, 7
nonfiction writing sample, 12, 229, 235
  acquiring editor, 230
  concern, 229
  creation, 231
    accuracy, 232
    agency requirements, 231
    content, 232
    feedback, 233
    multiple excerpts, 233
    number of chapters, 232
    originality, 232
    weak writing, 231
  enthusiasm, 230
  examples, 233-234
  major elements, 235
  next big thing, 230

O-P

online newsletter subscribers, 55
op-ed page, 193
originality, 8-9

platform creation, 13, 273-274
  branding, 13
  marketplace visibility, 13
  recognition, 14
  relationship building, 14
  website creation, 14
platform marketing section, 12, 189
  elements, 190
    continuous exposure, 193
    media experience, 190

    previous publications, 192
    product tie-ins, 192
    social media marketing, 191
    speaking engagements, 192
  example, 207
  ideas, 200
    blogs, 201
    branding, 205
    contributor, 202
    e-mail contacts, 204
    quotes, 205
    selling, 200
    social networking sites, 203
    speaking events, 202
    statistics counter, 201
    teaching, 203
    Toastmasters, 202
    website, 200
  importance, 189
  length, 207
  perspective, 197
  platform assembly, 193
  possible contacts, 206-207
  ready-made audience, 190
  self-promotion, 198
  social networking sites, 203-204
Poe, Edgar Allan, 249
point-of-purchase racks, 100
police procedural, 245
pop culture, 163
positioning, book proposal overview, 147
potential markets, 147
Precious, 90
primary market, 173
product tie-ins, 192
professional publications, 136
proposal. *See* book proposal
publicity, 14, 206, 271

publishers
  acquiring editor, 230
  direct query, 38
  Expanded Table of Contents,
    215
  snail mail preference, 57
Publishers Weekly, 92, 136, 266
publishing contract, self-
  publishing and, 267
publishing timeline, 269
  agency agreement, 270
  bottom line, 271
  contract negotiations, 271
  printed book, 271
  proposal finalizing, 270
  proposal submission, 270
  publishing contract executed,
    271
  query letter, 270
  request for materials, 270

Q

query letter, 6, 29
  benefit, 29
  challenge, 6
  checklist, 105
  competition, 36
  credentials of author, 34
  don'ts, 40-41
  early contact, 108-109
  elements, 30
    book title, 35
    close, 36
    competition, 35
    contacts, 37
    content, 33
    experience, 34
    hook, 31

  opening, 31
  pitch, 32
  enthusiasm, 40
  experience, 34
  feedback, 30, 112
  follow-up, 110-111
  importance, 30
  length, 107
  logbook, 40
  personalization, 37, 39
  publishing timeline, 270
  purpose, 5, 30
  referrals, 109
  stationery, 107
  submission list, 106
  waiting, 108-110
query letter, e-mail, 43-44
  content, 49
  do's and don'ts, 53-54
  first impressions, 43
  hook, 49
  professionalism, 47-49
  samples, 50
  sign of mass submission, 48
  subject line, 44-46
query letter, fiction, 89
  basics, 91
    agent, 92-93
    length, 91
    name, 92
    platform, 95
    proofreading, 94
    research, 91
    submission guidelines, 92
  elements, 90
  examples, 100
  genre, 98
    children's books, 98
    historical novels, 99
    mysteries and thrillers, 100
    romance novels, 98

science fiction/fantasy/
  horror novels, 99
 young adult books, 98
rules, 95-97
query letter, nonfiction, 69
 category, 71, 85
  biography, 76
  business book, 80
  coffee table book, 83
  cookbook, 74
  crafts, 80
  decorating, 80
  diet and health, 80
  financial book, 80
  gardening, 80
  history book, 76
  how-to or self-help book,
   79-81
  lifestyle, 80
  memoir, 71-72
  sports and fitness, 80
  travel book, 78
 fundamentals, 69
 highlights, 70
query letter, snail mail, 43, 57
 advantage, 57
 content, 60
 example, 61
 formatting, 58
 presentation, 66-67
 rules, 59
quick hook, 144-145

research and development, 3
 book proposal, 11
  About the Author, 12
  About the Market section,
   12
  components, 12
  description, 11
  difficulty writing, 12
  Expanded Table of
   Contents, 12
  nonfiction writing sample,
   12
  overview, 12
  platform marketing, 12
 clarity of book idea, 5
 credibility of author, 9-10
 elevator ride test, 5
 market, 10
 marketability, 4
 originality, 7-9
 platform creation, 13-14
 pre-query musts, 6-7
 query letter, 5-6
 reality, 4
 title, 15-17
resource books, 264
Robin Hood, 247
romance novels, 98, 246
Rosemary's Baby, 248
Rowling, J. K., 91
royalties, 122-123

R

Ramsey, JonBenet, 86
Random House, Inc., 80
referrals, 109
Regency romance novels, 244

S

sales
 information, 183
 materials, preparation, 271
 pitch, 32
 statistics, 181

sci-fi/fantasy/horror, writing
sample, 99, 247
Science Fiction & Fantasy
Writers of America, Inc., 248
Scott, Walter, 247
search engines, 26, 200
secondary markets, 178
self-publishing, 260
caveat, 267
claims, 267
decision, 266
definition of, 266
sales, 261
Selznick, David O., 14
shared remuneration, 7
Sherlock Holmes, 244, 249
Silence of the Lambs, The, 249
Simpson, O. J., 86
Sir Arthur Conan Doyle stories,
244
SiteMeter, 201
Skinny Bitch, 16
snail mail query letter, 57
advantage, 57
content, 60
example, 61
formatting, 58
presentation, 66-67
rules, 59
social media marketing, 14, 191
social networking sites, 203-204
Facebook, 47, 93, 155, 191, 203
LinkedIn, 37, 49, 94, 204
Twitter, 191, 204
YouTube, 203
Spaghetti Westerns, 250
speaking engagements, 192, 202
Star Trek, 247
StatCounter, 201
Stewart, Mary, 247
submission strategy, 106, 263
subsidiary rights, 123

T

tea-cozy mysteries, 245
teaching opportunities, 203
Tightwad Gazette, The, 267
To Kill a Mockingbird, 90
Toastmasters, 202
Tolkien, J. R. R., 247
trade magazines, 26
travel books, 78, 234
TV appearances, 71
Twilight series, 98

U–V

U.S. Mail. *See* snail mail query
letter

voicemail, 108

W–X–Y–Z

Wagon Train, 250
waiting, 269
platform building, 273-274
project advancement, 272-273
publishing timeline, 269
agency agreement, 270
bottom line, 271
contract negotiations, 271
printed book, 271
proposal finalizing, 270
proposal submission, 270
publishing contract exe-
cuted, 271
query letter, 270
request for materials, 270